UNDESIRABLE NEIGHBORS:

THE U.S. NAVAL BASE AT GUANTÁNAMO

UNDESIRABLE NEIGHBORS:
THE U.S. NAVAL BASE AT GUANTÁNAMO

Olga Miranda Bravo

Editorial José Martí

Original title in Spanish: *Vecinos indeseables: la Base yanqui en Guantánamo*
Editing: José H. Amieva Dalboys and Israel Fernández Pujol
Design: Enrique Mayol Amador
Desktop Publishing: Alberto F. Calienes

ISBN 959-09-0184-0

INSTITUTO CUBANO DEL LIBRO
Editorial José Martí
Publicaciones en Lenguas Extranjeras
Calzada No. 259 entre J e I, Vedado
Ciudad de La Habana, Cuba

To my nephews

OLGA MIRANDA BRAVO (Santiago de Cuba, 1934) graduated at the University of Havana in Diplomatic and Consular Law (1956) and Administrative Law (1956), and obtained a doctorate in Law (1960); she was awarded a scientific degree as Doctor in Juridical Sciences by the Academy of Sciences of the Republic of Cuba, and was appointed Honorable Member of the Cuban Jurists National Union (1997).

For almost three decades, Dr. Miranda was Juridical Director of the Cuban Ministry of Foreign Relations (1963-1992) with an ambassadorial rank, and later became Advisor to that same Ministry.

She has chaired and participated in various delegations at government, bilateral and multilateral meetings.

She is Arbiter and Vice-Chairperson of the Cuban Arbitrage Court for Foreign Commerce since its inception (1964), Vice-Chairperson of the Cuban International Law Society (1983), and Chairperson of the Permanent Tribunal that awards doctor's degrees in Juridical Sciences (1984). Since 1976, she is an Associate Professor at the Higher Institute of International Relations of Havana and member of the Court of Arbitration at The Hague.

Dr. Miranda has participated in numerous national and international conferences, colloquies and seminars and has lectured on international law and Cuba's international relations at home and abroad. Various newspapers and journals have published her articles. She authored the book *Cuba-USA. Nacionalizaciones y bloqueo (Cuba-U.S. Nationalizations and Blockade)* published in 1996.

Dr. Miranda is an associate consultant in various legal firms, a member of the technical advisory councils of several Cuban enterprises and institutions, and Legal Secretary of various mercantile associations.

I am grateful for the cooperation offered
by the women and the men, my companions one and all,
who rendered my research work for this book easier,
and specially to the Cuban Book Institute
that pledged me into writing it.

CONTENTS

I
CUBA: FROM A COLONY TO A PROTECTORATE

II
INTERVENTIONISM

III
THE BASE AND ITS TREATIES

IV
ILLEGALITY

V
THE AGGRESSIONS

VI
TERMINATION OF THE TREATY. VINDICATION OF THE OCCUPIED TERRITORY

ANNEXES

I

CUBA:
FROM A COLONY
TO A PROTECTORATE

THE LAST STEPS TAKEN BY THE UNITED STATES TO PREVENT CUBA'S INDEPENDENCE

The Wars of Independence

To understand the reasons for the undesirable presence of the U.S. Naval Base at Guantánamo, it is necessary to remember the Cuban process of independence from Spain and the opposition from the United States in that sense.

Just like the chameleon changes its colors. The United States of America struggled for decades (specially during the last five decades of the 19th century, but mainly in the 1890s) between its appearance of democracy and its imperial interests: on the one hand, it made passionate statements against Spanish colonialism, brimming with humanitarian feelings for the Cuban people, and on the other, conspired with Spain, merely playing their own game to hinder the island's independence and seize it when it was most convenient.

Much has been said about "geographic fatalism" to explain the United States' designs regarding Cuba. North Americans are permeated by an irrational fear when they remember that Cuba—an island barely ninety miles away from its coasts—was and could have been a pontoon used by the European powers to conquer their territory. But the roots are in the United States' imperialist nature when, after taking possession of Louisiana (1801), they expanded toward Florida and Mexico. Before that, in October, 1805, Thomas Jefferson declared that he considered Cuba indispensable for military defense. Jefferson was always obsessed with the annexation of Cuba, but he was not the only one: with more or less virulence, all the successive North American presidents, except for Abraham Lincoln, had targeted Cuba.

The men in the United States government were always worried about the independence of the American peoples under the Spanish yoke—consolidated during the first quarter of the 19th century—, because of the risk that they would assist in Cuba's emancipation, and not solely with their example. Spanish colonialism had weakened, and Spain could beat the mercy of the European powers and also of the most important emerging Hispanic-American nations, like Mexico and the Greater Colombia.

It was then, on December 2, 1823, that North American President James Monroe delivered his message to Congress announcing the imperialist doctrine named after him, that could be defined not as "America for the Americans," but as "America for the United States."

The seed of the Monroe Doctrine for imperialist expansion and hemispheric hegemony, was the fear of a Cuba they did not control; that prompted North Americans to develop a policy of interference and aggressions for almost two centuries, for Cuba was always a key piece for the United States policy and practice of expanding over and dominating the Americas as an empire.

In view of the ups and downs of Spanish domination over Cuba, and of the different political trends on the island, the United States took sides in order to safeguard their interests there.

In general terms, of all the European powers with colonies in America, Spain was the one the North Americans tolerated as the metropolis of the neighboring island of Cuba, for they considered it the weakest one. But when annexationist, reformist, autonomist or separatist disturbances broke out on the island, they used any weapon, be it denunciation, treason (as was the case of Narciso López and his followers in 1851), repeated attempts to buy it or, as they finally did in 1898, intervention.

This policy of keeping Cuba Spanish is evinced in Leland H. Jenks' comments based on U.S. Congress documents of that time: "In case any state should try to take this portion of territory from Spain, United States military and naval forces would assist (Spain) in keeping or recovering it."[1]

At the beginning of the second half of the 19th century, when the war against Mexico had already ended, California had been annexed and the United States already owned the Pacific, the eyes of the new American giant turned with a greater might toward the Caribbean and South America.

1. Leland H. Jenks, *Nuestra colonia en Cuba*, 41.

Some criollos, irked by the Spanish yoke, embraced the annexation to the United States as a solution to the critical situation in Cuba, but they were not far-sighted enough to understand that turning the island into a state of the American Confederation was only a way of changing owners. Therefore, in 1849, they founded the first Cuban Junta and organized several expeditions on American soil with soldiers and officers of various nationalities, with the sole purpose of defeating Spain and turning Cuba over to the new northern master.

The defeats suffered in the battlefield in 1850 and 1851 by Narciso López, denounced by his North American partners to the Spanish authorities on the island of Cuba, and the impassioned prose of the Cuban intellectual José Antonio Saco against the annexation to the United States, contributed to deal a fatal blow to annexationism, already cornered by its own aspirations. Before Saco, the Cuban priest Félix Varela, who had been elected as a delegate to the Spanish Courts in 1827, warned about the dangers of annexation and about them who thought about seceding from Spain by means of an invasion by foreign troops: "I am the first one to be against the island's union with any government, and I would like to see it as much of an island in its politics as she is in its nature."[2]

In 1848, José Antonio Saco stated in his document "Ideas About the Incorporation of Cuba to the United States": "Annexation would not be ultimately annexation, but the absorption of Cuba by the United States. It is true that, geographically considered, the island would not disappear from the Antilles group; but I wish that if Cuba would, in any event, separate itself from the trunk it belongs to, it always belonged to the Cubans and not to a foreign race [...]."[3] And he pursued his idea thus: "But I not only wish Cuba were rich, illustrious, moral and powerful, but that it were also a Cuban Cuba and not Anglo-American."[4]

Other political trends stirred the consciousness of some eminent Cubans. The changes that had taken place in Spain, and the reforms pro-

2. Hortensia Pichardo, *Documentos para la historia de Cuba*, I, 288.
3. José Antonio Saco, "Ideas sobre la incorporación de Cuba en los Estados Unidos," in *Contra la anexión*, 96.
4. Ibid., 97.

mised by General Serrano, head of the government in Madrid in his address to the Courts in 1865, encouraged the criollos in their quest for this formula to face the Cuban situation, focusing on three issues:

1. A reform of the tax and contributions system.

2. A Cuban representation to the Courts in Madrid.

3. The abolition of the slave trade.

In order to appease the Antilleans, Leopoldo O'Donnell's government presented two bills: one on the suppression of the slave trade and another on the creation of a Board for Overseas Information. Sixteen deputies from the Spanish Antilles were elected to the Board, twelve of whom were Cuban reformists, among whom outstood José Morales Lemus, Miguel Aldama, the Count of Pozos Dulces, José Manuel Mestre, José Antonio Echeverría, Manuel de Armas and José Antonio Saco.

Together with the four deputies from Puerto Rico, the Cubans waged harsh battles at the Madrid forum, but the Reform was agonizing without much ado. On April 30, 1867, on the last day of the Conference, the new Overseas Minister, Alejandro de Castro, closed the working sessions of the Board of Information and urged for a solution to the issues discussed. His inability to find it led to his resignation later on.

The failure of the Board of Information and the tightening of measures against reformist petitions implemented on the island by the Captain General Francisco Lersundi, exasperated the Cubans; and those who still waited for a last possibility of getting concessions from Spain, abandoned their ideas when faced by reality.

It can be said that both the annexationist and the reformist trends were foreign ideas that won some following in Cuba. Annexationism was nursed by the powerful and greedy northern neighbor. Reformism stemmed from Spanish ideas and their Antillean counterpart. But genuinely criollo separatism nurtured by the best South American doctrines of the advocates of the western hemisphere's indigenous peoples, and by the world's most advanced ideas on liberty, expressed itself truly in the Cubans' decision to be free or to die.

The alternative of waging a war of independence began to gain momentum. The reformist movement dissolved and many of its honest followers joined the conspiracies carried out in the Masonic lodges in the regions of Oriente and Camagüey to prepare the war for complete independence.

While Cubans were disillusioned because Spain did not carry out the reforms demanded from it, the United States was in the midst of its own struggles, among which slavery was an important issue, and as the Secession War raged on, the North American government headed by Lincoln approved the Emancipation Proclamation on January 1, 1863. The blood shed by blacks from the northern anti-slavery states contributed decisively to the outcome of the Secession War.

Lincoln lacked the time to look into the Cuban issue at that stage, but he had no cause to be upset about it either. However, the United States failed to notice that the depth of the now mature Cuban patriotic sentiments—supported by a nascent nationality—was not merely aimed at separating from Spain, but at being completely free and to master their own destiny. Thus, ninety miles away from the North American coast, a body of ideas began to gather strength, completely disregarding the island's already powerful northern neighbor.

Carlos Manuel de Céspedes, a bold and brave, intellectually mature man who was a landowner, a lawyer, a cultured, open-minded person imbued with the liberal ideas of the education he had received in France, Great Britain and Spain, launched the war of liberation together with a handful of thirty-seven men.

On October 10, 1868, the tolling of the bells of the sugar-mill "Demajagua" resounded with the songs of glory for the Cuban people and, at the same time, its echo must have reached the land of the powerful northern neighbor as a dismal omen of the end of is hidden designs on Cuba. From that moment on, they had no other choice but to take off their mask and reveal their aim of seizing the desired fruit by any possible means.

The rebel "mambí" bugle was already clearly heard across the Cuban countryside, answering the Motherland's demand: "Braves, swiftly take up arms," while in Havana, José Martí, a young man barely past puberty, feels his heart ablaze as he recites his sonnet *The 10th of October*:

> It is not a dream, it is true: a war cry
> From the enraged Cuban people,
> The people who has suffered for three centuries [...]

Lincoln's assassination one month before the end of the North American Secession War in 1865, and the involvement of Andrew Johnson, his successor, in serious conflicts with the Congress, rendered any concern about the Cuban issue untimely. General Ulysses Grant took over the Presidency in 1869, a few months after the beginning of the "mambí" war against Spain. The attitude of the United States in regard to Cuba's declaration of independence, while pharisaically seeming one of support, shows its true self in its disdain for the demands of the Cuban patriots, in the obstacles and hindrances it placed in the way of the emerging Cuban diplomacy that tried, by every possible means, to attain recognition for the belligerence of the island's rebels. It could not be lost upon the northern colossus that with the October 10 war cry, Cuba was not simply seeking to extricate itself from Spain, but was vying for a true independence that would mean the defeat of the North American Union's purpose to seize our country, availing itself of the possibility of definitively appropriating the island when conditions were ripe.

If, on the one hand, the United States did not acknowledge Cuba's belligerence, thus denying it the possibility of freely using the maritime ports to ship weapons to the patriots, on the other hand it permitted Spain to supply itself of North American weapons for its war in Cuba, and the Spanish government, headed by Prim, also received support from the government of the United States.

Carlos Manuel de Céspedes demanded from President Grant, to no avail, that the North Americans acknowledge the nature of the struggle in Cuba, but harkening the council of his advisor, Secretary of State Hamilton Fish, Grant refused to recognize the belligerence of the rebels and, furthermore, spoke against them and in favor of

Spain. In the proclamation of October 12, 1870, President Grant made public a document in which he qualified as criminal acts the efforts carried out by Cubans in North American territory to rally support for their struggle, and authorized all his military, naval and civil forces to arrest those who violated this decision.[5]

The diplomacy of the Republic-in-Arms attained some successes in Latin America during the Ten-Year War. In Mexico, President Benito Juárez ordered the admission to Mexican ports of ships under the Cuban flag, and authorized the Chamber of Deputies to acknowledge the belligerence of the Cuban Republic-in Arms. The governments of Chile, Venezuela and Bolivia also acknowledged the Cuban right of belligerence, the government of Peru did likewise and also officially recognized the Republic of Cuba and admitted its permanent diplomatic delegation. Thus, considered by Peru as an independent nation, Cuba was invited to participate in the American Congress of Jurists held in Lima, in 1877-1878; the Cuban delegate, Francisco de Paula Bravo, kept that post until the closing session of the Congress that took place after the end of the Ten-Year War.

The United States allowed Cuba to defend itself alone from Spain —then entangled in a war of attrition—as the powerful country waited for the convenient time to seize Cuba and deprive it from the victory over the Spanish yoke attained by dint of blood sweat, courage and machetes. The idea behind this sly policy explains why the North Americans did not acknowledge Cuba's belligerence. They did not want their hands tied up, not even by a mere declaration, in order to be able to carry out their plans for Cuba.

The agony of the end of the 1868 war led to the painful Zanjón Peace at the beginning of 1878. This writing shall not assess the critical situation that momentarily halted the Cuban armed struggle against Spanish colonialism.

The historic interview known as the honorable Baraguá Protest, held between the Cuban General Antonio Maceo Grajales and the Spanish General Arsenio Martínez Campos on March 15, 1878 at the Mangos de Baraguá—with negative results for the Spanish in-

5. Ramiro Guerra Sánchez, *La Guerra de los Diez Años*, 2, 59.

tentions, for Cubans wanted total independence—, ended with the renewal of the hostilities by the "mambises," although for a short time. Despite the way our glorious patricians felt, reality imposed a truce in order to better organize the struggle that must be pursued. Spanish had promised many things with the purpose of dazzling those who were responsible for watching over the country's destiny, but as expected, it did not fulfill its commitments.

Around mid-1879, the Cubans took up arms again, in what is known as the Short War, that lasted a little over a year. Its military chief, General Calixto García, fought again for Cuba's independence and also found the opposition of the government of the United States: the age-old hostility of Grant and Fish was still extant, and the ideas about purchase and annexation blossomed anew.

José Martí, banned from Cuba for the second time, stated in a speech delivered at Stack Hall, in New York, on January 24, 1880:

> The legend has not died. Indomitable and strong sons, be prepared to fearlessly repeat—and this time to put an end without a fault—the heroic feats of those brave and magnificent men who fed on roots; who seized from their enemies' belts the weapons for combat; who began a campaign that lasted ten years with three branches; who broke in the morning the horses they would into battle in the afternoon.
>
> That is a fact; despite conspiracies, fickleness and anathema; despite the treachery of a few, the fatigue of others and the persecution of our masters, war rages in Cuba [...][6]

Later on, the Cuban Apostle emphatically stated: "The southern sea will join the northern sea and a snake will be hatched from an eagle's egg before we desist from our pledge to make our Motherland free and prosperous [...]".[7]

6. José Martí, "Lectura en Steck Hall," in *Obras completas*, 4, 183.
7. Ibid., 211.

Cuban revolutionary clubs began to be organized in the United States; the spirit of independence had not even languished. A booklet published in Madrid, in 1884, by Juan Gualberto Gómez, glorifies patriotic feelings. But José Martí does not despair, and stresses that everything must be organized first and things must be done in order to avoid repeating the errors of the Ten-Year War; and he ceaselessly worked to that end.

Meanwhile, the North American media always alarmed and misinformed about the Cuban reality, supporting or rejecting annexation according to the prevailing trend among North American rulers, congressmen and businessmen.

In March, 1889, shortly after the new government headed by Republican President Benjamin Harrison had been sworn into office, certain circles in the United States commented that the government was readying to buy Cuban from Spain. On the 16th of that same month, the Philadelphia newspaper *The Manufacturer* published an article entitled "Do We Want Cuba?." On the one hand, it listed the economic advantages for North Americans if Cuba was added to the states of the Union, although the article doubted that those advantages—the fact that Cuba had the best tobacco in the world, all the sugar North America needed, tropical fruits that could not be frown in the United States and other products—would really be such, since it would also mean that the millionaire incomes that North American customs collected from those imports would cease. Besides, in order to assert their opinion that annexation would be completely disadvantageous for that enormous country that called itself a paradigm of freedom and order, the article mentioned how negative it would be for the United States to assimilate Cubans, both the white descendants from Spaniards, and the blacks, degrading our people in every sense, insulting it and slandering its values as honorable men, depicting Cubans as lazy, immoral, incapable, apathetic, unworthy of leading a government and of being on an equal footing with the illustrious sons of the North American Union.

A few days later, the New York paper *The Evening Post* not only took up the idea launched by the Philadelphia newspaper, but in its article "A Protectionist Opinion About the Annexation of Cuba," besides reproducing as valid all the offenses cast at the Cuban people by the previous article, thus echoing them, regretted that a newspaper like *The Manufacturer* had taken the lead in publishing such an article.

José Martí reacted immediately. On that same day, he wrote a long letter to the editor-in-chief of *The Evening Post*, whose unabridged version was published by the March 25 edition of the New York newspaper. Martí had entitled his letter "Vindication of Cuba." Some time later, Martí published a booklet under the title *Cuba and the United States*, printed in New York in 1889, where he included the three articles mentioned here, considering his letter as another article, for it had been published by the aforementioned newspaper.[8]

"Vindication of Cuba" is one of the most beautiful patriotic writings by the great José Martí. In it he expresses that there may be a group of Cubans who, because they abhor the despotic rule of the Spanish metropolis, consider the annexation to North America as a way out; but that the great majority of the Cuban people, a hard-working, educated and patriotic people, that knew how to behave civilly with the enemy during the war and was second to none in bravery, did not share that view. He clearly rejects all insults against our virile people, and recalls how, during the Ten-Year War, it had fought completely alone against a very powerful and ruthless enemy, armed to the teeth; he also recalls that our people requested the cooperation from the great North American nation, the land of freedom and order, but they were slighted; and he recalled, furthermore, that when the thirteen North American colonies fought for their own freedom, they had two European powers as their allies not because they were convinced about what freedom represented, but because of the enmity between their respective kings, and it remained to be seen what would have happened without the support of those allies in that emancipating war waged by North American warriors as illustrious as the Cuban patriots. Martí ends his letter by expressing: "Only with the end of life will our battle for freedom be over."[9]

Annexationism again gained momentum and had to be faced. The men of that generation of patriots prepared their spirits to liberate

8. José Martí, "Cuba y los Estados Unidos," in *Obras completas*, 1, 229 *Passim.*
9. Ibid., 241.

their beloved country from any oppressive yoke, be it Spanish or North American. In the banquet held in his honor at the Venus Hotel in Santiago de Cuba, on June 29, 1890, and after hearing the fatalist feelings expressed by one of the diners, José Joaquín Hernández, regarding Cuba's fate as another member of the North American nation, Antonio Maceo—one of those men whose thinking equaled in depth the blows dealt by his machete, convinced of the nature of the struggle the Cubans had undertaken in 1868, answered with the dignity and firmness that characterized him: "Although it seems impossible to me, I believe, young man, that that would be the only case in which I would perhaps take sides with the... Spaniards."[10]

On the other hand, Martí had renewed his endless struggle as a political organizer and so, on January 5, 1892, he founded the Cuban Revolutionary Party (CRP). It is stated in Article 1 of the Bases of the CRP that: "The Cuban Revolutionary Party is established to attain with the joint efforts of all men of good will, the absolute independence of the island of Cuba, and promote and assist that of Puerto Rico."[11]

José Martí had to travel and speak continuously in search of the unity among all officers and chiefs who had participated in the Ten-Year War, in order to impress on them the idea that success lies in unity, and not in regionalism. Martí's constant revolutionary and organizing activity, that always kept him traveling from one country to another. Wherever there were important communities of Cuban revolutionaries in exile, and organizing the "mambí" officers who had remained in Cuba was not an easy job, but never an impossible one, neither for someone who had a task as an Apostle, nor for the Cubans who welcomed him, anxious to see the independence of the island come true.

According to what was agreed, Martí authorized Juan Gualberto Gómez, who represented the Cuban Revolutionary Party in Cuba, to order the revolutionary and independentist uprising to all "mambí" chiefs committed to it on the island. The chosen date was Fe-

10. Manuel J. Granda, *La paz del manganeso* (Havana: 1939). Quoted by Raúl Roa García, *Aventuras, venturas y desventuras de un mambí*, 179.
11. Hortensia Pichardo, op. cit., I, 480.

bruary 24, 1895, and it was kept. One month later, on March 25, at the Dominican town of Montecristi, José Martí and Máximo Gómez, before returning to Cuba, signed the historic Manifesto that ratified the continuity of the struggle. Cuba had decided to be free and independent. That would be its fate.

The government of the United States knew that after a country has taken up arms to become independent from an oppressor, it would not give itself in to yet another. Years later, this certainty would make North Americans deprive Cubans of the victory and interfere in a war we had already won.

On April 11, Martí and Gómez landed at La Playita, in Cajobabo; a few days later, Maceo landed at Duaba; these two places are located in the easternmost region of the island. All military chiefs were then on the battlefield. Spain thought that General Arsenio Martínez Campos could convince the Cubans and pacify them again, and was sent to Cuba once more. On the insurgent side, the strategy for the war, that included the invasion of the western region of the island, was outlined at the meeting among Martí, Gómez and Maceo at the farm "La Mejorana."

José Martí's profound knowledge of North American ambitions in whatever guise for appropriating Cuba in order to dominate America said, on May 18, 1895 on the eve of his death on the battlefield fighting for the independence of Cuba, in an unfinished letter to his Mexican friend Manuel Mercado:

> I am now at risk of giving my life for my country and for my duty—since I understand it and have the courage to do so—of timely preventing, with the independence of Cuba, the United States from expanding across the Antilles and falling with that added might on our lands of America. All I have done until today and will continue to do, is to that end.
>
> . . . .
>
> I have lived within the monster and I know its entrails; and my sling is that of David.[12]

12. José Martí, "Carta a Manuel Mercado," in *Obras completas*, 20, 161.

Our eminent guide had probed the innards of the northern giant and was able to denounce how it looked upon and voraciously and greedily coveted the small island on the Florida Strait, as something that it had always considered its own, albeit it had no right to think about it as such. Of course, like a greedy merchant, it wanted to pay a cheap price for that gem, precious to its already imperialist interests. This history of a part of the just battle of the Cuban people, has shown the high costs of that ambition.

In his letter to Manuel Mercado, José Martí states that the North American correspondent Eugene Bryson had visited him at his camp in the Cuban countryside, and that he came to know through *The Herald's* journalist about the endeavors in the north to revive annexationism, as well as the opinion of Martínez Campos that: "without a doubt, when the time comes, Spain would much rather reach an understanding with the United States than to surrender the island to the Cubans."[13] Further on in the same letter Martí explains his anti-imperialist ideas to his friend Mercado: "The war in Cuba, a reality greater than the ambiguous and scattered wishes of Cuban and Spanish annexionists, that would only grant a relative power to their alliance with the government of Spain, has timely come to America to prevent, even against the overt use of all those forces, the annexation of Cuba to the United States."[14]

May 19, 1895 became a day of mourning for the Motherland, for Martí fell, facing the sun, at Dos Rios. His untimely death had consequences for the course of the war, but he had outlined the main political and organizational features so that the Revolution would not be lost.

Martínez Campos failed, the battle at Peralejo was the last blow, and the Spaniards appeared again to the bloodthirsty Valeriano Weyler, who was then sent to the largest of the Antilles as the colony's Captain General. His insanity caused inexpressible pain to the people of Cuba, decimating one-fourth of its population by hunger and sufferings; the mere memory of him hurts human sensitivity. In 1896,

13. Ibid., 162.
14. Ibid.

Weyler order the concentration of the island's peasants in the towns, a beastly act that could only be compared, years later, to Hitler's concentration camps.

The successive governments in the United States did not recognize Cuba's belligerence in 1895. Like Grant and Fish during the 1868 war, President Grover Cleveland refused to acknowledge it, and not precisely because he felt sympathy for Spain or due to indifference, but because he wanted to have his hands free to act in Cuba according to the old North American ambition.

Tomás Estrada Palma, responsible for the guidance of the Cuban Revolutionary Party, headquartered in the United States, encouraged intervention with his lobbying close to agents of the North American government, thus openly betraying José Martí's independentist ideas. Gómez and Maceo, the military chiefs that conducted the war on the island, were averse to it.

General Máximo Gómez, Commander-in-Chief of the Liberation Amy, wrote to Tomás Estrada Palma about this: "Much is said and written about the acknowledgement of belligerence by the North American government, and that would be quite convenient for U.S., but as we rose up in arms depending solely on our own strength and on the irrevocable decision to triumph, we will fearlessly go our own way."[15]

In his turn, and on the same subject, Antonio Maceo, Lieutenant General of the Liberation Army, refers thus to Estrada Palma; "We do not need such an intervention to attain victory sooner or later."[16]

In those days, Maceo also said to the correspondent of the *New York World*: "I would not want our neighbors to shed their blood for our freedom; we can do it by ourselves if, abiding by international law, we can rally all the elements we need to cast away from Cuba Spain's demolished power over America."[17]

After waging glorious combats on the island's eastern region, Lieutenant General Antonio Maceo fell on December 7, 1896, at Punta Brava; another irreparable loss, as was Martí's death, that also had major consequences on the outcome of the war.

15. Emilio Roig de Leuchsenring, *Ideario cubano: Máximo Gómez*, 51.
16. Leonardo Griñán Peralta, *Maceo*, 194.
17. Ibid., 195.

Autonomism, as the aspiration of some moderate strata of the Cuban population that did not want to face an open war against Spain or that did not have faith in the success of the independentist armed struggle, appeared in Cuba as an alternative, but was always firmly rejected by Martí, Gómez and other revolutionaries, because it was a false way out and also because it delayed the apogee of independence.

In his article "The Autonomist Agitation," published in *Patria* on March 19, 1892, José Martí said: "The continuation of the revolution cannot be the continuation of the methods and the spirit of autonomy, because autonomy was not born in Cuba as the daughter of the revolution, but as its opponent."[18]

On March 4, 1897, the republican William McKinley replaced the democrat Cleveland in the presidency of the United States; in his electoral campaign he had included the issue of Cuba, of restoring peace and giving the island its independence.

McKinley certainly came to bear on Spain to remove the bloodthirsty Weyler from the government of Cuba and to establish autonomism.

The international scandal around the cruel concentration ordered by Weyler, compelled the Regent Queen to sign, on November 24, 1897, the Decree by which an autonomous regime was established in Cuba. Previously, on October 31, 1897, Madrid had replaced Weyler by General Ramón Blanco.

It was shameful to establish autonomism in a country that had boldly risen up in arms and made the best Spanish generals bite the dust of defeat. Not even Weyler, with his plan to annihilate the peasants, had been able to defeat the independentist revolution. With autonomism, the key posts in Cuba's government went to those Cubans who, for lack of political far-sightedness, or in bad faith, played the game of both Spain—that finally managed to hold on to Cuba—and the United States, that did not want Cuba to be independent, waiting for the time when it would fall in its hands.

Máximo Gómez and all the Cuban patriots and revolutionaries opposed the autonomism decreed by Spain and the "mambises" pur-

18. José Martí, "La agitación autonomista," in *Obras completas*, 1, 332.

sued military actions, even though the new political situation was apparently "a change" that, in truth, was nothing but "the same dog with a different collar." That is why honorable Cubans continued to fight for total independence. The opposition of the Commander-in-Chief of the Liberation Army to the autonomism that Spain had decreed for Cuba was conclusive. It was so proclaimed in a Manifesto dated December 18, 1897, addressed to the "mambí" troops: "The independence of the country: Cuba for the Cubans. America for the Americans."[19]

This same expression was used by Máximo Gómez when answering the questions posed by the editor-in-chief of the *New York Herald* about the autonomist project for Cuba.

The Institutionalization of the Cuban Republic-in-Arms in the 1895 War

Like in the 1868 war, the Cuban Republic-in-Arms that stemmed from the 1895 war was organically structured, from a civilian viewpoint, by the fundamental laws that would rule it. The first was the Jimaguayú Constitution, named thus after the place in Camagüey where it was signed.

Also all along the process of the Republic-in-Arms, Cuba had acquired the juridical organization that, based on the Constitution, ruled penal procedures during the war. As an organized belligerent state, the Cuban Republic-in-Arms maintained links with foreign countries despite the efforts made to hinder them both by the United States and by Spain.

> The diplomacy developed by Martí and the chiefs of the 1895 Revolution was aimed, like in 1868, to attain recognition to Cuban belligerence from Latin American countries; but the results were quite different from the ones attained during the Ten-Year War. This time around, Spain used a different tactic.

19. Hortensia Pichardo, op. cit., 1, 293.

> Instead of resorting to threats and aggressions, it devoted itself to flattering Latin American governments. It was supported in this endeavor by the ruling oligarchies, under the influence of the rich Spanish merchants who had settled in their respective countries. The efforts made by the "mambí" diplomats were of little avail. Whereas the peoples showed their passionate sympathy for the Cuban cause, their rulers remained indifferent to the idea of cooperating with the new struggle undertaken by the Cuban patriots.
>
> The Republic in Arms bestowed diplomacy all the attention it deserved, and adequately organized its foreign service. Special representatives were appointed as well as general agents or *chargés d´affaires* in Washington, France, Great Britain, Chile, Peru, Bolivia, Colombia, Guatemala, Nicaragua, Honduras, Brazil, Uruguay, Argentina, Venezuela, Mexico, Costa Rica, El Salvador, Santo Domingo and Haiti.[20]

Article 24 of the Jimaguayú Constitution stated that the Charter would be in force for only two years. Thereafter, a new Constituent Assembly would be convened to approve another Constitution: the Constitution of La Yaya.

Thc last Constitution of the Cuban Republic-in-Arms, adopted on October 29, 1897 in La Yaya—where the government was then headquartered—in Camagüey, envisaged the end of the war and decreed the constitutional proceedings for the transit towards a Provisional Government until an definitive Constituent Assembly gathered. Let U.S. examine its articles 40 and 41:

> Article 40: If the government, according to clause 15 of the same Article 22, were to sign peace with Spain, it will summon an Assembly that would ratify the treaty. Such an Assembly will act *ad interim* on behalf of the regime and the govern-

20. Tomás Almodóvar Salas, *Apuntes del derecho diplomático y consular: Conferen ias de clases para el Instituto del Servicio Exterior,* 16-17.

> ment of the Republic until the definitive Constituent Assembly meets.
>
> Article 41: If Spain, without previous agreement with the Council of Government, were to evacuate the whole territory, an Assembly with the same faculties detailed in the second paragraph of the article above* will be summoned.
>
> This will be the case when the Cuban armies have permanently occupied all the territory of the Island, although the enemy still holds some fortresses.[21]

The aforementioned Article 22 referred to the attributions of the Council of Government and clause 15 granted that executive body the faculty of signing treaties with other powers and appointing commissioners to negotiate them. But the Council of Government retained its capacity to ratify treaties. The peace treaty with Spain, to be negotiated by the commissioners appointed to that effect by the Council of Government, should be ratified by the Assembly. But their negotiations could not even be initiated unless they were based on the absolute and immediate independence of Cuba as a whole.

Notwithstanding that Jose Martí had foreseen it long before, and had organized the 1895 war—assuming Cuba would be independent after a short struggle against Spain—to prevent the United States from getting hold of Cuba through peaceful and diplomatic means, which had not been foreseen even by Cuban supreme resolutions, it was like acting on the assumption that the North Americans would interfere in the Cuban struggle for its independence in order to get hold of it, least of all by blowing up the "Maine."

I will refer further on to the path the Government of the Cuban Republic was forced to take in the light of such events.

* "Second paragraph" meaning "second part, second sentence."

21. Hortensia Pichardo, op. cit., I, 506.

U.S. Interference to Prevent Cuba's Independence

The sensationalist media, the reports from U.S. consuls in Cuba and U.S. espionage, paved the way for the next chapter in their efforts to hinder Cuban independence: the incident of the warship "Maine."

U.S. consuls in Cuba played a significant role in U.S. decision-making concerning the emancipation struggle of the Cuban people against Spain hindering the attainment of full independence. Consul Williams advocated for annexation and Consul Lee, for intervention.

Spanish espionage against Cuban war operations had dramatic consequences. In 1897, 71 expeditions to Cuba were organized from the U.S., 37 of them were discovered by U.S. agents and only five by the Spaniards. These figures give an idea of the performance of espionage activities against the Cubans. Substitute consul Lee, worried about Cuban victories, Weyler´s failure and the shift in Spanish policy due to U.S. stand, persuaded his government about the preparedness of Spain for its war against the U.S.

Facing these circumstances, the Regent Queen of Spain, María Cristina of Hapsburg-Lorraine, asked the support of European powers in the light of the already evident direct confrontation with the U.S.

Consul Lee requested Washington U.S. warship fleets to be stationed in Key West, to protect the lives of U.S. citizens in Cuba. The "Maine" was among those ships. The "Maine" left U.S. shores December 23, 1897, and arrived at Havana's port on January 25, 1898. Its aim was clearly to threaten; in fact, its presence in Havana Bay caused extreme concern in Spain.

At 10:00 p.m., on February 15, 1898, the "Maine" blew up for allegedly unknown reasons, but the U.S. slanderously accused Spain. The toll was over 260 dead U.S. sailors, while Captain Sigsbee and many officers saved their lives because they "happened" to be ashore.

Then hysteria went rampant in the United States: "Remember the 'Maine'!" the U.S. media clamored, impelled by the obscure interests that sought to get hold of Cuba at any cost, even by declaring war to Spain.

In Spain, official statements and the media encouraged the euphoria of a victory against the United States. I recently read a chronicle in the Madrid-based journal *El Mundo*, dated February 16, 1998, entitled "February 16, 1898, the Year Spain Lost its Empire." The chronicle to an article published at that time in the daily *Poniente Solar*, which includes a fictitious talk between two people from Madrid. One of them says: "I was thinking about the Maine's explosion. We will pay for that... You'll see." The other replied: "But, are you among those who believe in a war with the United States? As soon as the government takes this seriously and sends a note, the pork dealers will come to reason... Spain is always Spain, and if they bite off more than they can chew, just by bombing their ports we reach the other shore..."[22]

The 20th century chronicle concluded: "The whole nation rested assure that a clash between U.S. and the North Americans would be an unquestionable victory."[23]

The Joint Resolution

John Quincy Adams, with his phrase about the "ripe fruit," considered that a break between Cuba and Spain would mean, by law of political gravity, Cuba's entrance into the North American Union.[24] And not only Cuba but also the Antilles, according to his idea about the "manifest destiny," could be an appendix of North America.[25]

On the other hand, the North Americans were not passively waiting for the fruits to fall into their clutches. To accelerate the ripening process they had their "gunboats" as the pretext of a continental defense against Europe.

22. Javier Figueroa and Carlos García Santa Cecilia, "16 de febrero de 1898, el año en que España perdió su Imperio," in *El Mundo*, 39.
23. Ibid.
24. "A fruit taken from its tree by the force of the wind, cannot, even if it wants it, avoid falling to the floor, thus Cuba, once separated from Spain (...) must inevitably gravitate toward the North American Union, and exclusively toward it..." John Quincy Adams, "Carta al Embajador de los Estados Unidos en España, de 28 de abril de 1823," in "Doctrina Monroe," in "Parte III. Glosario," in *Prontuario diplomático*, 271.
25. John Quincy Adams, op. cit., 270.

The so-called "doctrine of the ripe fruit," expounded in 1823, still ruled the North's appetite regarding Cuba. The point was to wait for a rupture of its bonds with Spain in order for it to begin gravitating toward the U.S. orbit.

However, the Cuban independence struggles as of 1868, and later with the outbreak of the 1895 war lead by Martí, Gómez and Maceo, dealt a harsh blow to the United States. Thus, they cunningly waited to steal our victory and interfered in a war the Cubans had already won.

The moment was chosen, and with the pretext of the explosion of the "Maine," the U.S. Congress passed the Joint Resolution on April 19, 1898, declaring that the Cuban people is and should be free and independent by law, and that the United States neither wished nor intended to exert its sovereignty, jurisdiction or domination over the Island. They only aimed at its pacification, and once it was attained, they would leave the government and rule of the island to its people.

The other not precisely humanitarian aims that lead the U.S. rulers and congressmen to support the Joint Resolution are not well known. True, a trend in U.S. public opinion favored Cuban independence, but it is also true that the Joint Resolution is an heir of the "ripe fruit" policy.

Neither selflessness nor sympathy, as U.S. governments have always boasted, were the real motives behind the Joint Resolution, for this declaration, furthermore, had to be paid for. Let U.S. review the case:[26]

One of the darkest episodes in U.S.-Cuba relations was the shameful deal that involved the plenipotentiary delegate of the Republic-in-Arms, Tomás Estrada Palma, and a group of lobbyists headed by the New York financial lawyer John McCook, a close friend of President McKinley, and Samuel M. Janney, representative of the Christy V. Janney bank of Wall Street. Estrada Palma, claiming the representation of the Cuban Republic-in-Arms, signed an agreement on August 5, 1896 according to which Janney would "implement a plan to buy the island of Cuba from Spain,"[27] committing himself to

26. See "Joint Resolution," in "Parte III. Glosario," in *Prontuario diplomático,* 317; and Emilio Roig de Leuchsenring, *Cuba no debe su independencia a los Estados Unidos,* 140-151.
27. Emilio Roig de Leuchsenring, Ibid., 142.

ask to and obtain from the U.S. government its compliance to act as a trustee, that is to say, as a guarantor in those operations. When McKinley's government agreed to act as such, Estrada Palma would pledge, in its turn, to hand "a certificate of 150 million pesos, in bonds, with a four percent annual interest rate, as a down payment abiding by the terms and conditions of that contract."[28] Those interests were to be paid weekly and the arrears in fifty years, and that amount was bound to compensate Spain for the loss of its sovereignty over the island, to pay the expenses derived from the execution of the covenant "and to compensate Mr. Janney and his associates' work."[29]

The negotiation failed, but the old partners insisted with another covenant signed by Estrada Palma and Janney on November 18, 1897, ensuring "the sum of 37 and a half million pesos in bonds, if the independence and evacuation of the island by the Spanish forces is achieved, and the sovereignty of the United States over the Republic of Cuba is recognized..."[30] But when on May 2, 1898 the last postponement granted to Janney by the Council of Government of the Revolution expired, he was notified that the aim of such a contract had in fact been revoked.

Nevertheless, Mr. Cook and Mr. Janney insisted that "the aim of the November 18, 1897 contract had been fulfilled since the Cuban people's independence had been recognized. Consequently, they deserved the retribution accorded by the contract."[31] But that demand was rejected by Estrada Palma who confronted the opposition of the lobbyists. Afterwards, the Delegate submitted the case to the Cuban Council of Government and recommended that those North American bargainers were taken into account because he claimed that, in effect, the Joint Resolution had proclaimed "that Cuba was *de facto* and *de jure* independent."[32]

28. Ibid., 143
29. Ibid.
30. Ibid., 145.
31. Ibid., 146.
32. Ibid., 147.

Thus, a few days later Estrada Palma obtained the accord of the council to confer Janney and his associates the amount of two million dollars in bonds from the Republic of Cuba as a compensation for their services. When the Republic was established in 1902 the holders of those bonds requested Estrada Palma to collect them. The payment took place immediately, in successive secret sessions by the Senate and the House of Representatives; the last one took place on January 11, 1912.

The Joint Resolution is not accountable for the sympathy or the lack of interest for the cause of Cuban independence. With its proclamation U.S. imperialism launched its hypocritical expansion policy, that consolidated its colonial empire worldwide and its economic dominion over Latin America.

Following the explosion of the "Maine," the U.S. Senate debated how to face the situation in Cuba around four standpoints:

1. The declaration of war against Spain.

2. The recognition of Cuban independence.

3. The expulsion from Cuba of the Spanish colonial rule

Empowering the president to pacify the island by expelling the Spaniards and guaranteeing the independence of Cuba.

Another typical factor of the conflict's final stage was the European powers' reluctance to support Spain. The German Empire, not wanting to jeopardize its flourishing commerce with the United States, declined the Spanish demand to head a European action against the United States in February, 1898. The French sympathized with Spain, and French capital had financed the struggle against the Cubans, but France was in favor of selling Cuba to the United States, thus allowing its debtor to honor its debt.

The Austro-Hungarian Empire, though with an anti-U.S. stand, did not agree with the Spanish proposal, conveying the idea that Spain resort to the Vatican. Spain did not receive the support of Russia or Great Britain. The former did not want to become an enemy of the

United States, and the latter had already outlined its collaboration with the United States.

Although the Vatican diplomacy was willing to mediate, it demanded as a prerequisite that Spain should give Cuba up. But Spain did not accept and the United States was not interested in such an undertaking. Despite the interest of the European powers mentioned above, they made a last joint attempt, and the Pope sent a plenipotentiary envoy to Washington, but to no avail.

On April 5 and 6, 1898, the European powers in Washington, at the initiative of the Austro-Hungarian Empire, forwarded a collective note to the U.S. government. They stated their trust in an agreement between Spain and the United States on the grounds of the "humanitarian feelings and moderation of the President and the American nation."[33] McKinley's ironical response was to hit back, claiming that such powers would praise their "selfless" efforts to put an end to the "unbearable" situation in Cuba.[34]

On April 6, 1898, although the Joint Resolution had not yet been approved, the U.S. naval fleet headed by Admiral Sampson, was ordered to blockade Cuba. On April 22 it showed up on our shores.

On April 10, the Spanish Regent Queen informed the U.S. government that she was about to announce an armistice, responding to previous U.S. demands. But it was too late, Spanish hesitation had allowed the United States to hone its intervention and occupation project because they did not really desire peace and independence for the neighbor they had coveted for so long.

On April 13, 1898, the U.S. House of Representatives adopted with little debate, and a vote of 342 against 19, a Resolution that empowered the President to intervene in Cuba and install an independent, stable government elected by the Cubans. The Senate, in its turn, wanted to include in the document that the Cubans should be and were by law, free and independent. The text passed by the House and the Senate had to be endorsed by a bicameral committee and, finally, after reaching a compromise, it was approved on April

33. V.P. Potemkin, *et al.*, *Historia de la diplomacia*, II, 300.
34. Ibid.

19, 1898: in the House, by 311 votes against 6; and in the Senate, by 43 votes against 35. The next day, McKinley signed the Joint Resolution of the House and the Senate: the war against Spain was a fact. (See Annex 1)

Senator Orville Platt was a character who later became "crucial" in the history of the humiliating relations imposed by the United States on Cuba. He opposed the senate formula that was more favorable for Cuba. Platt labeled the Joint Resolution as "silly," but he was finally defeated. However, a few years later he would override that defeat when he managed to impose the U.S. legislative amendment named after him.

On April 14, the U.S. consul in Havana, Mr. Lee, left the island together with the U.S. citizens living in Cuba. It was the prelude to the war.

In order to gain time until its war preparations were completed, avoiding any concrete reply to Spain's last proposal of good faith to save the critical situation, McKinley replied that the issue would be forwarded to Congress for examination. He did so, but not in order to move toward a peace negotiation but to demand that he be granted powers that allowed him to adopt measures to use the armed forces.

The degree of warmongering euphoria in Congress led them to consider the Spanish message as an unimportant and untimely gesture. *Alea jacta est*: on April 20, 1898 the Joint Resolution was proclaimed. At the same time, McKinley sent an open message to Spain, saying that if by noon, April 23, he had not received a satisfactory response to every proviso of the Joint Resolution, he would resort to the armed forces. Faced by such an insolent, overt ultimatum, the Spanish government broke diplomatic relations with the United States on April 23, because the Joint Resolution was in fact a declaration of war.

The Government of the Cuban Republic-in-Arms learned about the U.S. declaration of war to Spain on April 24, and not knowing any more details, for everything had been concocted behind its back, and considering that the Joint Resolution clearly expressed the thinking of the U.S. rulers, on May 10 the Cuban government instructed General-in-Chief Máximo Gómez and Lieutenant General

Calixto García to place themselves under the command of the U.S. military chiefs.

However, the Spanish government had previously published on April 12, 1898, in *Gaceta de La Habana* the halt to hostilities against the Cubans and, by various means, urged them to join Spain to fight the North Americans. This was rejected by the Council of Government of the Republic-in-Arms, because Spain had not granted Cuba its independence, which the Cubans had already conquered.

The military chief of the U.S. invasion was General William R. Shafter, who clearly lacked military skills to lead a campaign of such proportions. So much so that neither the landing in Daiquirí nor the victories in Loma de San Juan and El Caney in the outskirts of Santiago de Cuba would have been possible without the support of the Cuban troops headed by a seasoned general like Calixto García.

The U.S. "humanitarian" mission—albeit humanitarian only in name—, clearly responded to U.S. leaders' thinking concerning Cuba, evinced in a letter addressed y J.C. Brenckenridge to General M.A. Miles, dated October 24, 1897. Some of its paragraphs are abject and degrade its author: "The allied army will be constantly used in exploration and avant-garde actions, so they shall inescapably endure the burden of the war caught between two fires, and they will be assigned precisely all the most dangerous and desperate undertakings..."[35]

Mr. Brenckenridge's letter concretely summarized U.S. policy towards Cuba: "Our policy should always focus on supporting the weakest against the stronger, until the complete annihilation of both in order to achieve the annexation of the Pearl of the Antilles."[36]

Calixto García backed the landing of U.S. troops and fought with them until the Spanish army capitulated, but General Shafter, following the instructions of the aforementioned letter, prevented Calixto García and his troops from entering the city of Santiago de Cuba, that had surrendered to the U.S. army shortly after the Spanish fleet commanded by Admiral Cervera sank.

The Admiral of the Spanish fleet Don Pascual Cervera was the only one to appraise the seriousness of the events and the vulnerabi-

35. Hortensia Pichardo, op. cit., I, 513.
36. Ibid., 514.

lity of Madrid's fleet, when the High Command of the Spanish Navy sent him and his men to the slaughterhouse that was the naval battle of Santiago de Cuba.

The Spanish Admiral had received such irrational instructions from the high command of the Spanish *Armada*, that one can only think the main chiefs in Madrid contrived this absolutely quixotic episode to confront the power that the United States already represented, to seal with an arrogant gesture their defeat at the hands of the Cuban forces, disregarding the painful death toll of Spanish sailors.

General Calixto García, in a letter dated July 17, 1898, replied with a legitimate feeling of patriotic indignation to the ignoble attitude of United States military command that forbade the entry of Cuban troops into Santiago de Cuba. I quote several paragraphs from that letter, which I hope some day will be engraved in bronze at the Loma de San Juan, as an everlasting tribute to Cuban dignity and U.S. ignominy:

> Following the plans and obeying the instructions of the chiefs, I have done my best to fulfill my government's wishes having been to date one of your most loyal subordinates, and having the honor of carrying out your orders and instructions to the best of my abilities [...]
>
> General, there is a rumor so absurd that it deserves no credit; that the order of preventing my army's entry into Santiago de Cuba was due to the fear of revenge and reprisals against the Spaniards. Allow me to protest against the slightest trace of such a thought. We are not savage people who ignores the principles of a civilized war. We are a poor and ragged army, so poor and ragged as the army of your ancestors during the noble war for the independence of the United States. But, like the heroes of Saratoga and Yorktown, we respect our cause too much so as to desecrate it with barbarism and cowardice.[37]

37. Ibid., 516-517.

On the other hand, an even greater infamy circulated together with all the outrageous dirty work against the Cuban troops carried out by U.S. officers in the battlefield: the U.S. media and the reports of their troops stationed in Havana attempted to depict "mambí" soldiers as apathetic for the struggle, although the Cubans' courage and bravery in combat was more than proven. According to data of that time, the Cubans had suffered more than 10,000 fatalities in battle from February 1895 until August 1898. This also evinces the response of the Spanish army in combat.

On July 16, 1898, at the Loma de San Juan, the capitulation of the Spanish colonial rule over Santiago de Cuba was signed. On the following day, U.S. troops headed by General Shafter and Admiral Sampson entered the second most important city on the island. General McGibbons, appointed Military Governor, was replaced on July 18 by Leonard Wood, who behaved as if Santiago de Cuba were an independent republic. That behavior concurred with his idea that the capitulation of the city meant that it belonged to the United States, and he took the measures required to that end. Consequently, he imposed upon the vanquished city the Provisional Constitution of October 20, 1898.

The autonomy vested by Spain upon Puerto Rico was not among U.S. plans, that is why a few days after the "Maine's" explosion, the U.S. fleet bombed San Juan, the Puerto Rican capital. And on July, 1898, U.S. General Nelson A. Miles occupied the island. Thus, this maneuver allowed Puerto Rico to be considered as war booty by the Treaty of Paris.

Philippine nationalist chiefs had declared the independence of the Archipelago on June 12, 1898, but it was not included in U.S. plans either. The North Americans hastened their attack against the Spanish fleet in Cavite; shortly after, the Spaniards capitulated and the Philippines also became a part of the war booty, although it was denied its independence because allegedly its people was not mature to govern itself consequently and needed U.S. tutelage. The Treaty of Paris endorsed the U.S. tutelage for that nation also.

Following the capitulation of Santiago de Cuba, Madrid proposed to Washington that it cease hostilities. On August 12, 1898, the preliminary protocol for peace negotiations to be held in Paris between the United States and Spain was signed in the U.S. capital. The ambassadors present were Jules Cambon, French ambassador to Washington, appointed by the Regent Queen, and William R. Day, Secretary of State, appointed in its turn by President McKinley.

In this case, the signing of the preliminary protocol to put an end to U.S.-Spanish hostilities on August 12, 1898, and the subsequent endorsement of a Peace Treaty, as in the cases of the Joint Resolution and the Declaration of War against Spain, the Cubans were not invited as they should have been. Nevertheless, the Council of Government of the Cuban Republic-in-Arms acquiesced to the suspension of hostilities on Cuban soil during the session held on August 25, 1898.

Emilio Roig de Leuchsenring, in his work *Historia de la Enmienda Platt* (*History of the Platt Amendment*) quoted a telegram dated October 6, 1898 sent by the Spanish Minister of State, Duke of Almodóvar del Río, to the president of the Spanish Senate and also the Chairman of the Spanish Peace Commission in Paris, Eugenio Montero Ríos. It read:

> Since the message to the President of the Republic opening peace negotiations, the Spanish government has sought to agree with that of the United States a definitive political status for the Republic of Cuba. During the negotiations an identical aim has been upheld. It has even been suggested that the interests of loyal Spaniards and islanders would be best served if the American Republic were annexed to the Island (...) Whether through annexation or with a protectorate status, it is essential that the United States accept to relinquish sovereignty on their behalf, clearly and expressly determining in the treaty the mutual rights and obligations arising from Spain's refusal to its sovereignty and other rights.[38]

38. Documents presented to the Court in the 1898 Legislature by the Minister of State (Duke of Almodóvar del Río), Madrid, 1899, Document number 20, p. 26. Quoted by Emilio Roig de Leuchsenring, *Historia de la Enmienda Platt*, 60.

Towards the end of its rule in Cuba and disregarding the traditional magnanimity of the Spanish people, the ruling elite of the decaying kingdom rejected and opposed Cuba's independence.

The Spanish persistent refusal to accept its defeat by the "mambí" Army and the intervention forces' promise of future large profits, led Spain to an ominous abdication of the island to the United States and the North Americans, sheltered by the "grape leaf" of "occupation" to evade the Joint Resolution, would actually accept the transference of the dominion and property of the island, acting with the conceit and arrogance typical of the owners and masters.

The Spanish troops began to concentrate in the villages and fortresses, except for the already occupied Santiago de Cuba, allowing the evacuation of the island. The road was paved for the Treaty of Paris. The Council of Government of the Assembly of the Cuban Republic-in-Arms learned, on October 23, 1898, that Tomás Estrada Palma had accepted an armistice without previous consultation with the Cuban government: Estrada Palma was once more ignoring the Cubans.

THE CONSPIRACY AGAINST CUBAN INDEPENDENCE

The Treaty of Paris

The first session of the Paris conference, summoned to negotiate a peace treaty, was held on October 1st, 1898. Spain arrived utterly defeated at the negotiation table with the United States. Nonetheless, Spain demanded the return of the Philippines facing a blatant U.S. denial. Then, apparently, Spain became interested about Cuban independence; however Spain truly intended to make Cuba pay the debts acquired by a squandering administration that had burdened the Cuban public treasury with all the expenses of its colonial adventure. In 1898, the amount of that debt was estimated at 500 million dollars owed by Spain to various countries and banks.

The Spanish rulers' idea was to transfer the debt to Cuba via the United States. That would have meant an unbearable indebtedness for the newly born republic. Likewise, the United States, showing its disregard for Cuban independence, sought to charge the debt to Spain, in order to demand its payment and satisfy its imperial aspirations.

Spain also wanted a statement establishing its innocence in regard to the explosion of the "Maine." It also sought privileges for the Catholic Church in the Spanish colonies, now under U.S. rule.

Finally, as it had been already stated by some Spanish chiefs in several occasions, the stately Spain of the Bourbons of the late 19th century, powerless vis-à-vis its imminent defeat at Cuban hands, laid down its arms to the United States, preferring to hand the island over to the North Americans rather than to the Cuban Liberation Army. Moreover, ignoring the Cubans *de facto* and *de jure*, the United States signed the peace with Spain, thus consecrating its war booty. The Peace Treaty between the two countries was signed in Paris on December 10, 1898. It is usually known as the Treaty of Paris. (See Annex 2)

Among the provisos of the Treaty of Paris, there are two particularly significant articles, closely related to Cuba: articles numbers 1 and 16, which I will comment below:

Article 1 stipulates that Spain would renounce all rights of sovereignty and property over Cuba. It also reads that, once evacuated by Spain, the United States would occupy the island, while such an occupation lasted, the latter would assume and fulfill the obligations for the protection of lives and property enforced by International Law.

Article 16 of the same treaty specifies that any obligation acknowledged by the United States regarding Cuba in the Treaty was thereby confined to the period of occupation of the island. But once completed, the United States would advise the government established in Cuba to accept those same liabilities.

Through the Treaty of Paris, the United States inherited an empire, and the war with Cuba only implied around 200 million dollars in expenses and a few hundred fatalities during the war plus 5000 men killed by the diseases that plagued the unsanitary encampments.

As a result of the Peace Treaty between Spain and the United States, the latter's empire was founded at the expense of the former. The new American colonial power swallowed Puerto Rico and some small neighboring islands, like Guam and the Philippines. Regarding Cuba, the Platt Amendment, the naval bases, the right to intervene, the permanent political and economic burden would stem from temporary occupation rights; that is to say, a curtailed sovereignty, an occupied territory and an indebted Motherland.

The 1898 Treaty of Paris that deprived Cuba of its independence, encroached U.S. hegemony in the Caribbean and Central America. It also gave the U.S. command over the area where the Inter-Oceanic Panama Canal would be built, enabling the U.S. to open its doors to China and to Asia at large.

Since then, Cuba and Panama became a part of the U.S. expansionist policy. The Panama Canal and the Guantánamo U.S. Naval Base are lacerating expressions of that imperialist stroke.

The pact between the United States and Spain that put an end to the 1895 war, begun and won by the Cubans, was the defeated Spain's reward for the U.S. government, that reaped not only its occupation rights over the island but also compensations and the spoils of war mentioned above.

The Treaty of Paris recognized neither Cuban independence nor the Cuban struggle to accomplish it. It was as if 30 years of struggle were wiped out from history. But the peoples have very good memory. This affront cannot be forgotten.

The Sad End of the Republic-in-Arms

As has already been said, the U.S. declaration of war against Spain took place behind the Cubans' backs, a deceit supposedly mitigated by the interventionist power's unfulfilled promise of the "humanitarian aims" of the Joint Resolution.

The United States struck a deal with Spain. Cuba was ignored and did not take part in the Treaty of Paris. The Cuban Government Council, presided over by Bartolomé Masó, was not recognized by the North American occupation, that is why the Assembly had to head the government. The Assembly—also chaired by Bartolomé Masó—would deal with everything related to the mandate conferred by Articles 40 and 41 of the aforementioned La Yaya Constitution. It met at Santa Cruz del Sur—hence it is known as the Santa Cruz Assembly—, and succeeded in perceiving the U.S. treachery.

The alleged "humanitarian aims" of the Joint Resolution appeased numerous Cubans, even some of the most illustrious. This is shown by the naïve thinking of Bartolomé Masó, the president of the Santa Cruz Assembly, in his message dated October 24, 1898, from which I quote the following excerpt:

> The concrete and expected agreement with the U.S. government could not be reached, but the solemn statements of the U.S. Congress about the fact that the Cuban people is and should be free and independent by law; that Spain should renounce its sovereignty over the island; that U.S. maritime and terrestrial operations are aimed at expelling the Spanish troops from Cuban soil and waters; that the U.S. government will not exert its sovereignty, rule or administration over Cuba, restraining its actions to the pacification of the island in order to subsequently hand over to the Cuban people the free management of its affairs, obviously unveiled the end* of armed intervention and naturally pointed out the only course the Cubans should take in the battle waged between the United States and Spain on our behalf.[39]

The time when the United States wanted to seize Cuba to turn it into its colony had been left behind. The emerging strategy was based on the thesis of the protectorate and the neo-colony, more subtle and subduing domination mechanisms to allowed it to exercise its incipient imperial policy.

At the time, Cuba's situation, placed between two armies—one of them defeated and the other, a self-declared winner—, was some-

* "End" meaning "aim."

39. Hortensia Pichardo, op. cit., 1, 529.

how relieved when finally, on January 1st, 1899, the Spanish colonial government withdrew and the last Captain General, Adolfo Jiménez Castellano, handed over power to the North American Military Governor, General John R. Brooke. Spain left behind a devastated country, entire families killed and others brutally mistreated. A new struggle against a new enemy—U.S. military occupation—began for the Cuban people, from which it would emerge victorious.

La Yaya Constitution had established the procedure for the organization of the country once the war was over—the aforementioned Articles 40 and 41. That Constitution was still in force; so much so that, in keeping with Article 48, only a new constitution could repeal it.

Thus, completely ignored by U.S. occupation forces, the Santa Cruz Assembly first met in the province of Camagüey province, subsequently moved to Marianao, a town near Havana, and later to Calzada del Cerro, in a neighborhood in Havana proper. Since then, it came to be known as the "Asamblea del Cerro." On April 4, 1899 it closed down due to illogical divisions that mislead the Cuban assembly members.

The U.S. Intervener Government

The North American military intervention government created a cabinet made up by Cubans but made room in it mainly for several spokesmen of autonomism. This was another blow below the belt against the independentists who had waged three wars to finally corner the troops of the proud Spain in the large Cuban towns, the only places on the island where they were safe; a blow below the belt against those who had defeated Spain. But it was not the worst blow, for North Americans were readying for an even dirtier blow: to create a protectorate, a neo-colony in Cuba, and to thus deprive it from the independence they were obliged to grant it by the Joint Resolution and the Treaty of Paris, birthing an operetta republic that would gladly submit to U.S. rulings.

Order 301 issued on July 25, 1900 by J.B. Hickey, Chief of Staff at the General Headquarters of the U.S. Occupation Forces in Cuba, ignored the Constitution of La Yaya and in practice repealed it, albeit he was not mandated to do that. Likewise, he rejected the Joint Resolution that stated:

> That the people of the island of Cuba are, and of right ought to be, free and independent.;
>
> That the United States dismiss every desire and intention to exercise sovereignty, jurisdiction or domination over the Island, unless it is aimed at pacifying it, and declare they are determined, when such pacification is carried out, to leave the government of and dominion over the Island to its people.
>
> Since the people of the Island of Cuba has established municipal governments that derive their authority from the popular vote, granted under just and egalitarian laws, it is ready to establish a general government that will have sovereignty, jurisdiction and domination over the Island.
>
> Therefore, it is ordered that a general election be held on the Island of Cuba on the third Saturday of September, 1900, to elect delegates to the Convention that will convene in the city of Havana, at 12 noon on the first Monday of November, 1900, to draft and adopt a Constitution for the people of Cuba and, as a part of it, to reach an agreement with the Government of the United States about the relations that will exist between that Government and the Cuban Government, and to provide, by means of popular elections, the officials that such Constitution establishes, and the transfer of the Government to the officials elected...[40]

It is also interesting to call the attention on some paragraphs of the speech delivered by the then U.S. military governor Leonard Wood at the opening of the first session of the Constituent Assembly—made up of 31 delegates from the six Cuban provinces—, on November 5, 1900.

40. Emilio Roig de Leuchsenring, *Historia de la Enmienda Platt*, 381.

The contents of this speech became Military Order No. 455:

> It will be your duty, first, to frame and adopt a constitution for Cuba, and, when that has been done, to formulate what, in your opinion, ought to be the relations between Cuba and the United States.
>
> . . . .
>
> When you have formulated the relations which, in your opinion, ought to exist between Cuba and the United States, the Government of the United States will doubtless take such action on its part as shall lead to a final and authoritative agreement between the people of the two countries to the promotion of their common interests.
>
> . . . .
>
> Under the order pursuant to which you have been elected and convened you have no duty and no authority to take part in the present government of the island. Your powers are strictly limited by the terms of that order.[41]

It must be emphasized that U.S. military intervention granted a mandate to the delegates to the Constituent Assembly to design a relationship completely alien to what they were directly going to do, over which the members of the assembly had no authority. In fact, the Government of the United States was already hatching what would be later known as the "Platt Amendment," irrespective of the text the Constituent Assembly adopted to regulate the relations between the two countries. It seems that paragraph in General Wood's speech was only aimed at entertaining the Convention, but was not to be taken seriously. The following days and the debates by the Cuban delegates who tried to prevent the imposition of the plattist yoke, show the mandate lacked seriousness for the good faith of the one who ordered it was burdened by its ignoble origin.

Thus, the U.S. Secretary of War, Elihu Root, sent General Wood the Report dated February 9, 1901, where he included five points

41. Ibid., 383.

that summarized the conditions of the U.S. Executive regarding the guidelines to be included in the Cuban Constitution as the regulations to be borne in mind regarding the relations of the future Cuban state with the United States. Wood secretly summoned the members of the assembly and made the document known to them.

But the Cuban members of the assembly did not readily cast aside their efforts to establish a free and sovereign Republic and, therefore, drafted and approved "their" own five points about the future relations between Cuba and the United States, rejecting the provisos of the memorandum Wood had given them, and declaring it was a document that did not have a "definitive and legal character" and that could only be considered as "the opinions from the Executive Department," adding that some of those provisos were unacceptable because they "violated Cuba's independence and sovereignty." On February 27, the Assembly approved what its delegates deemed corresponded with the mandate granted by the Military Order No. 455.[42]

And it was thus that, in fact, under the guise of a "pacifying occupation" U.S. imperialism entered Cuba, violating its own statement in the Joint Resolution of April 20, 1898—that was finally repealed and replaced by the Platt Amendment, for it was the formal obstacle for legalizing colonial domination over a *capitis diminutio* republic; that is to say, a republic that had diminished or no civil capacity—about not having an appetite for political, economic or territorial domination over Cuba.

The Platt Amendment

In the book of that illustrious Cuban Emilio Roig de Leuchsenring entitled *Historia de la Enmienda Platt* (*The History of the Platt Amendment*), a writing to be consulted by those interested in this thorny issue, it is expounded in detail everything regarding the debate about the Amendment by the Congress of the United States. On February 25, 1901, during the debate on the bill about the concession of cre-

42. Ibid., 392.

dits for the expenses of the United States Army during the fiscal year that ended June 30, 1902, the text of the law that would define the relations between the United States and the future Republic of Cuba would also be examined. That text, prepared by the Secretary of War Elihu Root, was submitted then by Senator Orville H. Platt to be included as an amendment in the law on credits for the army, as allowed by U.S. legislature.

The said amendment was discussed by the Senate on the 26th and the 27th, and the draft presented was approved without modification on that last day by 43 to 20 mainly republican votes; it was then submitted to the House that passed it likewise by 159 to 134 mainly republican votes, and it finally became a law despite some congressmen's opposition.

The following paragraph is taken from the aforementioned book by Emilio Roig de Leuchsenring:

> The swiftness in taking the vote and approving the Platt Law was due to the fact that the North American legislative term was about to end, and President McKinley wanted to profit from the dependable majority he could count upon in the two legislative bodies to have the much mentioned amendment approved without hindrances, despite the opposition that could—and did—come from some congressmen; thus, by March 4, when he was sworn into his second term in office, [the amendment] would have already become an Act of the Union.[43]

Roig's learned comment on the above paragraph is included next:

> Surely the Cuban members of the Constituent Assembly were not acquainted with or failed to appreciate the extraordinary and transcendental value of the criteria against the amendment presented by senators Morgan, Bacon, Foraker, Pettus, Teller, Culberson, Mallory, Clay, Berry, Tillman and Jones (from

43. Ibid., 70.

> Arkansas), because if they had known it and accurately assessed and appraised it, they would have not given their final approval to the amendment, and would have resisted the impositions of President McKinley, Secretary Root and the Congress. The establishment of the Republic would have naturally been delayed, but when was established months or years later, it would have not been afflicted by the congenital ailment of the limitations to its sovereignty brought about by the amendment, plus its sequels of North American intrusion and intervention in Cuban affairs, and of submission of the Cuban politicians and rulers to North American interests and needs. And that conscious attitude of resistance, based on a high esteem for civil decorum, and a broad overview of Cuban political problems, would have been the best way to prepare for self-government.
>
> . . . .
>
> What a difficult situation would McKinley's government have faced vis-à-vis its own people and the world at large, if he had been compelled by the Cuban rejection of the amendment to indefinitely pursue the military occupation of the island, thus delaying and violating the solemn commitments contracted by the North American state in regard to Cuba in the Joint Resolution of April 20, 1898!"[44]

The democratic Senator Morgan's arguments opposing the amendment stood out from all others; he was given the floor several times and examined articles included in the draft. In his aforementioned book, Emilio Roig conveys this important legal notion Morgan presented at the debates in the Senate:

> Senator Morgan also believed it was absurd to include the amendment's articles in a permanent treaty, "as if there had been in this world, in the public law of nations, a permanent treaty, unless it were a treaty that transferred a deed and, in

44. Ibid., 70-71.

> that case, its permanence does not depend from the fact that it is a treaty and is called a permanent treaty, but it depends from the fact that a treaty of this nature cannot be revoked by demanding the return of whatever has been transferred by its provisos."[45]

But Morgan went even further with amazing courage:

> [...] Senator Morgan asked himself whether Cuba would ever be an independent state while clause 3 remains in its Constitution or in a treaty signed with the United States. And he answered that question thus: "No. It is a false pretense. It is an act of hypocrisy on the part of the Congress of the United States to make such a declaration and, at the same time, to say it is carrying out and fulfilling the Congress's aim and promise that that country will be free, sovereign and independent..."[46]

Finally, Senator Morgan said: "I would be shamed..."[47]

For his part, Senator Bacon, who had an outstanding participation in the 1898 congressional debates about the United States' intervention in the Spanish-Cuban conflict, addressed the issue in his speech, clearly and without unnecessary rhetoric: "If we are determined to violate our promise, why are we stopping halfway? In that case, we should go all the way and seize the Island without any reservation whatsoever."[48]

During the debate, Senator Jones also opposed the amendment and said: "I confess that for many months I have feared that the deliberate intention of the majority here is to absolutely ignore our promises to the world and to Cuba when we declared war against Spain, and to maintain a control of absolute supervision of the Island."[49]

45. Ibid., 88.
46. Ibid.
47. Ibid., 89.
48. Ibid., 90.
49. Ibid., 90-91.

Further on, Senator Jones decisively stated: "It seems to me that to reserve for the United States the right to maintain a government, when it is the United States the one that decides the adequate type of government to protect life and property, is tantamount to reserving for the United States the right to maintain or to oust the government of Cuba when it deems it convenient."[50]

On March 1rst the amendment was discussed and approved by the House of Representatives of the United States. Its approval was so important for McKinley, that he went to the extreme of presenting an "urgency motion" to prevent a debate in the House. However, several democratic representatives took the floor against the amendment; De Armond and Richardson deserve a special mention. Roig said "Richardson defended the right of the Cubans to their freedom and their independence, rejected by the United States' amendment."[51]

Furthermore, four republican representatives—Drescal, Lond, Manu and MacCall—were also against it. The republican representative MacCall, from Massachusetts, stated in his speech: "And, in this case, the glory of the American victory over the Spanish arms would end in national shame and dishonor for all centuries to come."[52]

However, the way the North American Government thought and acted was quite different. On March 2, 1901, the day after the Platt Amendment was approved by the Senate and the House of Representatives, President McKinley ratified the Act, thus immediately enforcing the amendment which he immediately sent to the U.S. Military Governor in Cuba so that he could notify the Constituent Assembly. (See Annex 3)

It is evident that it was the Executive who imposed upon the Congress its policy toward Cuba. The McKinley Administration craftily manipulated its majority in Congress and managed to make the Legislative Power ratify its policy.

50. Ibid., 91.
51. Ibid., 96.
52. Ibid., 97.

The Platt Amendment as an Appendix of the Cuban Constitution

The final text of the Constitution drafted by the Constituent Assembly was made known on February 21, 1901; only the issue of the relations with the United States was pending. As it was mentioned above, when Wood notified the members of the Assembly about the five points Root wanted to include in the Cuban Constitution—that would later be included in the Platt Amendment—, the Cuban representatives drafted "their own" five provisos to that end, which were approved by the Convention on February 27, but as those points did not satisfy the interests of the occupant, they were rejected by the North Americans. As we have already seen, this interest was to underhandedly annex Cuba. The North Americans had already completed a detailed text to that end: the Platt Amendment.

On March 2, 1901, the North American military governor, General Leonard Wood, informed the Chairman of the Cuban Constituent Assembly about the approval of the Platt Amendment by the Congress and the Executive of the United States, and emphasized that the document had already been enforced in the United States and that, consequently, President McKinley was waiting for the Constituent Convention to act according to that law's provisos.[53]

The Cubans refused to accept the Platt Amendment and demanded from the North Americans the respect due to the 1898 Joint Resolution. Coercion, intimidation, blackmail, in short, aggression, loomed over the future republic.

One of the delegates to the Constituent Assembly, who always remained staunchly opposed to the acceptance of the Platt Amendment, was José Martí's great friend, the patrician Juan Gualberto Gómez, to whom the Apostle had entrusted organizing in Cuba the 1895 revolutionary uprising. Gómez was one of the five members of the Commission of the Constituent Assembly elected to rule about the Platt Amendment as soon as the Assembly received the message of the U.S. Executive. Juan Gualberto Gómez then proposed a dig-

53. Ibid., 99.

nified response to the United States in a long paper presented before the Convention, where he expressed:

> And the first thing one thinks is that there must have been a regrettable change in the concept that, regarding their rights and obligations towards Cuba, is currently upheld by the powers that be in the United States, if compared with what they said three years ago when they stated Cuba was and should be an independent people. Currently Cuba seems a defeated country upon which the victor's imposes conditions before evacuating it; that must be exactly fulfilled or it will continue to be under the rule of the victor. And, in the present case, those conditions are harsh, cumbersome, humiliating: limitation of independence and sovereignty, power to intervene and territorial cessions. There is all of that in the Agreement of the Congress of the United States reported to U.S.... [54]

Popular outrage ensued, and a public protest against the amendment marched through the streets of Havana and down the Paseo del Prado, and from there to the Martí Theater, where the Constituent Assembly held its working sessions. In this act of repudiation a declaration was distributed addressed to the American people demanding: "Absolute independence, total sovereignty—the former without limits, the latter without deceptions—, were and are the eternal, unbreakable and indomitable aspiration of the Cuban Motherland."[55]

Antonio Bravo Correoso, one of the members of the 1901 Constituent Assembly, tells about his conversation with General Leonard Wood, during the interview the U.S. Governor held with several Cuban representatives to the Assembly at the Government Palace in Havana. At a given moment, Bravo Correoso reminded Wood that: "the United States, according to the April, 1898 Joint Resolution of the North American Congress, disclaimed all interested motives for their involvement in the war but, however, they had acquired Puer-

54. Ibid., 407.
55. Ibid., 109.

to Rico and the Philippines, an archipelago that did not affect North American traditional politics, while claiming they would not acquire territories thus, without popular consensus."[56] Bravo Correoso says that General Wood replied, baffling those present, that the North Americans had not received much, and quotes his words: "North Americans even showed their generosity by allowing Santiago—whose Spanish garrison had capitulated to the intervening army, and therefore belonged to it as a war booty—to continue being a part of the Cuban territory."[57]

A commission of delegates from the Constituent Assembly traveled to the United States to speak with President McKinley, but to no avail. The delegates left Havana on April 20, 1901 and returned empty-handed on May 6.

On May 31, 1901 faced by the Cuban's refusal, Root notified Wood that the president would withdraw the occupation troops only when a government was established in Cuba under a Constitution that included either in its text or as an appendix, the provisos of the Platt Amendment. That was an unthinkable act of force, as the treatise writer Leland H. Jenks defined it: "This is an ultimatum, a legislative ultimatum for Cuba."[58] The U.S. Congress and the U.S. government considered that the amendment ensured the continuity of North American sovereignty over Cuba that had to be imposed at any cost.

The Convention met in late May to discuss the report from the Commission that had returned from Washington. That document proposed to the Convention the approval of the Platt Amendment as an appendix to the Constitution, but with various clarifications that purported to render the amendment's provisos less harmful the sovereignty of the future republic. When a vote on the report was taken, it was approved by 15 in favor of the report and 14 against it. When they cast their vote, some of the members of the Constituent Assembly also established their positions. There were some giving ups, like Manuel Sanguily's, who argued he voted for the report that accepted

56. Antonio Bravo Correoso, *Cómo se hizo la Constitución de Cuba*, 79.
57. Ibid.
58. Leland H. Jenks, op. cit., 97.

the Draconian Platt Amendment "because there is none other, although I am afraid that the Government of the United States will find it very ambiguous and will reject it,"[59] and Gonzalo de Quesada's "because I understand that only by accepting the report and with it, the Platt Amendment with its clarifications, will the Republic be created,"[60] but there were other completely independentist stances from the indomitable anti-Plattists, like Salvador Cisneros Betancourt, Marquis of Saint Lucia, the patrician from Camagüey who twice presided the Republic-in-Arms in the 1868 war and the 1895 war: "the Platt Amendment is opposed to our absolute independence [...] forever enslaving the fate of future generations of Cubans."[61]

It must be emphasized that among those who voted for the acceptance of the Platt Amendment there were proven revolutionaries, like Manuel Sanguily, who favored achieving what he understood was best: an independent republic albeit bound to the neighboring imperial colossus, rather than accepting the only other option left by the North American controllers: to continue the military occupation of the island. But it must also be borne in mind that the Convention was under pressure from the most conservative elements in the Cuban economy and politics, besides the Spanish property owners who had remained in Cuba and still had all their economic might. Thus, the associations of estate owners, of landowners, of merchants and of manufacturers living in Cuba, wrote to the Convention proposing that the amendment be accepted with the purpose of attaining economic advantages from the United States; furthermore, the Republican Party of Oriente, founded in Cuba's easternmost region, also campaigned in the media for the amendment to be accepted and "compensation for our main products"[62] requested from the North Americans, and that Cuban group added, referring to the northern giant that "this definitive rupture [...] will lead U.S. to chaos."[63]

59. Emilio Roig de Leuchsenring, *Historia de la Enmienda Platt*, 159.
60. Ibid.
61. Ibid.
62. Ibid., 154.
63. Ibid.

Naturally, McKinley did not accept the Cuban Constituent Assembly's agreement, and thus the ultimatum arrived, delivered by the U.S. Military Governor to the Assembly on June 8. General Wood sent a copy of the report about the impossibility of modifying the terms of the Platt Amendment by the U.S. Executive that Mr. Root, the Secretary of War had sent him, "for being a statute agreed upon by the Legislative Power [...] it is mandatory to carry it out as is."[64] And he added that the President of the United States "cannot change or modify it, make additions or deletions."[65] Lastly, he said that the President was unable to withdraws the troops from Cuba because the Platt Amendment had not been included in the Cuban Constitution.

Bearing in mind the ultimatum from the President of the United States, the Constituent Assembly decided to take a vote to include in an appendix to the Constitution the chapter about the future relations of Cuba with the United States, copying all the articles of the Platt Amendment, without modifications or explanations. This meeting was held on June 12, 1901; 27 of the 31 members of the Convention attended, and the final result was 16 votes in favor and 11 against.

The general explanation for the favorable votes from the delegates who decided to include the amendment as a constitutional appendix, was that it was the only way to establish the republic. Among those delegates was Manuel Sanguily, who said: "above all, because it is an imposition by the United States against which all resistance would be definitively unfortunate for Cuban aspirations."[66]

Thus, once the Platt Amendment became an Appendix of the Cuban Constitution, the promise the United States demanded in order to pave the way for the establishment of a "republic" that was a veritable North American protectorate was fulfilled.

64. Ibid., 160.
65. Ibid.
66. Ibid., 162.

II

INTERVENTIONISM

TREATIES, ACCORDS, REGULATIONS AND BLACKMAIL

The Platt Amendment Dons Its Third Disguise: The 1903 Permanent Treaty of Relations

The Republic of Cuba, for whose advent the Cuban people had fought since 1868, was not born on May 20, 1902. The Platt Amendment that became a Constitutional Appendix and later a Treaty of Relations, aborted it, to give way to a State subjugated to the North American Empire.

After the approval of the 1901 Constitution and the blessing of the North Americans with the inclusion of the Platt Amendment, the U.S. military governor in Cuba arranged the holding of elections for the Presidency and the Vice-presidency of the Republic as well as for the Senate and the House of Representatives.

The 1901 Constitution established in its Article 65 the requirements to be elected President of the Republic, which were: to be Cuban by birth or naturalization—in the latter case, it was necessary to have fought for Cuba in its wars of independence for no less than 10 years,—to be 40 years of age and to fully enjoy civil and political rights.

I would like to highlight the fact that a naturalized Cuban could aspire to the presidency of the Republic, including the many brothers from other countries who fought in our wars of independence against Spanish colonial rule for more than 10 years. A specific case was that of the General-in-Chief of the Liberation Army, Dominican by birth, who was one of the favorite candidates among the "mambises" for that high-ranking post.

However, Máximo Gómez declined the offer. Then other two candidates came through: Don Tomás Estrada Palma, and General Bartolomé Masó Márquez. Estrada Palma—the favorite U.S. candidate—was known for his support for the North Americans rather than for the Cubans. The electoral process suffered various irregularities and Masó withdrew. That is how Cuba had its first president elect who was entrusted to receive the "independent" Republic from the hands of the U.S. intervention forces on May 20, 1902.

The Estrada Palma administration was fateful. Its main concern was to pay back dutifully the U.S. loans, even when it implied cuts in basic public expenditures like education, in a country devastated by the war. He was unable, vis-à-vis the people's demands, to amend his errors, and fell into the arms of the conservatives. He even welcomed to his cabinet some enemies of the independence and notorious autonomists. He allowed fraud to be carried out on the 1906 elections, when he ran for a second term in office, but fearing an armed uprising against him, he opted to hand the country back to the United States. But I will refer to that embarrassing episode further on.

We have seen how the United States, taking advantage of its temporary right of occupation and in violation of the Treaty of Paris and the principles of the 1898 Joint Resolution, obliged the Cuban constituents to approve the Platt Amendment as an appendix to the Cuban Constitution, on June 12, 1901.

Among the first actions taken by the Republic of Cuba as a U.S. protectorate were the compliance with two items included in the Platt Amendment as well as in the Constitutional Appendix: the agreement on the coaling stations and the naval bases of February 16/23, 1903 and the Permanent Treaty of Relations dated May 22, 1903.

The 1903 Permanent Treaty of Relations signed by the Republic of Cuba and the United States of America is the same text of the Amendment/Appendix. The United States had obliged the Cubans to include the Platt Amendment (See Annex 3) in the 1901 Cuban Constitution and both the Amendment and the Appendix called for the signing of a treaty. Thus, conditions were ripe to ensure the U.S. permanence on the island, for the Constitution could be modified by the Cubans, and the Treaty could only be altered by the United States.

This 1903 Permanent Treaty of Relations contains a preamble that ratifies the Platt Amendment and deceitfully resembles the Joint Resolution. The rest of the Treaty includes the same eight clauses in the Amendment/Appendix. The preamble, that is to say, the following paragraph, deserves no comment:

> WHEREAS the Congress of the United States of America by an Act approved march 2, 1901, provided as follows:
>
> Provided further. That in fulfillment of the declaration contained in the joint resolution approved April twentieth, eighteen hundred and ninety-eight, entitled. "That it is the duty of the United States to demand, and the Government of the United States does hereby demand, that the Government of Spain at once relinquish its authority and government in the island of Cuba, and to withdraw its land and naval forces from Cuba and Cuban waters, and directing the President of the United States to use the land and naval forces of the United States to carry these resolutions into effect," the President is hereby authorized to "leave the government and control of the island to its people" so soon as a government shall have been established in said island under a constitution which, either as a part thereof or in accordance appended thereto, shall define the future relations of the United Sates with Cuba, substantially as follows:

Next, the text of the Treaty reproduces the eight clauses of the Amendment, and further on it refers to its history as the new Constitutional Appendix:

> WHEREAS the Constitutional Convention of Cuba, on June 12, 1901, adopted a Resolution adding to the Constitution of the Republic of Cuba which was adopted on the twenty-first of February 1901, an appendix in the words and letters of the eight enumerated articles of the above cited act of the Congress of the United States:
>
> AND WHEREAS, by the establishment of the independence and sovereign government of the Republic of Cuba, under the constitution promulgated on the 20th. of May 1902, which embraced the foregoing conditions, and by the withdrawal

> of the Government of the United States as an intervening power, on the same date, it becomes necessary to embody the above cited provisions in a permanent treaty between the United States of America and the Republic of Cuba.[1]

The Treaty includes once again the same eight clauses, naming them "articles" and changes clause VIII for a new "Article VIII," in correspondence with the characteristics of a Treaty, that was written as follows:

> Article VIII. The present convention shall be ratified by each party in conformity with the respective Constitutions of the two countries and the ratifications shall be exchanged in the City of Washington within eight moths from this date (as soon as possible.)[2]

The Permanent Treaty of Relations between the Republic of Cuba and the United States of America was signed in Havana on May 22, 1903. It was signed for the Cuban side by the Secretary of State and Justice, Carlos de Zaldo, and for the U.S. side, by the special envoy and Minister Plenipotentiary, Herbert G. Squiers.

The U.S. Senate approved the Treaty on March 22, 1904, while the Cuban Senate approved it on June 8, 1904. The exchange of the documents ratifying the Treaty took place in Washington on July 2, 1904.

The Agreement on coaling stations and naval bases (See Annex 4) was not drafted on the basis of the provisos in the 1903 Permanent Treaty of Relations, but according to clause VII of the Amendment/Appendix which was, of course, identical to Article VII of the aforementioned Treaty, signed and enforced months after the signing of the Agreement on the coaling stations and the naval bases.

In America, the principles proscribing the use of force, the lack of validity of territorial acquisition by this means, date back to the 1826 Congress of Panama, to the first 1847 Congress of Lima, to the 1856

1. Archive of the Ministry of Foreign Affairs of the Republic of Cuba.
2. Ibid.

Pact of Washington, to the 1864 Second Congress of Lima, to the first 1883 Bolivarian Congress and to the first 1889 Pan-American Conference, all of which held prior to the signing of the Platt Amendment, that has been but the expression of coercion, pressure, and force.

A work of paramount importance such as the *Tratado de derecho internacional público* (*Public International Law Treatise*) by the noted Argentinean jurist, Daniel Antokoletz, makes various references to the impact of the Platt Amendment on issues such as international leasing, the international protectorates resulting from treaties and the international protectorates created without treaties.

When referring to international leasing by means of which one State obtains certain rights over the territory of another, Antokoletz notes that this is in fact an act of annexation or "a disguised territorial cession, especially if it is a lease in perpetuity."[3]

Among the many international protectorates resulting from treaties mentioned by Antokoletz's book is that of the United States in Cuba that stemmed from a U.S. law—the Platt Amendment—, imposed on a militarily occupied nation to be included as an Appendix to its Constitution, thus obliging the emerging republic to later ratify that imposition by the 1903 Permanent Treaty, in such a way that Cuba could not alienate its independence, nor obtain foreign loans beyond its own resources; and the United States could intervene in Cuba to guarantee internal order and use its territory in the event of a war with a foreign power.[4]

Anyone who analyzes the situation of total dependence of the Republic of Cuba from United States' designs, could only inquire: "What sort of independent republic is that?"

When Antokoletz referred to protectorates that emerge without the previous existence of a treaty, the Argentinean jurist mentions the relation of the United States with Cuba through the Platt Amendment, for those provisos for dependence behave the same without needing the 1903 Treaty, for they were unilaterally approved by an external act and imposed under coercion.

3. Daniel Antokoletz, *Tratado de Derecho Internacional Público*, II, 310.
4. Ibid., I, 537.

Actually, Cuba never ceased to be a colony. It was rather a mere change of metropolis, for a unilateral notice suffices to establish a protectorate. That is what the Platt Amendment was: a simple notification of a decision adopted by the U.S. Congress and ratified by the President of the United States.

The 1902 Commercial Treaty

The first treaty signed by the recently inaugurated Republic of Cuba with the United States of America was the December 11, 1902 Treaty of Commercial Reciprocity, that was "reciprocal" only in name since it was totally unfavorable to Cuba and tailored to protect U.S. interests and favor the introduction of U.S. capital on the island.

The treaty comprised three lists or types of U.S. products. Class A included products that would be admitted with a 25 % tariff cut, like manufactured copper and other alloys products, iron, steel, glass, ships, vehicles, food stuffs and even whisky. Class B listed the products from the United States whose tariffs would be cut by 30%; the list included butter, flour, non-alcoholic beverages, etc. And class C encompassed U.S. products whose tariffs would be cut by 40%, like cotton textiles and cotton manufactures, paper pulp, and perfumes and toiletries.

Cuba, in return, would get a 20% tariffs cut in the U.S. for its agricultural produce like sugar cane, coffee, tobacco or industrial products like various types of rum, etc.

This unequal exchange prevailed until the signing of the new Commercial Treaty in 1934 that, in fact, furthered increased the inequalities in bilateral trade. The 1902 Commercial Treaty—shortened to "Reciprocity Treaty"—was approved by the U.S. Senate on March 19, 1903 and by the Cuban Senate on March 11 and 28, 1903. The ratification documents were exchanged in Washington on March 31 of that same year.

The Isle of Pines: Another Sample of Blackmail

The Isle of Pines had always been part of the territory Spain called its "colony of the island of Cuba." However, the United States purposefully questioned its integration to the Cuban archipelago and attempted to include it among the territories relinquished by Spain, as stipulated in Article II of the Treaty of Paris. These territories were considered a part of the "West Indies" mentioned in it. West Indies was the name first given to America.

Article II of the Treaty of Paris says: "Spain relinquishes the island of Puerto Rico to the United States and the others now under its sovereignty in the West Indies, as well as the Island of Guam in the archipelago of Las Marianas or Ladronas." Article I of the same Treaty says: "Spain renounces all its rights of sovereignty and property over Cuba." If in 1898, Spain only possessed the islands of Cuba and Puerto Rico and other small ones surrounding them, it can be asked which are "the others" mentioned in Article II? Where did this bad faith come from, the North Americans or the Spaniards? Or perhaps the two parties were agreed?

The Isle of Pines had always been administered by the Spaniards as a part of the colony of the island of Cuba, and when the province of Havana was created, it became one of its municipalities. However, the United States ignored this fact and considered that the Isle of Pines had been relinquished by Spain.

In addition to the Isle's economic interest, Senator Platt thought it could help in the defense of the United States in the Caribbean; hence its inclusion in his notorious amendment. But the issue must be examined from a different angle: Blackmail. According to Article VI of the Platt Amendment, the Isle of Pines was, at the same time, a token and a guarantee for the concessions that Cuba should grant to the United States for establishing coaling stations and naval bases once its "independence" was declared.

Since the beginning of the U.S. military occupation of Cuba, the Isle of Pines the presence of North Americans settlers became noticeable. Several plots of land were sold to U.S. buyers. The Isle of Pines Company was founded in 1901 by various U.S. speculators who sold thousands of hectares of land there for insignificant amounts of money. Meanwhile, other similar businesses flourished with the creation of real state companies like the Santa Fe Land Company and the San José Company. Once the land was divided into lots, hotels and gardens were built. The Isle was advertised as a paradise linked to the mythical Treasure Island. It was even said that it was the latest land purchased by the United States..

That is how the United States, sheltered by the distorted definition in Article II of the Treaty of Paris, omitted the Isle of Pines from Cuba's boundaries and left the discussion of its ownership to a future agreement, as specified in Article VI of the Platt Amendment. For that reason, a new Treaty was drafted and signed by Cuba and the United States on March 2, 1904, but it needed the U.S. Congress ratification. (See Annex 6)

In addition to various U.S. presidents, the settlers who were exploiting the land on the Isle of Pines refused to accept the fact that it belonged to Cuba. So they availed themselves of all their political resources to keep it under the flag of the occupant nation. It was estimated at the time that some 300 U.S. citizens were living on the Isle of Pines, and it must be brought to mind that Washington considered it as an excellent place for a naval base.

There was a strong opposition in the United States to return the Isle to its legitimate owner: the Republic of Cuba. To prevent it, the same diabolical maneuvers were staged. On November 4, 1905 news were spread that a "revolution" had broken out on the Isle and that the "revolutionaries" were demanding that the Isle be separated from Cuba and annexed to the United States. *The New York Herald* echoed the news on its November 15 issue. Undoubtedly, the move was aimed at blocking the implementation of the treaty signed some months before and the U.S. Congress's delay in ratifying it was becoming a cause of concern. The 1904 Treaty was not ratified until 1925, that is to say, 21 years later.

A legal malfeasance, to give it some name, is found in the March 2, 1904 Treaty on the Isle of Pines. Article I of this Treaty, by which the United States renounce the Isle of Pines, invoked articles I and II of the Treaty of Paris. Invoking Article II was obvious, but invoking

Article I, which gave the U.S. the right to occupy the island, was not fitting for on that date with the Platt Amendment already in place, the occupation of Cuba should end.

Actually, the United States had reserved a new modality for the Isle of Pines, not precisely that of a coaling station or a naval base but colonization by means of North American settlements. These settlers, according to Article III of the 1904 Treaty, would maintain certain rights and privileges. That article stated that—and this was the trap—until the Treaty's ratification, the rights and privileges acquired by U.S. citizens who lived or owned property on the Isle, before the date on which the documents ratifying it were exchanged, would not be affected. It further explained that such U.S. citizens could stay or leave the Isle of Pines without losing their rights over their properties or dispose of them or of their products as they saw fit. Finally, it said that they were entitled to practice their trades or professions according to the Cuban laws applicable to foreigners.

In tune with the U.S. plans to colonize the Isle of Pines, and considering that the settlers were protected until the signing of the Treaty, 21 years simply elapsed. On March 13, 1925, the U.S. Senate acknowledged and consented to ratify the 1904 Treaty, albeit with the following two reservations:

- The first one established that all clauses or stipulations of existing or future treaties between the United States and Cuba, including the 1903 Permanent Treaty of Relations, announced on July 2, 1904, would be applicable to the territory and the inhabitants of the Isle of Pines.

- The second one specified that Article III of the Treaty on the Isle of Pines uses the term "other foreigners," that should be interpreted as "foreigners who are granted the most favorable treatment by the Cuban Government." (See Annex 6)

Finally, the U.S.-Cuba Protocol of Exchange to ratify the March 2, 1904 Treaty establishing the property over the Isle of Pines was signed in Washington on March 23, 1925.

The North American settlements on the Isle of Pine did not prosper for various reasons, the main one being the Cuban people's rejection to the theft of part of their territory. This led to the signing of the Treaty and to its ratification, albeit two decades later. Many of these settlers returned to their places of origin, and of those who stayed, only a few mixed with the Cuban population.

But history had something better in store for the Isle of Pines. Years after the triumph of the Cuban Revolution its name was changed to Isle of Youth, and the imagined Treasure Island became the site of a beautiful solidarity program for thousands of young Africans, Latin-Americans and Asians whose intellectual capacities were educated and trained so that they will, availing themselves of their talents and their professions, contribute with the development of their respective countries.

U.S. INTERVENTIONISM IN CUBA FROM 1902 TO 1934

The Second U.S. Military Intervention

The 1906 U.S. military intervention of Cuba was another shameful episode for the Republic.

President Estrada Palma opted for a second term in office and decided to present his candidacy, representing the conservative Partido Moderado (Moderate Party) at the 1905 November general elections. To top it all, autonomism re-emerged with Rafael Montoro, Eliseo Giberga and others, and took refuge in the Moderate Party striking an alliance with Estrada Palma and his followers Ricardo Dolz and Domingo Méndez Capote.

The National Liberal Party, whose electoral platform was drafted by Juan Gualberto Gómez and whose main figure was Alfredo Zayas, proclaimed they would strive for a clean voting. Bartolomé Masó and Máximo Gómez supported the Liberal Party and were outraged by the autonomist revival. The struggle for the presidential was between moderates and liberals.

The opposition Liberal Party denounced the electoral fraud that allowed Estrada Palma's reelection and using that as a pretext—for the real aim was to appropriate for themselves a slice of the budget and other perks enjoyed by those in power—decided to overthrow Estrada Palma.

On May 20, 1906, Tomás Estrada Palma began his second term in office.

On August 19, 1906, in a move that resembled a comedy more than a tragedy, the plotters in the Liberal Party rose up in arms. Estrada Palma was frightened and asked for Washington to intervene militarily, by requesting the implementation of Article III of the Platt Amendment. Estrada Palma's preference was well known: better the North Americans than the Liberals.

The U.S. Consul General to Cuba, Frank Steinhart, head of that country's Mission in Havana sent the following message to Washington:

> Cuban Foreign Minister asked me on behalf of President Palma, to beg President Roosevelt to immediately send two ships to Havana and Cienfuegos. They must arrive at once. Government forces cannot quench rebellion. Government impotent to protect lives and properties. President Palma will summon the Senate next Friday to ask for our strongest intervention. Palma's request should be kept secret and confidential. Except for the president, the minister and myself, no one else knows here.
>
> We await prompt reply.[5]

On September 12, the ships "Denver" and "Marietta" docked in Havana and Cienfuegos respectively with the trite order to protect U.S. lives and properties, but they did not land. On September 19, the U.S. Secretary of War, William Taft and the Undersecretary of State, Robert Bacon arrived in Havana. Taft waited for the resigna-

5. Leland H. Jenks, op. cit., 107.

tion of Estrada Palma and his cabinet on September 28 and on the following day proclaimed himself Governor General of the Republic of Cuba by virtue of Article III of the Platt Amendment.

On October 12, 1906 Charles E. Magoon, a corrupted character, former governor of the Panama Canal Zone, took over as Governor of Cuba, a post he occupied until January 28, 1909. On that date, he transferred power to José Miguel Gómez who, as the candidate for the Liberal Party, had been elected to the Presidency on November 14, 1908. This second U.S. intervention sparked the annexationist interests that had been dormant in some figures of the pseudo-republic the United States forced U.S. to maintain.

Other Military and Political Interventions

The blacks and mulattos who accounted for a high percentage of the members of the Cuban Liberation Army, were discriminated against firstly by the U.S. military occupation and afterwards during the "republic" established on May 2, 1902. To confront this discrimination, a group of them founded the Partido de los Independientes de Color (Independent Colored People's Party), but it was soon declared illegal by a law passed to that end in 1910.

All efforts that political party made to abort the ruling banning it, were fruitless. In an attempt to stage an "armed protest," the leaders of the Independent Colored People's Party—Evaristo Estenoz and Pedro Ivonet—rose up in arms on May 20, 1912, a decade after the eestablishment of the "republic." Even though the uprising almost succeeded in spreading throughout the island, its most important scenario was the former eastern province of Oriente, mainly in the territory between the cities of San Luis and Guantánamo, where a high number of blacks and mulattos was concentrated.

The U.S. marines acted "to protect U.S. interests." On May 25, Washington sent the following message to Havana:

> The "Nebraska" will arrive in Havana tomorrow and an important naval force will concentrate in a strategic point, pro-

> bably Key West. A gunboat will be sent to the bay of Nipe. Please inform the Cuban Government that if it cannot protect the lives and properties of North American citizens, the Government of the United States, according to what it invariably does in these cases, will land the necessary forces to protect them. This will not mean intervention.[6]

But the rebellion continued and, on May 30, U.S. marines landed in Daiquirí to protect the properties of the Spanish American Iron Company. U.S. Secretary of State, Knox ordered to keep a regular force of 200 men at Daiquirí and Firmeza, and 50 men at El Cobre, to protect the Spanish- American companies Juraguá and Cuban Copper.

On June 5500 U.S. marines occupied the city of Guantánamo and 4 armored ships left Key West for Cuba carrying 5000 U.S. soldiers, ready for action. The El Cobre copper mines were seized and 7 companies of U.S. troops were distributed among various sugar-cane mills, and along the railroad lines of the Guantánamo and Western Railroad Company, that naturally belonged to the United States.

The United States sent more forces. On June 10, U.S. marines clashed against the rebel forces in El Cuero, near the town of Imías, in the former province of Oriente. U.S. Ambassador Beaupré requested that a man-of-war be sent immediately to Havana. Tension mounted between the Cuban Government and the North American administration. The intervention was so blatantly overt that after the landing of U.S. troops in the Oriente province, President José Miguel Gómez sent U.S. President Taft the following telegram:

> A decision of such serious nature alarms and hurts the feelings of a people so proud of their independence, even more when these measures have not been agreed upon by the two governments, thus placing the Cuban Government in a position of humiliating inferiority, holding its national rights in contempt and discrediting it both at home and abroad.[7]

6. Ibid., 128.
7. Ibid., 130.

I have cited these examples to illustrate some cases of the permanent U.S. intervention in our internal affairs. But these were not the only interventions; there were many more landings of U.S. troops in Cuba.

There were always illegal business under way during the pseudo-Republic, but the aforementioned examples suffice to illustrate that at no time was there any change in the North American stance after its troops landed and they claimed it did not mean an intervention.

Raúl Roa's incisive prose best characterized the gloomy period of Gerardo Machado's dictatorship and his overthrow. In his article "Tiene la palabra camarada Máuser"[8] ("Comerade Mauser Has The Floor"), he shows the impact of these interventions. In another article, "La generación inmolada" ("The Sacrificed Generation"), Roa explained that as soon as the North Americans saw their economic interests in danger, they immediately tried to make changes in the leadership of the "republic" or, as he called it, "the overseas trading post:"

> In February 1933, Hamilton Fish demanded, in the Houses of Representatives, immediate intervention in Cuba by the Government in Washington, in order to protect U.S. interests. The formerly pampered "manager" of the "overseas trading post" was already a hindrance for investors, businessmen and politicians avid for a more favorable political climate for their pockets.[9]

Raúl Roa goes on to comment the historical experiences of the times when U.S. imperialism tried once again to snatch away from the Cuban people its opportunity to seize power. At the worst moment faced by Machado's pro-imperialist dictatorship due to the successes of the revolutionary movement, the United States propitiated the so called "mediation," which was nothing but activating all the bourgeois parties to snatch the victory from the Cuban people, as it finally happened first in August, 1933 and later, in January, 1934.

8. Raúl Roa García, "Tiene la palabra camarada Máuser," in *La Revolución del 30 se fue a bolina*, 71-75.
9. Raúl Roa García, "La generación inmolada," in *La Revolución del 30 se fue a bolina*, 294.

Next, another fragment of the aforementioned article "La generación inmolada:"

> The new U.S. Ambassador to Cuba, Benjamin Sumner Welles, arrives in Havana invested with full powers to "resolve" the Cuban crisis. Mediation made its way into the courts with its notorious round table (...) The mediator's maneuver will fool no one: His aim is to undermine the revolutionary movement to benefit the Foreign Ministry and the U.S. banks, and to get rid of Machado without altering the basis or the structure of the "machadato"...[10]

In his article "El alba de la efebocracia," ("The Dawn of Ephebocracy)" Roa commented on the "change" sponsored by the United States behind the back of the Cuban people: "After the hasty escape of the tyrant and the implacable revenge, Carlos Manuel de Céspedes acted as President but the Mediator was truly in charge. Machado had left, but the "machadato" remained..."[11]

Further on, Raúl Roa expressed: "The formidable national and social liberation movements that had already tilled the land of a new destiny was, on the other hand, experiencing, thanks to a *coup de main* plotted by Summer Welles and the mere transfer of power to the ABC and the old mediating caudillos, the most abominable filch recorded by our republican history..."[12]

With a few strokes of his pen, Roa's vibrant prose depicts the situation in Cuba after the empire's diplomatic intervention. Summer Welles, U.S. Ambassador and mediator, forced dictator Machado to flee the country and imposed a docile functionary from the "machadato:" a sad mission for the offspring of Cuba's founding father, named Carlos Manuel de Céspedes after him. He was accepted by the mediation supporters, that is to say, by the bourgeois parties politicians and by the ABC, a fascist-style organization whose main figures were the clique chosen by the United States to snatch away the

10. Ibid., 295.
11. Raúl Roa García, "El alba de la efebocracia," in *La Revolución del 30 se fue a bolina*, 296.
12. Ibid.

victory from the revolutionaries who had not only made Machado's regime stagger but had also succeeded in making the country ungovernable.

Cuba: A Center for U.S. Capital

Even before the U.S. intervention in 1898, Washington's investments in and trade with the island were significant. Examples abound: millionaire businessman Edwin F. Atkins and his Boston Company in Cienfuegos; the Rionda family in Sancti Spíritus and Bethlehem from Pennsylvania in Santiago de Cuba's mining areas.

Among the string of lies under which U.S. rulers buried the Cubans in order to white-wash the image of the Platt Amendment, were the much publicized "benefits" that Cuba received according to the 1902 Commercial Treaty, that granted Cuban products sent to the United States 20% tariff cut, but in fact because Cuba, in exchange, granted a tariff cut from 20% to 40%, according to the goods in question, to imports from the United States. This unequal relations plunged the nation into indebtedness and prevented its development.

Sugar-cane was the Achilles' heel of the Cuban economy because its market was controlled by the United States. In 1929 it suffered a serious setback when tariffs were set at two cents the pound, which practically cut to one half the island's participation in the U.S. sugar market. This triggered a crisis that affected the fragile Cuban economy in the early 1930's. That, together with the political crisis brought about by Machado's dictatorship, placed the country in a very difficult financial situation vis-à-vis the United States.

As I have already pointed out, after the U.S. military forces left Cuba and the second intervention ended, the United States permanently threatened the successive Cuba governments so that they agreed to protect U.S. interests on the island. Albeit Cuba did not formally acknowledge the interpretation of the Platt Amendment that prevented a sovereign country to do business freely; the U.S. governments did exert the right to veto in their protectorate over Cuba.

It was always notorious that the U.S. sent its gunboats with the purpose of intimidation under any pretext, and exerted diplomatic pressures and threats via its pro-consuls accredited as ambassadors, to prevent any business deals with any foreign power.

I could bear witness to many cases, but I am just going to mention some:

The Platt Amendment ensured the hegemony of U.S. capital in Cuba, and on the sly, implemented the Monroe Doctrine. However, in the case of Cuba, contrary to other Latin American countries, this Doctrine was part of a document imposed on a state that emerged from a national liberation war. The Platt Amendment was not merely a reference to an alleged U.S. permanent right to intervene in all of the island's internal affairs, but was actually going to be exercised in Cuba by and during the successive U.S. administrations.

U.S. President Taft gave the Amendment a preventive interpretation that would prevent an overt intervention in Cuba. An example can be found in their strong opposition to any investment by any European and even Cuban capitals on the island, and the maneuvers and pressures that the United States exerted over the complying Cuban rulers via their Embassy in Havana.

To better illustrate the above, we can cite a funny yet painful example. On June 1, 1912, Cuban President José Miguel Gómez signed a decree granting the Compañía Agricultora de Zapata the exclusive privilege of exploiting the forestry resources and the swamplands at the Zapata Swamp, in the south of Cuba. The U.S. Embassy learned about it through the protests that appeared in the Cuban media; the Ambassador, without going deeper into the matter, reported to his country that this exploitation would affect the interests of the Cuban people, a pharisaic concern, for he did not know at the time that U.S. interests were involved in that business deal.

Washington's message was prompt, and when the United States did not approve the aforementioned concession, President Gómez repealed the decree. However, the North American contractor Isaac K. Champion, who was interested in the project, complained before the U.S. State Department which in turn called for an investigation to be carried out in Cuba. Finally, it was ruled that this indiscriminate exploitation that would affect the nation's ecology, would not be harmful to the Cuban people. Thus, the interdiction was lifted. As a result, the complying and solicitous Cuban President Gómez had a new decree drafted, grating the concession to the U.S. company.

Another example was the concession of the Nuevitas-Camagüey Railroad when, on March 5, 1912, the U.S. Ambassador to Havana, Beaupré, was instructed by his country to notify the Cuban president about their displeasure for the possible presence of British capital in the project. Obviously, the U.S. capital won the contract. A simple telephone call, a mere diplomatic note or a threatening comment from the U.S. ambassador sufficed to return the stray sheep to the U.S. master's flock. The instructions received by Ambassador Beaupré said:

> News received by this Ministry have led U.S. to believe it is a renewal of a project of British capitalists to extol from the Cuban Congress the concession of the Nuevitas-Caibarién railroad. You must make the President see the convenience of postponing the final solution to buy time for a full investigation and debate, insisting on the burden that favoring capitals other than North American or Cuban would impose upon the Cuban Treasure.[13]

The Cuban government wanted to grant a concession and a subsidy to Cuban Colonel José Tarafa who was associated with the Frenchman Regino R. Truffin and with Martin Littleton and Roland R. Conklin, from New York. The British interests were opposed to this business deal for, at the time, controlled most of Cuba's railroads. The opposition ceased after Mr. Littleton spoke with the prime minister in London and publicly announced that the loan granted to Tarafa to build a railroad that crossed the land he owned would be issued by London. These are the circumstances that led to the

13. Leland H. Jenks, op. cit., 125.

U.S. intervention in the matter.

Another serious irregularity in the concession of public works contracts at that time, was the construction of Havana's sewage system and street paving, and the building of the aqueduct system in Cienfuegos, all obtained by the same maneuverings and pressures.

In the chapter "La diplomacia del dólar y la política preventiva" ("The Dollar Diplomacy and Preventive Politics") of Leland H. Jenks's book *Nuestra colonia en Cuba*, numerous examples of the preventive implementation of the Platt Amendment can be found.[14]

From the Big Stick to the Good Neighbor Policy

In 1933, Franklin Delano Roosevelt became President of the United States and the Democrats replaced the Republicans who had been in power for three terms in a row: 1920, 1924 and 1928 under the presidency of Warren Harding, Calvin Coolidge and Herbert C. Hoover respectively. The U.S. economic crisis tipped the electoral balance to the Democrats' side because 1932, the year the elections were held, was the most critical since the beginning of the crisis in 1929.

The Big Stick policy was not useful anymore to Washington's new interests in Latin America, the region that would play an important role in the United States economic recovery. The Democratic administration had to change the Big Stick policy for Roosevelt's Good Neighbor's as explained on his inaugural speech. Even though it was meant to have an international connotation, it only applied to Latin America: "I shall commit this nation to a policy of Good Neighbor—a neighbor who respects himself and therefore respects the rights of others—, a neighbor that respects his obligations and the sanctity of accords in and for a world of neighbors."[15]

14. Ibid., 120-137.
15. Franklin Delano Roosevelt, Inauguration speech at his swearing in ceremony on March 4, 1933, in "Buen Vecino," in "Parte III. Glosario," in *Prontuario Diplomático*, 211.

Actually, there was no change of policy but a change of method aimed at achieving the same interventionist and aggressive goals. The first quarter of the 20th century witnessed with horror how the marines' boots trampled the soil of our sister Latin American republics, but such a fearsome image must be obliterated for the sake of the United States, not for the sake of the assaulted.

Roosevelt's New Deal, the basis of his government policy, was aimed at putting back on track the battered capitalist economy. But "the backyard"—as the U.S. has always regarded its Latin American neighbors—was experiencing economic and political turmoil. Several Latin American nations, unable to honor the loans they had received, causing U.S. exports to plummet, went bankrupt due to the crisis. Meanwhile, the revolutionary movement acted as a catalyst within the ranks of the oppressed as an anti-imperialist sentiment grew.

It was, therefore, necessary to change that image, to win the trust and give "proof of friendship" to Latin America in order to redesign the economic relations under the guise of the Good Neighbor policy. To that end, new reciprocity treaties were signed with Brazil, Haiti, Colombia, Honduras, Nicaragua, Guatemala, Costa Rica, El Salvador, Ecuador, Venezuela, and also Cuba.

In Cuba, 1933 marked the overthrow of the U.S.-backed tyranny of Gerardo Machado. In Nicaragua in 1934 Augusto César Sandino was assassinated with the complicity of the U.S. government. At the time, the United States maintained close relations with dictators like Anastasio Somoza in Nicaragua, Rafael Trujillo in the Dominican Republic, and Jorge Ubico in Guatemala. On the other hand, Washington reacted violently against the government of Mexican President Lázaro Cárdenas, even applying economic sanctions in reprisal for the nationalization of Mexican oil. Nothing had really changed. The pretext for exchanging the Big Stick for the Good Neighbor policy was free trade, that meant plunging Latin America even further into underdevelopment, hunger, and hopelessness.

An expression of the Good Neighbor policy was the so-called repealing of the Platt Amendment, no longer needed to keep the island's economy under control. On the other hand, it served their purpose of projecting a new image in Latin America and reaped economic benefits, low tariffs, and reopened Cuban ports for their surplus products, while taxing Cuban goods with high tariffs to protect U.S. goods.

In Cuba, the Good Neighbor policy required two premises: Firstly, as Machado's dictatorship was in the way of the new U.S. plans, it was necessary to get rid of it and put in its place a docile government with no history yet of criminal atrocities against the people; it was equally important to keep under strict control the people's revolutionary fervor to prevent them from taking over power. Secondly, the signing of a new commercial treaty to replace the 1902 treaty, that would fit in with the New Deal's design.

U.S. NEO-COLONIAL DOMINATION IN CUBA FROM 1934 TO 1958

The Good Neighbor's Claws

The two U.S. military occupations of Cuba, 1898-1902 and 1906-1909, allowed Washington to transform the island from a Spanish colony into a U.S. neo-colony. After more than 30 years of pseudo-republic, the cosmetic changes in U.S. foreign policy—that is to say, Roosevelt's New Deal's statement that the era of military intervention would be left behind—only meant more control over Cuba's economy, politics, culture, education and the mass media with the systematic purpose of deforming our people's consciousness.

The year 1934 marked a turning point in the history of the relations between the United States and Cuba. Fulgencio Batista y Zaldívar had emerged from a movement of Army sergeants driven by purely economic reasons, that took place on September 4, 1933, with the support of the petite-bourgeoisie opposed to the government imposed by the U.S. Ambassador on August 12, 1933, right after the overthrow of Gerardo Machado's dictatorship (1925-1933). That is how Batista became the head of the Army. But he immediately sought the complicity of the U.S. Ambassador and, January 1,

1934, overthrew Ramón Grau San Martín's self-styled "revolutionary" government that in fact, could be considered thus to a certain extent, given the times and the satisfactory performance of some of its ministers.

Since then, Fulgencio Batista placed and replaced one president after another, always backed by the U.S. Embassy. It was the time when the 1934 Commercial and Permanent Treaties were signed. The latter under the guise of invalidating the sinister Platt Amendment, while in fact leaving untouched former arrangements regarding the U.S. Naval Base at Guantánamo.

The illusion about the repealing of the Platt Amendment, presented as a gift from President Roosevelt's Democrat administration, concealed this policy's true roots that, in fact, preserved the U.S. intervention in Cuba under various disguises since 1934 on, and established the U.S. Naval Base at Guantánamo.

The U.S. media saw clearly President's Roosevelt's real objectives regarding the "repeal of the Platt Amendment." An editorial in the daily *New York Times*, dated May 31, 1934 said: "renouncing to that privilege in Cuba (...) is rather a concession to the Latin temperament than a refusal of a fundamental international right."[16]

This period witnessed the increase of unrestrained corruption of public officials, headed by Batista himself and his gang of assassins and thieves. That was also the time when the Italian-American Mafia arrived in Cuba and made their best business deals linked to gambling and prostitution.

In 1934 began the time when it was attempted more violently and viciously to quench Cuban popular and revolutionary movements, while the doors were opened wide to U.S. monopolies so that they could plunder the people and the nation's resources.

Commercial Relations

16. Francisca López Civeira, "La política del Buen Vecino y su aplicación en Cuba," in *Historia de las relaciones de EE.UU. con Cuba. Selección de lecturas*, 440.

The 1934 Treaty of Commercial Reciprocity signed by Cuba and the United States, that replaced the 1902 Treaty of Commercial Reciprocity, maintained the same inequalities than its predecessor. In exchange for some improvement in the tariffs for Cuban sugar in the U.S. market, we had to make new concessions regarding a group of 400 U.S. goods, reducing import tariffs by 60%. In addition the new Treaty opened the era of the system of quotas for the purchase of Cuban sugar by the United States.

The trade control by the United States became stable during and after World War II, when Cuban purchases averaged 80%; at the same time the sales of Cuban goods to U.S. market also increased during the war reaching nearly 90%, but fell down abruptly after the war to 52%, although they went up gradually, reaching 68% toward 1958.

When analyzing the 1948-1958 U.S.-Cuba commercial relations, the Cuban economist and professor Jacinto Torras noted:

> From our brief analysis of U.S.-Cuba economic and commercial relations entirely based on official Cuban and North American statistics we can reach the following conclusions:
>
> There is an acute imbalance, a complete lack of reciprocity, in the commercial and economic relations between the United States and Cuba, even if this phenomenon were analyzed taking 1948 as a starting point. This lack of equilibrium is shown by:
>
> a) A 558 million-dollar deficit in the period analyzed (1948-1957) in our commercial exchanges with North America.
>
> b) A 952 million-dollar deficit in the period 1948-1958 in the

17. Jacinto Torras, "Las relaciones comerciales y económicas entre Cuba y los Estados Unidos de América," in *Revista de Comercio Exterior*, 12.

balance of payments on our current account with that country.[17]

The 1952 Coup d'Etat and Its Background

Early during World War II, when Nazi and Fascist forces began to terrify the world and the Soviet Union and the Western powers headed by the United States agreed that the first task was to jointly confront the Nazi beasts, in Cuba, like in many other countries, there appeared, on the one hand, a tendency to democratize public management and, on the other, to create a common front with the revolutionary forces against the Nazis.

That was when the 1940 Cuban Constitution was born—one of the most progressive of the world at the time. This was followed by a stage of relatively stable bourgeois democracy, although accompanied by the already known and new social evils, like gangsterism backed by the successive governments. But with the end of the war in 1945, the so-called "cold war" appeared, and the United States fostered a mounting wave of repression against the popular and revolutionary movements, although undoubtedly—and this was proved by the votes cast in the always fraudulent bourgeois elections—that at the time the strength of the working class and the masses became increasingly evident in Cuba.

Thus, when the 1952 general elections were nearing, the victory of the Partido del Pueblo Cubano Ortodoxo (The Cuban People's Orthodox Party) seemed imminent. It had already been announced that it could count upon the votes of the already important Partido Socialista Popular (Popular Socialist Party). But the United Stated decided to put an end to the much publicized and defended representative democracy, for albeit that formula had always served so well the interests of Cuba's reactionary forces allied to U.S. interests for so long, in a few months time, could grievously hurt those same pro-imperialists at the ballots. Therefore, the U.S. set a plan in motion to seize again the victory from the hands of the Cuban people before the June, 1952 elections. The chosen instrument was Fulgencio Batista, their loyal pawn, who did away with the democratic system by staging a coup d'état on March 10, 1952, obeying his U.S. masters.

If Washington had been behind Machado's dictatorship and later in the mediation, it was clear that it was also behind the cunning coup of March 10, 1952. The fear for a revolutionary process on the island due to the people's disappointment and hopelessness prompted Washington to back a military coup in Cuba as it had happened before in several other Latin American nations.

There is proof gathered by comrade Blas Roca—who was Secretary General of Cuba's Popular Socialist Party until the triumph of the Revolution and who later chaired Cuba's People's Power National Assembly. In his article "El golpe de Estado del 10 de marzo" ("The March 10 Coup d'Etat"), Roca denounced that two U.S. officers from the Guantánamo Naval Base were seen in the Santiago de Cuba garrison on March 10, 1952, since daybreak until the putschists seized military command.[18]

A visit to Cuba, days before the coup d'état of the enigmatic Mr. Elliot Roosevelt, also aroused suspicions. He allegedly arrived in Havana to buy the "RHC Cadena Azul" radio station—the second most important in the country at the time. It surfaced that this man phoned Washington saying that "everything had turned out as planned."[19] On the day Batista took position in the Presidential Palace, Roosevelt paid him a visit but, according to press reports, they just greeted each other. It was also revealed that since the early hours of the events that led to the March 10 coup d'Etat, at the very same place where the action was taking place—the military garrison at Columbia—, there was a U.S. officer.[20] Comrade Blas Roca stressed in his article that the March 10 coup d'état was not triggered by domestic politics but sponsored by the reactionary interests of U.S. imperialists.[21]

18. Blas Roca Calderío, "El golpe de Estado del 10 de marzo," in Francisca López Civeira, *Historia de las relaciones de EE.UU. con Cuba, Selección de lecturas*, 507.
19. Ibid., 506-507.
20. Ibid., 507.
21. Ibid., 508

III

THE BASE AND ITS TREATIES

THE FIRST TREATIES

The Coaling Stations Agreements

Clause VII of the Amendment/Appendix, falsely derived from the right of occupation granted to the United States by the Treaty of Paris in regard to the island of Cuba, stated: "That to enable the United States to maintain independence of Cuba and protect the people thereof as well as for its own defense, the Government of Cuba will sell or lease to United States the lands necessary for coaling or naval stations at certain specified points to be agreed upon with the President of the United States." (See Annex 3)

When President Roosevelt announced the U.S. Senate that May 20, 1902 would be the date when Tomás Estrada Palma would assume the Presidency of the Republic of Cuba, President Theodore Roosevelt expressed that Cuba had joined in the United States' international political system thanks to the Platt Amendment, and thus it was urgent to demand from the island the fulfillment of clause VII of the Amendment, a key piece in the U.S. hegemonic projection in the Caribbean.

On November 8, 1902, the U.S. Secretary of State requested the Government of Cuba to cede in perpetuity tracts of land for four naval stations at Guantánamo and Cienfuegos, on the island's southern coast, and at Nipe and Bahía Honda on the northern coast. The Cuban response requested a postponement of this issue until the signing of the trade agreement, which took place late in 1902.

The U.S. Navy Department also intended to have a naval base in Havana. However, there is no document in the historical archives of the Ministry of Foreign Affairs of Cuba proving that the Government of the United States had considered making such a request.

Lastly, the United States accepted tracts of land to establish two naval bases in Cuba, one in Guantánamo and another in Bahía Honda, and changed their opinion in regard to the duration of the bases from perpetuity to a lease without date of expiry. They later insisted, demanding the solution of the issue of the coaling stations, and set March 4, 1903 as the date for its conclusion, for that was the time when the U.S. Senate closed its working sessions.

The February 16/23, 1903 Agreement

The agreement on the two coaling and naval stations was signed, under the aforementioned North American pressures, in Havana on February 16, 1903, and on March 23 in Washington by presidents Tomás Estrada Palma and Theodore Roosevelt, respectively. Their lease "for as long as they are needed," as stated in Article I, (See Annex 4) camouflaged perpetuity.

The preamble of the agreement on coaling stations and naval bases is Article VII of the amendment and the appendix; it also has three further articles:

Article I of the Agreement says that the Republic of Cuba leases two territories to the United States—the document says "the extensions of land and water" and that the lease would be "for as long as they are needed and with the purpose of establishing there coaling or naval stations," and immediately goes on to specify the extension of land and water of each of those territories, respectively located at Guantánamo and Bahía Honda.

Ultimately, the legal term used was lease, for Article VII of the amendment/appendix/treaty established the alternative of selling or leasing.

The above sentences enclosed in quotation marks should be specially borne in mind: the agreed time for the lease was "as long as they are needed" by the United States and, according to such an agreement, they were leased "with the purpose of establishing coaling or naval stations on them."

Article II determines the right of the United States of America to use and to occupy the waters adjoining the area defined by the geographic coordinates specified in Article I, and grants the North Americans both comprehensive and limited powers to do "all that is necessary to outfit those places so they can be used *exclusively* as coaling or naval stations, and for no other purpose." I emphasize the word "exclusively" so that one of the many violations of the agreement can be verified, for the United States has put to other uses the territories leased.

Article III of this same agreement specifies that the United States acknowledged the definitive sovereignty of the Republic of Cuba over the extensions of land and water of the aforementioned coaling and naval stations whereas Cuba consented to the agreement's provisos in the sense that, while the United States occupies those areas, they would be under the North American nation's full jurisdiction and domination.

The 1903 Complementary Agreement

The Plattist, interventionist February 16/23, 1903 Agreement was regulated by the Complementary Agreement signed in Havana on July 2, 1903. José M. García Montes, Secretary of Finance and interim Secretary of State and Justice signed on behalf of the Republic of Cuba, and Herbert G. Squiers, Minister Plenipotentiary in Havana signed on behalf of the United States (See Annex 5). The Complementary Agreement stipulated that:

- The United States would give Cuba, as the yearly price of the lease, the amount of 2000 U.S. gold dollars (currently some 4085 U.S. dollars).
- Such areas would be defined.
- No criminal or fugitive from Cuban laws would find shelter or sanctuary in the territory of the base.
- Other clauses refer to the uses of the base.

About Approvals and Ratification

As the approval of the Senate of the Republic of Cuba was needed prior to the ratification of the February 16/12, 1903 Agreement, President Estrada Palma submitted it on the following March 3 and, according to the Senate's *Working Sessions Journal*, the Agreement was read on March 6, causing an outraged comment from the Marquis of Saint

Lucia, who refused to participate in the voting, saying that if he had opposed the Platt Amendment as a delegate to the 1901 Constituent Assembly, he was also against this handing over of Cuban soil.

Finally, the document was ratified on July 16, 1903 by 12 votes to 4, and on that same afternoon the Complementary Agreement, signed on July 2, 1903, was also approved. The President of the United States ratified the Agreement on October 2, 1903; Estrada Palma had already done so on August 17 of that same year. The documents of ratification were exchanged in Washington on October 6, and published in the *Gaceta Oficial de la República de Cuba* on October 12 of that same year.

The Non-Ratified 1912 Agreement

The so-called "August Warlet" took place in Cuba in 1906. That prompted President Estrada Palma, always so eager to have the North Americans in Cuba, to pave the way for the second U.S. intervention that began in 1906 and lasted until 1909. The epigraph "The Second U.S. Military Intervention" in chapter II offers more details about this issue. A new president, José Miguel Gómez, came to power in Cuba in 1909. Another civil confrontation took place in 1912, the so-called "Negroes' War" that ended in a massacre. U.S. troops came into Cuba again on that same year; in chapter II, I have commented some episodes and given certain examples of U.S. interventionism on the Cuban economic and political life, and of some of that year's happenings.

Furthermore, a development related to the coaling and naval stations took place in 1912. Late that year, in December, the United States and Cuba signed a new Agreement where the following was stipulated:

- The section about the Naval Base at Bahía Honda was rescinded.

- New limits were fixed to broaden the perimeter of the base at Guantánamo, pushing them to the middle of the Yateras river and the Guantánamo Bay outlet.

- The payment for the lease rose to 5000 U.S. gold dollars, thus covering for all of the base's territory, both the one included in the 1903 Agreement and the parcels added by the 1912 Agreement.

- Cuba would buy from their respective owners any private parcels located within the new limits of the territory to be leased to the United States according to this Agreement, to include them in the area of the base at Guantánamo.

- The United States would pay Cuba in advance so that it could purchase those parcels. The amounts advanced would be deducted from the lease's payment.

The Agreement, signed on December 27, 1912 in Havana, was not approved by Senate of the United States or by the Senate of the Republic of Cuba. The agreement specified that it had to be ratified within six months for, on the contrary, the treaty would be null and void.

The issue of the naval base at Guantánamo was once again submitted to a treaty: the 1934 Relations Treaty, to which I will refer further on.

It is worth explaining that when Cuban experts refer to "the Base Treaties," we are really referring to the two 1903 agreements, as well as to the base at Guantánamo, for the 1934 Relations Treaty included the 1903 agreements in regard to the naval base at Guantánamo and did not include the naval base at Bahía Honda.

Why Guantánamo?

Cuban author Gerardo Castellanos in his book *Paseos efímeros* (*Ephemeral Promenades*), published in 1930, offers certain facts about Guantánamo Bay and how convenient it was for the North Americans to have picked it up as the site for a base:

> When Christopher Columbus visited it on April 29, 1494, during his second trip, he called it Puerto Grande "because its

girth amazed him." Castellanos describes that bay thus:

> Its almost hidden, quite narrow entrance, and then the bay itself with numerous coves, inlets and inner ports, all of them sufficiently deep; the keys, the beautiful rivers that flow into it, the adjacent salt marshes, in short, complex labyrinths good for hiding and even for watching, made it the strategic meeting-place of pirates and buccaneers. They were in fact the first to acknowledge the advantages it offered as a lookout from where to begin the hunt and hide in the blink of an eye [...] undoubtedly the best maritime hiding place on these coasts [...] Immense. Eleven miles deep and twenty-seven around. A navigable river that runs to the north. Heights that can be fortified to an advantage. Beyond its outlet, the deep, open sea [...].[1]

The background of the Marine Corps of the United States is the British Royal Marines, created on October 28, 1664. In the early 1740s, England created four 3000-strong battalions to serve against Spain; these men were known as "Gooch's Marines" after their chief, Colonel William Gooch.

In 1741 British troops commanded by Admiral Edward Vernon occupied Guantánamo Bay and the adjoining areas for some time, naming the place Cumberland, as a tribute to the famous British marine who fought against Philip II of Spain's Invincible Armada. Gooch's Marines watched over the bay that served as a base for the British Fleet.

George Washington's older brother, named Leicester Washington, from the troops of the Thirteen North American Colonies, was among the British troops that occupied Guantánamo at the time: a numerous squad and over 5000 men. It is said that when he returned home he named his properties "Mount Vernon" as a tribute to his chief, Admiral Edward Vernon.

In the months before Spaniards and Cubans definitively drove them back, and before they left on July 18, 1742, the Britons studied the

1. Gerardo Castellanos, *Paseos efímeros* (Havana: 1930). Quoted by Emilio Roig de Leuchsenring, *Historia de la Enmienda Platt*, 293.

flora and the fauna in Guantánamo and also explored the broad bay, thus determining its strategic importance for controlling the Caribbean.

But the city of Guantánamo, to the rear end of the bay, was not founded until almost one century later, during the third decade of the 19th century, on orders of the island's colonial government.

The U.S. Marines, who already knew the terrain and its location, landed at Guantánamo on June 9, 1898, in the midst of the military operations against Spain, and since then kept watch over the Guantánamo bay and the adjacent area.

They remained there since then until the Cuban Government, according to the Platt Amendment, was obliged to lease that area indefinitely to the United States.

In 1898—the year of the Joint Resolution and the Treaty of Paris—, long before the Platt Amendment was approved on March 2, 1901 by United States President McKinley, a commission of experts in hydrography made up by officers from the gunboat "Eagle" of the U.S. Navy, spent several months in Guantánamo taking various measurements and fathoming the bay. The accuracy of this commission's work was fully verified by the mixed commission that marked the limits of the future base.[2]

Gerardo Castellano's view about the U.S. base at Guantánamo, contained in his aforementioned book referring to the Guantánamo bay and to the base was the following, at the time it was published in 1930:

> An observatory, an insuperable watch tower from where watching neighboring Haiti and Saint Domingo, where Uncle Sam has already set foot, is easy and economical. To the south, the entrances to the Panama Canal and to the canal soon to be built in Nicaragua. Almost to the other side, the island of Puerto Rico. To the rear, the rich land of Cuba, whose government is a mandatory ally. With a narrow mouth impossible to take by storm due to the dangers posed by the modern batteries placed on the

2. Act of the operations carried out to mark the limits of the Naval Station at Guantánamo, signed on board the cruiser "Olympia" in the Bay of Guantánamo, on July 8, 1903. Archives of the Ministry of Foreign Affairs of the Republic of Cuba.

> Leeward and Windward tips. It can easily shelter several squads with all their auxiliary means and scores of hydroplanes.[3]

The Transfer of the Territory to be Occupied by the Base at Guantánamo

The transfer of the land where the North American Base would be established according to the Plattist plot, caused concern even to President Estrada Palma who was not characterized precisely by his ill-will for U.S. rulers. There are some documents in the archives of the Ministry of Foreign Affairs that historically mark the initial and permanent repudiation from the Cuban people to the mutilation of its territory to establish an imposed naval base.

On February 16, 1903, the Secretary of State of the Republic of Cuba sent a letter to Herbert S. Squiers, Minister Plenipotentiary of the Embassy of the United States in Cuba, accompanying the Agreement for coaling and naval stations signed by President Estrada Palma on that same day. One of its paragraphs is one proof more of the force used by the U.S. Government to seize the territory for the base. The Cuban Secretary of State begins by saying to Mr. Squiers, according to the protocol used at the time, that he had been entrusted by the Cuban president to make it known to him that the

> President expresses to the North American minister that he has signed that document in the understanding that, according to what it establishes, Cuba has fulfilled the provisos in Article 7th of the Constitutional Appendix and, therefore, the Government of the United States will not request other naval or coaling stations. At the same time, he points out, on behalf of the president, that the Cuban people will be satisfied if the Government of the United States, matching the behavior observed by the Government of Cuba in regard to this issue, begins to transfer the North American troops that occupy Cuban fortresses to

3. Gerardo Castellanos, op. cit., in Emilio Roig de Leuchsenring, *Historia de la Enmienda Platt*, 293.

> the places assigned them as soon as the complementary agreement to which he previously referred, is completed.[4]

On October 28, 1903, the Secretary of State of the Republic of Cuba sent a note to Gonzalo de Quesada, the Cuban Minister Plenipotentiary in Washington, referring to the fact that he has learned about the intentions of the North American Government to rally a large number of warships to witness the ceremony to hand over the naval base, and instructs him to present to the State Department the following consideration: "That the Cuban Government, interpreting the people's patriotic sentiments, would appreciate that such a ceremony was not highly publicized or turned into a festivity by the United States."[5]

The aforementioned note from the Cuban Secretary of State goes on to say that: "You know perfectly well that the cession of adequate places for the establishment of naval or coaling stations has been agreed upon by the Republic fulfilling an unavoidable commitment; but in no way whatsoever is it a pleasant happening for the people of Cuba who, for that reason, cannot associate with any demonstration of joy for that cession."[6]

The result of that action was a cablegram from Minister Gonzalo de Quesada, dated in Washington, November 9, 1903, and addressed to the Cuban secretary of State in Havana, saying:

> I spoke with the secretary of the Navy and got assurances that what you deem convenient will be done. Send cable informing me adequate way for transference Government determines. Could simply be an American salute to Cuban flag when hauled down, as sign of respect and consideration; and a salute to America flag when hoisted.

4. Olga Miranda Bravo, "Algunas consideraciones histórico-jurídicas sobre la ocupación ilegal del territorio cubano de la base naval yanqui en Guantánamo," in *Revista Cubana de Derecho*, 38 (Havana: 1989): 153.
5. Ibid.
6. Ibid.

> The Secretary suggests parade by American Marines; I think it can be omitted."[7]

Finally, Note No. 1222, dated December 9, 1903, from the Cuban Mission in Washington, Minister Gonzalo de Quesada informed the Cuban Secretariat of State that Rear-Admiral Albert S. Baker, who commanded the U.S. North Atlantic squad, had informed him on the previous day that:

> The "Kearsage," the "Alabama," the "Illinois," the "Massachusetts" and the "Scorpion" had left Guantánamo.
>
> The transfer of the base to North American hands will be effective on the 10th according to the simple program agreed upon.
>
> The "Vixen" will remain in Guantánamo and its Captain, Lieutenant Commander W.H. Allen, will be the first commander of the naval station.[8]

On December 10, 1903, the chief engineer of the Santiago de Cuba district went to Caimanera early in the morning, boarding the battle-ship "Kearsage," the North American flag-ship, to meet Rear-Admiral Baker. At noon, 21 volleys were fired and, while the Cuban national anthem was played, the Cuban flag on the "Kearsage" was lowered, and the North American flag was immediately hoisted on land, at Playa del Este, accompanied by an equal number of volleys. Thus concluded the ceremony.

According to the 1903 Complementary Treaty, the purchase of privately-owned land in the area to be occupied by the Guantánamo Naval Base would be funded by the Cuban Government with money from the U.S. Navy Department, and those amounts would be deducted from the annual payments of the lease made to Cuba by the United States.

7. Ibid., 153-154.
8. Ibid., 154.

It is stated in the notes dated September 18, 1903, exchanged between the U.S. Minister Plenipotentiary in Cuba, H. P. Squiers, and Carlos de Zaldo, Cuban Secretary of State and Justice—now in the archives of the Ministry of Foreign Affairs of the Republic of Cuba—, that the U.S. Navy Department informed that 100,000 dollars were available for that purchase, and offered to pay the rest with a credit approved by the Congress.

The estates El Cuero, El Ocujal, El Boquerón, El Cuzco, Punta de Caracoles and Mata Abajo would be transferred to the Cuban state to be handed over to the United States for the lease of land and water mentioned in the 1903 Agreement. The 24 keys in the Guantánamo bay, the Guantánamo lighthouse, the lighthouse keepers' houses, the buoys and the markers, all of which belong to the Cuban state, would also be transferred to the United States.

All these properties totaled 591,662 "caballerías" (1 "caballería" = 33 acres) and should be made available to the United States on December 10, 1903, the date fixed by them for the transference ceremony; according to the lease, those properties would be occupied by the United States "for as long as they need them."

However, not all of these privately-owned estates were available on the date fixed; there are several notes in the archives of the Ministry of Foreign Affairs about various issues related to the receipt of money and the payment of properties, like the ones dated July 7, 8 and 25, September 6 and December 20 and 22, 1904 about the partial payment of $35,577.55 to purchase the farm El Cuzco; the notes dated May 16, December 19, 1905, January 24 and February 10, 1906 about the receipt of $44,192.78 to pay for the Punta Caracoles and El Cuero farms, and about the buildings located near Fisherman Point and Tres Piedras. On February 20, 1906 a U.S. money order for 23,116.70 payable to Cuba was sent to pay for the bulk of the farm El Ocujal.

It may be assumed that a good part of the money involved in those transactions ended up fattening the pockets of corrupt rulers.

The Limits of the Base at Guantánamo

Article II of the 1903 Complementary Agreement rules that the land leased for the Base would be permanently and precisely fenced off. The United States would pay for the building and maintenance of all those fences.

Although the site was well known, in compliance with the February 16/23, 1903 Agreement a bipartite commission was established to mark the limits of the land destined for the naval station at Guantánamo. It was formed by Captain Lyon, Lieutenant Commander Lean and Lieutenant Benham for the U.S. side, and by the Director of Public Works José Primelles and the Engineer in Public Works Agustín Gordillo for the Cuban side.

Measurement of the land began on May 28, 1903, and the limits were thus established:

- East border, from a site on the coast 4.37 maritime miles from the lighthouse located at Windward Point according to Article I of the Agreement.

- North border, from the northern end of the East border, 5.87 maritime miles to the west.

- Northeast border, from the west end of the North border, 3.31 maritime miles to the southwest.

- West border, from the southwest end of the Northeast border, along the line that runs southward to the coast.

"Rectangular prism-like concrete boundary markers made of one part of cement, two parts of sand and four parts of chopped stone, were made to mark out the boundaries…"[9]; their upper part resembled a pyramid. The five boundary markers placed on the Nor-

9. Act of operations carried out to mark the borders of the Naval Station at Guantánamo, signed on board the cruiser "Olympia" on the Guantánamo Bay, on July 8, 1903. Archives of the Ministry of Foreign Affairs of the Republic of Cuba.

theast, Northwest and Southwest borders, and where the East and West borders touch the coast are taller than the intermediate ones, with 1.60 meters and 1.20 meters respectively. Each marker has the letter H (for the Spanish word "hito" = boundary marker) and a number, from 1 to 25. H-1 is on the coast, on the south end of the east border; H-3 is on the north corner and runs through the north border; H-14 to the east of the bay and H-15 to the west, H-17 on the northwest corner and along this border to the southwest corner and, lastly, H-25 on the southern point of the west border.

The intermediate markers were placed in such a way that they can be clearly seen from one main marker to the next.

The total area of the Naval Base is 117.6 *sq. km*, and comprises 79.4 *sq. km* of land and 37,21 *sq. km* of water. Given that the site is swampy, its considered that there are 39.9 *sq. km* of sea, 29.4 *sq. km* of swamps and 49.5 *sq. km* of terra firma.

The base's limits were ratified by the May 29, 1904 Treaty, whose Article III states: "While the United States of America does not abandon the aforementioned naval station at Guantánamo, or while the two governments do not agree to modify its current limits, it will continue to have the territorial extension it now occupies, with the limits extant on the date this Treaty is signed."

Maritime Traffic

According to Article II of the February 16/23, 1903 Treaty, and to the way of implementing it due to the contiguity of the occupied (leased) areas and the rest of the Cuban national territory, articles V and VI of the July 2, 1903 Complementary Agreement that regulated the former implementation, ruled in detail the aforementioned maritime traffic as follows:

Article II of the February 16/23, 1903 Agreement begins by saying: "The concession on the previous Article," and refers to what was stated in Article I, to wit, the extensions of land leased by Cuba to the United States, according to the description. Article II expresses that such concession would also include the right to use and occupy the waters adjacent to those extensions of land and water, and to improve and deepen the entrances of those bays, and their anchoring grounds and, in general terms, to do what is deemed necessary to make those places available for their use as coaling or naval stations exclusively, and for none other purpose. The second and last paragraph of Article II states: "The ships devoted to trading with Cuba will be able to pass freely through the waters included in this concession."

On the other hand, the Complementary Agreement dated July 2, 1903, that regulated the Agreement on coaling and naval stations signed a few months earlier, devoted its articles V and VI to the maritime traffic in the North American bases. Article V states that all types of goods, like merchandise, war equipment and ammunition imported by such areas for their exclusive use and consumption, would not have to pay customs duties or any other cargo duties. In regard to the ships transporting these goods, they would not have to pay harbor, tonnage, anchorage, or other duties, save when they were unloaded outside the boundaries of the areas where the bases would stand. Then it goes on to clarify that such ships would not be unloaded outside the limits of the areas under lease save at ports authorized by the Republic of Cuba, in whose case, both the cargo and the ships would be subject to Cuban custom's laws and regulations, and would have to pay the corresponding duties.

The second and last paragraph of Article V of the Complementary Agreement stipulates that the goods, merchandise, equipment and ammunition referred to in the previous paragraph would not be transported from the area occupied by the bases to Cuban territory.

Article VI of the aforementioned Complementary Agreement expressly states that "excepting what is instructed by the previous article"—referring to Article VI already commented—and provided that they are within the limits of the Cuban territory, the ships going in or out of the bay of Guantánamo Bay or Bahía Honda will be exclusively accountable to Cuban laws and authorities in regard to Cuban port authorities, customs and sanitation. Lastly, Article VI states that U.S. authorities will not place any obstacle whatsoever to the entry and exit of the aforementioned ships, but the document makes an exception regarding the latter: "except in a state of war."

The February 16/23, 1903 Agreement on coaling and naval stations and the July 2, 1903 Complementary Agreement refer to the concessions of territory in the Cuban areas of Guantánamo and Bahía Honda but, as I had already said and will expound further on, the concession for a base at Bahía Honda was not ratified by the Treaty signed in 1934. (See Annex 7)

It must also be noted that, as the naval base at Guantánamo is located at the entry of the great bay, from whose coasts it penetrates for 4.25 maritime miles to the north, it was logical to foresee the rules to which the ships that needed to cross the waters adjacent to the naval station to load or unload within the bay, on whose shores important Cuban towns like Boquerón and Caimaneras are located, would be subjected, for the station completely controls the aforementioned entrance to the bay. Thus the agreement ensures both the free access to the bay and the full jurisdiction over the ships that enter it and are not carrying goods, merchandise or war equipment for the naval station.

The last sentence in Article VI cannot be dismissed, for it grants the United States the right to unilaterally hinder maritime traffic "during a state of war." It could be asked what two parties would wage that war. Could it be a war between the United States and Cuba, or could it be a war between the United States and another country, in whose context Cuba would have declared allegiance to the United States or its neutrality in the conflict?

Such a clause could drag or involve Cuba in a war extraneous to it, and close the doors of the Guantánamo bay to its normal trade. The Agreement is plagued by those hegemonic dictates for, although the United States did not—and still does not—have sovereign rights, they can in fact exercise full domination.

Some Preliminary Legal Considerations

I deem it pertinent at this point to comment some legal issues, and make certain comparisons that I will expound further in the next chapter.

I must emphasize that due to the fact that contracts are the expression of coinciding wills in the creation of a legal link, free consent from both parties is essential to its perfection. For such reason, in the case of the agreements imposed upon Cuba for it to allow the establishment of bases on its territory, that consent was defective by the coercion exerted upon Cuba.

It is known that some people in our country have been confused by or are not acquainted with the timeframe of the lease of the land where the base at Guantánamo is located. Therefore, it must be clarified that the timeframe of this lease is not fixed in years, but by the will of the lessee, in this case, the United States.

There are another cases regarding various treaties on naval bases. For example, on September 2, 1940, the United States signed with the United Kingdom an agreement for the lease of several territories in some British colonies, to be used as naval and air bases for a term of 99 years: in Terranova, on the Avalón Peninsula, to the south and on the east coast; in Bermudas, on the Great Bay coast. It also included lands to the east of the Bahamas, south of Jamaica, east of Saint Lucia, in Trinidad—in the Gulf of Paria—, in Antigua and in British Guyana. I will deal with the case of these leases later on.

Naturally, it was an agreement with Great Britain, that was not, like Cuba, occupied or subjected to the coercion and the intervention of its sovereign values. The 99-year term was fixed according to British laws that recognize leases for that maximum span of time.

In 1913, the United States signed a 99-year lease with Nicaragua in order to establish, operate and keep a naval base in the Nicaraguan territory bordering the Gulf of Fonseca, in the sites chosen by the United States. But as Nicaragua is not the United Kingdom but, in North American criteria, part of the U.S. back yard, North American imperialism appropriated in that treaty the right to opt for its renovation for another 99 years when the previous treaty expired. Ultimately, the coastal Gulf states objected to the Treaty.

Perhaps issues like the aforementioned contributed to make some Cubans, among others, realize that the 99-year limit was also applied to the Agreement on coaling and naval stations.

In regard to the naval base at Guantánamo, the *Digest of International Law* published by the U.S. State Department says: "In the Agreement between Cuba and the United States, signed by Cuba February 16 and by the United States February 23, 1903, to lease in Guantánamo and in Bahía Honda, 'for the time required for the purposes of coaling and naval stations'."[10]

In 1903, the United States did not consider Cuba a sovereign state, for the treatment it bestowed to the emerging Cuban republic was that of an occupied territory, of a war booty, given its ancestral wish to seize Cuba, but having to observe certain formalities by means of a legal lease, that does not imply a perpetual right but a temporary one, they opted for keeping to themselves the setting of that timeframe in regard to the base, that is to say, "for as long as they need it."

THE LAST TREATY

The Circumstances Surrounding the Treaty's Signature

I already said that U.S. imperialism's new face was purportedly presented to Latin America and to the world as the caricature of a promoter of non-intervention by the Democratic Party under Franklin Delano Roosevelt's presidency. This new face exhibited the aforementioned Good Neighbor policy whose most important expressions were the signing of the Convention About the Rights and the Duties of States, approved at the Pan-American Conference held in Montevideo, in Uruguay, in 1933, which proclaimed non-intervention, the withdrawal of U.S. interventionist troops in Haiti and, regarding Cuba, the false repeal of the Platt Amendment and the signature of new treaties on relations and trade.

Vis-à-vis this circumstances, Cuban and North American figures began to lobby during Roosevelt's government in order to bring about a formal change in U.S. policy toward Cuba.

In a message to Congress explaining the motives that had prompted another message sent to 54 nations, President Roosevelt, with the purpose of showing his pacifist policy, said: "It is the time when we

10. *Digest of International Law*, 2, 1216.

and every nation understand the simple fact that the invasion of any country, or the destruction of a national sovereignty can be prevented only with the complete elimination of the weapons that render such a thing possible."[11]

It was late 1933 and the media spread the news that in Washington a new trade reciprocity treaty was in the making, and that the Platt Amendment would be repealed and its demands obliterated.

Due to the developments of September 4, 1933 in Cuba, the U.S. Government faced the issue of its protectorate in a two-fold manner: it sent 19 men-of-war from the Atlantic Fleet to Cuba by way of a military action and, as a diplomatic measure, it stated its non-recognition to the Provisional Government headed by Ramón Grau San Martín. The well-known mediation of the U.S. presidential envoy, Jefferson Caffery, already in connivance with the man who would be his most loyal ally, the then chief of the Cuban army, Fulgencio Batista, forced President Grau to resign thus paving the way to the formation of a servile government presided by Colonel Carlos Mendieta, to whom Washington's recognition was immediately granted.

Thus we find ourselves before an evident contradiction within the North American Government in regard to its Good Neighbor policy: on the one hand, its declaration about its much publicized non-interventionism and, on the other, the dispatch of warships to Cuban coasts; political pressure was another variant of interventionism as well. Rather than a contradiction, the North American behavior regarding these developments confirm that it was nothing but a pharisaic declaration of non-interventionism by the government in Washington.

Once the "machadista" tyranny was overthrown, the U.S. media commented that the repeal of the Platt Amendment must wait until Colonel Mendieta's Government had stabilized itself in power. Thus, the 1934 Relations Treaty (See Annex 7) was quietly negotiated between the United States and its Cuban acolytes headed by Batista and Mendieta. These negotiations did not leak to the media and they were concluded in a hasty fashion. Emilio Roig de Leuchsenring, in his *Historia de la Enmienda Platt* (*History of the Platt Amendment*) com-

11. Emilio Roig de Leuchsenring, *Historia de la Enmienda Platt*, 282.

ments what the media said at the time about that issue, and quotes a note that appeared on May 30, 1934:

> As an example, we will quote the comments from the daily *Ahora*. "Yesterday afternoon, Havana unexpectedly learned about the repeal of the Platt Amendment [...] The news was front-paged by the evening papers, the public was amazed by it [...] many comments among which those made by foreigners, even more surprised by the news than the Cubans themselves. A few hours after the news was spread, there were surprised comments at not seeing the multitude take to the streets shouting in joy. Why? Perchance because we learned about it unexpectedly, without giving U.S. time to greet it with the expected hurrahs...?[12]

What were the reasons for this concealment and this haste? Perhaps they were due to the fact that on May 27 an attempt against the life of the North American Ambassador Jefferson Caffery had taken place and, on the following day, another attempt against H. Freeman Matthews, First Secretary of that same Embassy, occurred. These two developments could explain to North American authorities that the domestic situation in Cuba could involve them and prevent them from enjoying their new image.[13]

The Government of the United States wanted to give this new treaty as much publicity as possible and appointed no less than the Secretary of State Cordell Hull and the Under-Secretary of State, Sumner Welles to sign it; Welles' signature was not required, for the signature of the Secretary—who headed the Secretariat—sufficed, more so when the Cuban side was only represented by its Ambassador to Washington, Manuel Márquez Sterling.[14]

The United States purported with the signing of this treaty to erase the blemish of coercion, imposition and interference that had stained the signing of the 1903 Permanent Relations Treaty; but the 1934

12. *Ahora*, (May 30, 1934). Quoted by Emilio Roig de Leuchsenring, Ibid., 294-295.
13. Emilio Roig de Leuchsenring, Ibid., 295-296.
14. Ibid., 297.

Relations treaty was in fact signed under coercion, for it must be borne in mind that warships were sent to Cuba and that a government like the one headed by Grau in 1933, that had ample popular support, had not been recognized. Therefore, coercion and blackmail continued to be present, and the naval base at the Guantánamo bay also continued to be present.

The 1934 Treaty

The Treaty on Relations of May 29, 1934 signed between the United States and the Republic of Cuba states that its aim is to invalidate the 1903 Permanent Treaty of Relations, that is to say, the Platt Amendment, that were one and the same thing. But the North Americans hastened to ratify by the 1934 Treaty their hold over the naval base at Guantánamo, for the February 16/23, 1903 Agreement on the lease of the territory for the bases was previous to the May 22, 1903 Permanent Treaty of Relations, and the Agreement is based on clause VII of the Platt Amendment rather than on Article VII of the aforementioned Permanent Treaty of Relations that did not exist at that date. Therefore, the 1934 Treaty does not repeal the Platt Amendment, nor the 1903 Permanent Treaty of Relations regarding the base.

The heading of the Treaty on Relations dated May 29, 1934, establishes the following: "The Republic of Cuba and the United States of America, prompted by the desire to strengthen the links of friendship between the two countries, and to modify to that end the relations established between them by the Treaty of Relations signed in Havana on May 22, 1903…"

The five articles included in this Treaty are listed next. They refer to the following issues:

Article I expresses that the Permanent Treaty of Relations dated May 22, 1903 became invalid and was repealed as of the date in which the new Treaty of Relations was enforced. That date was June 9, 1934.

Article II establishes the validity of all the actions carried out in Cuba by the United States of America during its military occupation until May 20, 1902.

Article III states that, while "the two contracting parties fail to agree to modify or repeal the Agreement's provisos"—referring to the Agreement on coaling and naval stations signed February 16/23, 1903 first by the president of the Republic of Cuba and then by the president of the United States of America—"in regard to leasing land in Cuba to the United States of America" for the aforementioned coaling or naval stations—and it is this point in Article III that clearly establishes the base's status quo after the 1934 Treaty was enforced, like it was established by the 1903 document—, "that agreement's provisos will continue to be in effect regarding the naval station at Guantánamo."

Further on, and clearly referring to the Complementary Agreement, it states that: "In regard to that naval station, the supplementary agreement referring to naval or coaling stations concluded between the two governments on July 2, 1903 will also continue to be in force in the same manner and under the same conditions." However, Article III also says that the United States will keep the base at Guantánamo for as long as they stay in it.

As a consequence of the fact that the 1934 Treaty did not ratify what had been agreed upon in paragraph 2, Article I of the February 16/23, 1903 Agreement on coaling and naval stations, in regard to the North American right to establish a coaling and naval station in Bahía Honda, what remains of the territorial demands imposed by the United States upon Cuba according to the Platt Amendment is the territory they still occupy in Guantánamo.

Regarding the base at Bahía Honda, the twin of the naval base at Guantánamo according to the 1903 Treaty, it must be borne in mind that the United States had already made know their intentions of leaving it in the 1912 Treaty that, as we already saw, was never ratified; the 1934 Treaty of Relations does not include that issue. Note that the North Americans did not expressly renounce the base at Bahía Honda: they simply abandoned it. It appears to be their habit not to renounce to what they deem is theirs, although it is useless to them or harmful to their interests.

According to Article IV of the 1934 Treaty, the reciprocal suspension of trade among the ports in the two countries was established if any contagious disease broke out in the future in any of them, albeit not considering that suspension as an unfriendly act. This article is not written in the blatantly interfering style that characterizes Article V of the 1903 Treaty.

Article V of the 1934 document refers to the procedures to ratify the Treaty and to other formalities.

It has been frequently said that the 1934 Treaty repealed the Platt Amendment, but it can be seen by literally reading this Treaty, that the Platt Amendment was and continues to be alive and underhandedly implemented.

It is an accepted legal axiom that to derogate a law is to oppose it with something, and to repeal a law is to entirely destroy it. The Platt Amendment was not repealed, for it was extant in the 1934 Treaty in regard to the naval base at Guantánamo.

Regarding the concept of "perpetuity" that has been occasionally used—that in fact is tantamount to the indetermination or to the lack of a date of expiry for the 1903 Permanent Treaty of Relations and the 1903 Agreement on coaling and naval stations—, I must point out the importance of the fact that the 1934 Treaty of Relations derogated the 1903 Permanent Treaty of Relations and that a clause (Article III) was necessary to indicate that "the provisos in that Agreement regarding the naval station at Guantánamo will continue to be in effect."

Note that the 1903 Agreement refers to "coaling and naval stations," but that the 1934 Treaty changed the name to "naval station."

If we make a careful reading of Article III of the 1934 Treaty we will verify that the February 16/23, 1903 Agreement and its Complementary Agreement dated July 2, 1903 is still in force regarding the naval base at Guantánamo; therefore, the 1934 Treaty only derogates and replaces the 1903 Permanent Treaty of Relations, but the February 16/23, 1903 Agreement is based on clause VII of the Amendment/Appendix and not on the aforementioned 1903 Treaty. Consequently, the *null ab initio* of the February 16/23, 1903 persist and are not affected by the 1934 Treaty because they are derived, as we have already pointed out, from the Constitutional Amendment/Appendix.

I believe that the fate of the 1903 Agreement on coaling and naval stations was not the same than that of the 1903 Permanent Treaty of

Relations, for the 1934 Treaty of Relations modifies the latter, but not the former.

The February 16/23, 1903 Agreement on coaling and naval stations, and the May 22, 1903 Permanent Treaty of Relations were plagued by grounds for invalidation. There was no freedom of consent on the part of Cuba, for the United States coerced it by the use of force and the constant threat of intervention. Do we not remember Leonard Wood's report to the members of the1901 Constituent Assembly, and the arrogance of the North American Government, as well as the humiliation to General Calixto García when he was not allowed to enter Santiago de Cuba in 1898? There was no good faith on the part of the United States since the Joint Resolution.

In order for the norm *pacta sunt servanda* to be fulfilled, a bilateral treaty must be the result of an agreement between two wills and not the prevalence of one of them. Likewise, this norm is no longer mandatory when one of the parties acts contrary to the obligations agreed upon and, consequently, the other party can consider itself released from its commitment.

A treaty *null ab initio* like the Agreement for coaling and naval stations dated February 16/23,1903, cannot be validated by the simple fact that time has elapsed, but only when the cause of the invalidity has ceased to be, and such a cause was the lack of will from the Cuban people to relinquish that portion of its territory.

It is not about applying the norm *rebus sic stantibus* (every treaty in force is binding upon the parties to it and it must be performed by them in good faith)—and I refer to that in detail in chapter IV—to the February 16/23, 1903 Agreement on coaling and naval stations for the lease of the naval station, for that treaty did not come to be, that treaty is not licit, it does not stem from a legitimate obligation: a unilateral decision was imposed upon Cuba; thus, the occupation of the territory where the naval base at Guantánamo stands is unlawful. Therefore, the 1934 Treaty of Relations cannot be validated by the lease imposed.

The 1934 Treaty Benefited Only One of the Signatories

The 1934 Treaty of Relations did not really benefit the people of Cuba nor did it address its interests. The beneficiary was the Government of the United States. However, it achieved nothing by means of the naked coercion and threat it had exerted in 1901, but by showing the latent threat of intervention, of interference, of aggression.

Only the naval base at Guantánamo needed an evident, unequivocal ratification in the context of the U.S. right to intervene in Cuba, established in the amendment/appendix/treaty, for the remaining interests that benefited the North Americans in the amendment/appendix/treaty had been fully ensured by the *de facto* domination exerted by the United States over the Cuban economy and politics.

I will explain in further detail the last issue in the previous paragraph. The situation related to Cuban sovereignty over the Isle of Pines (Article VI of the Platt Amendment) had been resolved by the 1904/1925 Treaty. The right to intervene (Article III of the Platt Amendment) contradicted the avowed North American Good Neighbor policy—based in non-intervention—reaffirmed at the Pan-American Conference held in Montevideo in 1933 and, therefore, the United States could not uphold the right to intervene in Cuba's case alone. Also they did not need it any more, for the neo-colonial domination was exercised without hindrances, and the Cuban economy was totally dependent from the powerful northern empire. The United States did not need to preserve Cuba's limitations to sign treaties with other nations and to contract public works (articles I and II of the Platt Amendment), for the implementation of its policy, availing itself of successive puppet governments, did not require such a contradictory instrument with a republic whose attributes of independence were reflected in the exercise of its external policy.

The new 1934 Commercial Treaty granted the United States a preferential reduction of between 35% and 60% in the tariffs for 487 groups and sub-groups of North American goods coming into Cuba, thus displacing European goods. Cuba had to accept the sugar quotas, an issue that limited its exports to the United States, albeit the 1934 Treaty granted Cuba a tariff reduction of 90 cents (0.90 dollars) for sugar and some other products like rum, fruits and vegetables; such reductions would only be made during the seasons when those products were neither produced nor harvested in the United States.

While these preferences benefited the United States, the Castigan-Jones Act—establishing the sugar quotas—impaired Cuba, since Cuban sugar exports to the U.S. market in 1922 were 56.7% and in 1934 it was fixed at 29.40%, upon the average of the last three years, which were the worst ones in the history of the trade between Cuba and the United Sates.

Although the mediation of the U.S. Ambassador Sumner Wells to try to save the tyrant Gerardo Machado was fruitless, a new stage in the relations with the United States began with the signing of the 1934 Treaty, burdened still by the sequels of the protectorate. That is why those relations would continue to be relations of dependence. On that same year, the structural changes required to face the economic crisis on the island, in the United States and in the world at large, began to be introduced in the semi-colony or Plattist Republic of Cuba.

Since then, U.S. interventionism adopted another style, for the Platt Amendment would no longer be wielded, but the method would rather be the use of the successive puppet governments and the dominance of foreign capital over Cuba. The naval base at Guantánamo, the only really valid thing in the outdated Platt Amendment, was what remained from the apparent renunciation of U.S. rights over the Cuban republic

The 1934 Relations Treaty cannot conceal the aims foreseen by U.S. policy toward Cuba since 1805. When he presented the Treaty for ratification by the Senate, President Roosevelt said:

> I have publicly declared "that the policy defined by the United States is, as of now, opposed to armed intervention." In this new treaty with Cuba the right to intervene in Cuba, granted to the United States by the previous 1903 Treaty, is abolished and, furthermore, other rights equally granted to the

> United States by the aforementioned document—that is to say, participation in determining the Republic of Cuba's foreign policy regarding finances and public health—are omitted. By signing this [new] treaty, our government makes it clear that it not only opposes the policy of armed intervention, but that it renounces those rights to intervene and interfere in Cuba granted by the treaty.[15]

Immediately, the President added in his speech to the Senate:

> Our relations with Cuba have been and must always be specially close ones. They are based not only in geographic proximity, but also on the fact that American blood and Cuban blood were shed to attain the freedom of the Cuban people and establish the Republic of Cuba as an independent power within the family of nations. I believe this treaty will further uphold those good relations based on the lasting foundations of sovereign equality and friendship between the two peoples and, consequently I recommend its ratification by the Senate.[16]

The history of these relations is a flat denial of that assertion.

We know that the relations, characterized as "specially close" by the United States, that according to them must prevail to justify their presence at the Guantánamo Naval Base, never existed. Much less can they exist now when diplomatic relations between the Government of the United States and Cuba were severed in 1961. Therefore, it is a fact of life that the naval base at Guantánamo is kept by the United States despite the lack of legal norms that validate it, just by asserting a policy of force. On January 4, 1961, on the day after the United States announced the severance of diplomatic relations with Cuba, the U.S. State Department hastened to state that "breaking relations with Cuba does not affect the status of our naval station at Guantánamo."[17]

15. Ibid., 298-299.
16. Ibid., 299.
17. "Cronología de agresiones," in *Agresiones de Estados Unidos a Cuba Revolucionaria*, 224.

Restructuring the Base

After the signing of the 1934 Treaty of Relations, the territory of the "naval station" was gradually fortified and arranged until, in the spring of 1941, the base became established as a naval station for operations with the following structure: naval station, air-sea station, base for the Marine Corps and warehouses.

The expansion continued and, around 1943 they contracted the construction of other facilities with the firm Frederick Snare Co., that hired some 9000 civilian workers, many of whom were Cubans.

Nineteen fifty-one was also a year of hard work in the expansion of the military and civil facilities at the base. Streets and roads were given names like Sherman Avenue, Deer Point Road, Boat Sked Road. The names in the area most frequented by Cuban civilians were Martí, Gómez and Maceo and others like McCalla Hill, Bargo and Villamar, Baker Pier.

In 1952, the U.S. Navy Secretary decided to change the name U.S. Naval Operating Base for U.S. Naval Base. By then, the base was already organized to include the Training Center.

A report that appeared late in 1997 on Internet said that the aim of the naval base at Guantánamo is to "give logistic support to operations in the Caribbean, train joint forces and carry out humanitarian operations." No further comment is necessary, for this stated purpose is contrary to the letter of the treaties analyzed so far.

That report includes data from 1996 regarding the base's staff. There were 116 officers; 1315 ground crew; 71 essential personnel and 640 civilian employees.

Likewise, and seemingly to reassert their limitless permanence on Cuban territory, that report says: "There is no fixed date or number of years for the lease to expire. It was agreed that the land must be handed over to Cuba if it were abandoned or by mutual accord. None of this has happened."

The entry to the base is the place called Leeward Side and the boats that transport staff go in through the place called Windward Side, that includes the blocks of houses, the temporary lodgings, schools, family services and recreation facilities, the naval hospital, the bank, the post office, shops and other facilities. Fishing is allowed in the occupied territory, but hunting is forbidden to the marines and their families.

In an unusual piece of information that serves to reaffirm that the base is located on part of our territory, Internet's report says that a birth certificate or a passport are required to travel to the base.

Drinking Water at the Base

On June 6, 1934, the U.S. Senate passed a law that authorized the Navy Secretariat to sign a long-term contract with a company that committed itself to supply drinking water to the naval base at Guantánamo. But before that, U.S. plans existed to build an aqueduct that supplied the base with water from the Yateras river.

According to documents from the archives of the Cuban Ministry of Foreign Affairs, Cuba's acting Secretary of State in 1932 confirmed on that date such plans and negotiations between the Embassy of the United States and the Ministry of Foreign Affairs, as well as the authorization granted by the Cuban Council of Secretaries on July 13, 1934 to a group of engineers that would carry out a feasibility study so that the base could use the water of the Yateras river, and the consent for those works to be carried out by whatever contractors the U.S. Government entrusted them. Furthermore, authorization was granted for the Cuban Public Works Secretary to facilitate their task to the engineers that would carry out those studies.

Although the U.S. Secretary of State conveyed his criteria to the Secretariat of State of the Republic of Cuba that the building of the aqueduct in question did not expand the territory the United States occupied in Cuba, he added that his government had suggested to the Cuban Government when it had requested authorization for the aqueduct to be built that, in case of war, the 6-mile long aqueduct was to be guarded by the U.S. Marines.

That aqueduct, planned and built by the Government of the United States, was in fact, according to the new 1934 Treaty of Relations, an expansion of the limits of the naval base, for the U.S. Government would exercise the same control over the aqueduct and the land where it stood, that it exercised over the land comprised within the base's limits. It was thus until the triumph of the Revolution, when the U.S. Marines had to withdraw from the aforementioned aqueduct.

However, just after the incident of the fishermen kidnapped on February 2, 1964, taken to the Key West Naval Base by units of the U.S. Navy and imprisoned at the jail in Monroe County, in Florida, the Revolutionary Government of Cuba decided on February 6, 1964, to suspend the water supply from the Yateras river to the Guantánamo Naval Base. I will discuss this issue at length in chapter V under the title "Labor Aggressions."

Payments and Checks

Due to the fact that it is a land lease, the payment established for the Guantánamo Naval Base is naturally symbolic. Article I of the Complementary Agreement dated July 2, 1903 fixed 2000 pesos a year in U.S. gold mint, as the amount to be paid for as long as the United States occupy and use such areas according to the February 16/23, 1903 Agreement on coaling and naval stations.

In 1934, when U.S. gold coins were no longer issued, the value of the old U.S. gold dollar was fixed at $1693.25 in legal tender. That is why the Treasury Department issued yearly checks for $3386.25 dollars until 1972, when the value of the old U.S. gold dollar was readjusted at $1838.25. Thus, the checks issued then were valued at $3676.50. In 1973 a new correction of the value of the old U.S. gold dollar was introduced and, since then, the value was fixed at $2042.50. Therefore, the value of the checks was modified and fixed at $4085.00. The checks issued by the U.S. Treasury Department are charged to the U.S. Navy, responsible for the operation of the naval base.

The checks issued by the Government of the United States of America as payment for the lease of the aforementioned naval base are addressed to the Treasurer General of the Republic of Cuba, an institution and a post that have ceased to be a part of the government structure in Cuba for many years.

These checks are sent annually by diplomatic pouch. The one issued in 1959 was mechanically cashed due to confusion. The checks issued since 1960 to date have not been cashed. As General Raúl Castro has said, they have been put away to exhibit them on the day when, once the occupied land is returned, a museum is build to show what that offending North American base really was.

Undoubtedly, the fact that the checks were neither cashed nor returned means that Cuba does not accept the payment of the repudiated lease. The mere issue or the mere receipt of the check does not mean that payment has been effected.

From the viewpoint of private law, the United States law is not applicable for, according to the doctrine of the "weight proof," in the fulfillment of the contract to determine the jurisdiction applicable, it is unquestionable that it is Cuba's, given that the object of the contract (the base) is in Cuba, and that Cuba is also the creditor. The mere handing over by the debtor to the creditor is not sufficient, for the latter has rejected that contract, and it is required that the creditor makes another gesture as an unequivocal sign of its acceptance, and not a mere reception. For that reason, in this case payment in cash would be required instead of a check.

Cuba's intention evinced by the retaining and not cashing the checks is consistent with the non-acceptance of the lease: such a lease is not in force.

Usually, the silence of the check's receiver is not considered tantamount to its acceptance and, in this case, after the repeated public denunciations by the Cuban side, this cannot lead the issuer to think that the payment has been accepted.

But even in the hypothetical case that someone considers those checks have been accepted, this can be denied by saying those checks have expired and cannot, therefore, be cashed.

IV

ILLEGALITY

MILITARY BASES AS A COLONIAL MONSTROSITY

The U.S. Naval Base on Cuban Soil Is a Colonial Enclave

Almost four decades ago, on the occasion of the debate during the XV Period of Sessions of the United Nations Organization General Assembly about the issue of the "Declaration on the Concession of Independence to Colonial Countries and Peoples"—also known as the "Declaration Against Colonialism"—, just as UNO members were about to approve Resolution 1514 (XV), the head of the Cuban delegation, the Chancellor of Dignity Raúl Roa García, in his December 6, 1960 speech, presented the case of the naval base at Guantánamo as a colonial fact and stated:

> Under this colonialist doctrine, the United States, with the close cooperation of Latin American dictators and oligarchies, paved the way to its merchants, its bankers and its corporations for the exploitation of our underdeveloped, defenseless and disunited peoples. Regarding Cuba, I point out the Platt Amendment, the Permanent Treaty of Relations, the compulsive lease of the naval base at Guantánamo, the reciprocity treaties, the law about sugar, and the monopolies of the public services and the mining concessions among those corollaries...[1]

Further on, in that same speech, the Cuban Minister of Foreign Affairs, Dr. Roa, addressed some specific facts about the history of the usurpation of the Cuban territory illegally occupied by the United States: the base at Guantánamo, the nullity of the imposed treaty, the violation of international norms, the contempt for the sovereign will of the Cuban people, who rejected and repudiated since its inception this colonial enclave on their country's soil, and has never given up its willingness to vindicate it. It was at that point of his important speech before the world gathering, that Roa clearly and

1. Raúl Roa García, *Retorno a la alborada*, II, 365.

firmly demanded that the case of the U.S. naval base in Cuba be included in the voting, and said:

> The Revolutionary Government of Cuba reiterates before the United Nations that it does not purport to seize by force the portion of national territory occupied by the naval base at Guantánamo; but it also reiterates, with equal solemnity, that it intends to claim its return when it deems it appropriate, within the canons of international law. Therefore, it assumes that this claim is included in the terms of the proposed Declaration...[2]

Resolution 1514 (XV), approved on December 14, 1960, was the first in a series of resolutions condemning colonialism and other forms of colonial dependence all along these years. Each of those resolutions emphasized the urgent need to put an end to every form of colonialism for the sake of international peace and security.

It is true that the United Nations has made urgent calls against colonialism, and that this organization has devoted its best efforts to eradicate colonial situations contrary to the purposes and principles of the UNO Charter and the "General Declaration on Human Rights", but the struggle against colonialism is more complex, and Resolution 1514 (XV) says so when referring to every manifestation of colonialism. The aforementioned Resolution established that colonialism also is:

- All acts contrary to or that violate totally or partially a country's territorial integrity.

- All armed action or repressive measure of any kind aimed at violating or preventing the free right to self-determination, sovereignty and territorial integrity.

- All interference in the internal affairs of other states to violate the people's sovereign rights and their territorial integrity.

2. Ibid., 366-367.

In the preamble of Resolution 1514 (XV) it is stated that the United States are convinced that "all peoples have the inalienable right to absolute freedom, to exercising their sovereignty and to the integrity of their national territory."

Article 3 of the February 16/23, 1903 Agreement imposed upon Cuba by the United States, establishes that the United States will exercise full jurisdiction or dominion over the land leased for coaling or naval stations in Cuba and, albeit that treaty ultimately acknowledges Cuba's sovereignty over such tracts of land according to the legal concept used—lease—, the effective domination has been exercised by the United States. Let it be known: that the U.S. naval base at Guantánamo is a form of colonial domination exerted by the United States. It is undoubtedly comprised, as a military base, in the other forms of foreign domination that the "Declaration Against Colonialism" (Resolution 1514 [XV]) expressly forbids.

During the first Summit Conference of Non-Aligned Countries held in Belgrade, September 1-6, 1961, the head of the Cuban delegation, and President of the Republic of Cuba, Dr. Osvaldo Dorticós Torrado, asserted:

> Cuba can speak at this Conference prompted by its own painful experience. When our country was militarily occupied by United States' forces (...) the obligation was imposed upon it to tolerate the military base at Guantánamo and, after the triumph of the Revolution on January 1, 1959, that base has been kept on our national territory against the will of the people and of the Revolutionary Government of Cuba. That base is not even relevant to the strategic aims of the military defense of the United States. It has only served to hurt our nation's dignity, to shelter counterrevolutionary forces, to introduce arms in our country with which to fight against the liberating Revolution, to concentrate troops whenever liberation movements in Caribbean countries have threatened imperialist domination.[3]

3. Osvaldo Dorticós Torrado, Speech by the Cuban President at the Belgrade Conference. September 1-6, 1961, Archives of the Ministry of Foreign Affairs of the Republic of Cuba.

Further on, the then President Dorticós pointed out the origin of the aggressions against Cuba: "Our national independence and our historical revolutionary achievements daily suffer the threats of military aggression from and organized by the United States of America or in the territory of that military base..."[4]

Finally, the President of the Republic of Cuba requested in his speech that the Conference went on record against this type of facilities on foreign soil:

> (...) we urge this Conference to adopt a firm resolution demanding the immediate dismantling of all military bases established in countries whose peoples and governments do not consent to them. This would be a decision that could be boldly advanced during the next General Assembly of the United Nations, and would be a great step forward on the way to disarmament.[5]

The first Summit Conference of Non-Aligned Countries also considered the linkage between military bases imposed upon certain countries as an expression of colonialism, and demanded the immediate end of this territorial occupation. Such a declaration has been reiterated throughout the fruitful history of the Non-Aligned Movement for the consolidation of peace and peaceful cooperation among the peoples.

Two of the most important agreements taken in that direction, included in the "Declaration of the 1961 Belgrade Summit Conference", are expressed in its paragraphs 11 and 12:

> 11. The participants consider that the establishment of foreign military bases in the territory of other countries against the will of those concerned is a violation of national sovereignty. They likewise denounce the colonial problems that force the countries that seek their independence to pay the price of ha-

4. Ibid.
5. Ibid.

ving foreign military bases on their territories in exchange for their freedom. They declare their full support for the countries that want to be freed of foreign military bases and call upon the countries that keep such bases to proceed to their suppression as a contribution to world peace.

12. They also acknowledge that the North American military base at Guantánamo, in Cuba, to whose permanence the Government and the people of Cuba are opposed, is harmful to the sovereignty and the territorial integrity of that country.

Another of the agreements taken in Belgrade and included in paragraph 5 of the "Declaration of the 1961 Summit Conference", says: "The participants in the Conference request the immediate end of all occupation of a colonial nature, and the restoration of the territorial integrity to the legitimate peoples in the countries of Asia, Africa and Latin America where it has been violated, and the withdrawal of foreign forces from their national territory."

According to these Non-Aligned sentiments, undoubtedly the U.S. naval base at Guantánamo is the booty of a war that the United States neither waged nor won with Spain, and the price of domination, threat and coercion against a people that, after three wars waged throughout 30 years of struggle against Spanish colonialism—that fiercely and tenaciously defended Cuba, its rich colonial possession in America—, was weary, but also anxious to begin its republican life, despite the fact that it was acquainted with the voracious appetite of its powerful neighbor, and was compelled to hand over that portion of its territory.

Thus, the U.S. naval base at Guantánamo is the first example of what the Non-Aligned countries declared in Belgrade in 1961 about "paying the price of having foreign military bases on their territory in exchange for their freedom." Perhaps that is why the Non-Aligned acknowledgment of this fact had pride of place in paragraph 12 of the aforementioned Declaration, followed by their consideration about military bases, which I now reproduce: "They also acknowledge that the North American military base at Guantánamo, in Cuba, to whose permanence the Government and the people of Cuba are opposed, harms the sovereignty and the territorial integrity of that country." It is evident that the presence of imposed foreign military bases harms the territorial integrity of the countries that suffer from it and, in fact, is an expression of colonialism.

Later, during the XVI Period of Sessions of the UN General Assembly, Resolution 1654 (XVI) was approved on November 27, 1961. It created the Special Committee, with 17 members at the time, now increased to 24, to examine the issue of colonial territories and apply Resolution 1514 (XV) dated December 14, 1960. This Special Committee is also known as the "Decolonization Committee" and later as the "Committee of 24."

Paragraph 11 of Resolution. 2189 (XXI)—passed by the UN General Assembly on December 13, 1966, related to the implementation of the "Declaration Against Colonialism" [Resolution 1514 (XV)] and based on the report of the Special Committee regarding the fulfillment of its tasks in 1966—, requests colonial powers to dismantle their bases and military facilities in colonial territories, to abstain from establishing other new ones, and from using those still extant to hinder the liberation of the peoples of colonial territories exercising their legitimate rights to freedom and independence.

Cuba, of course, is not a colonial state since the dawn of January 1, 1959, but it would be appropriate to ask whether the undesired presence of the U.S. base at Guantánamo has hindered or purported to hinder the people of Cuba from exercising its full sovereignty, and whether this colonial enclave has been used by the Government of the United States to attack our country.

Military bases have continued to be analyzed as a colonial issue, but what has been the United States' stance regarding this matter? At all times, North Americans express their reluctance to hand over the territory and dismantle the bases when they have been compelled to do so in compliance with UN rulings.

It is interesting to comment a recent case as an example. I am referring to the military bases on the Bermuda Islands, a British colony whose territory comprises some 150 isles or islets located on the western portion of the Atlantic Ocean, some 900 kilometers east of Cape

Hatteras, on the United States' coast. Of all foreign bases on Bermuda, the Canadian base at Daniel's Head, was closed in 1993 and the British base at Malbar, in 1995. But the United States have leased approximately one-tenth of the territory of Bermuda for military purposes, and there lies the conflict: problems have arisen with the North Americans, who do not want to leave the naval base at Southampton and the air and naval base at Cooper, both in Bermuda.

The following comments were taken from the report of the Special Committee responsible for settling the problems regarding the implementation of the "Declaration on the Concession of Independence to Colonial Countries and Peoples", in reference to the case of Bermuda:

> During the negotiations held on December, 1994 between the Government of Bermuda and the representatives of the United States in regard to the fate of the ground bases vacated by the Navy of the United States, the Government (of Bermuda) requested the complete environmental rehabilitation of the land and rejected the assertion by the North American negotiators according to which the value of the assets held by the air and naval base and by the naval facility of the United States amounted to 140 millions Bermudan dollars. Furthermore, the Government of Bermuda added there was nothing in the treaties and laws in effect that supported the assertion by the Government of the United States that it had the right to be compensated for the value of capital assets, for example, the buildings constructed within the bases during North American tenure. The Government of the Territory of Bermuda rejected the viewpoint of the United States Navy regarding the fact that when cleaning the base only "imminent and serious risks to human health and safety" should be eliminated. In regard to the issue of the tracts of land, the representative of the United States stated in conversation with the Government (of Bermuda) that the contract subscribed in 1941 with the Government of the United Kingdom of Great Britain and Northern Ireland regarding the use for 99 years exempt of

> payment of rents should be kept in effect, after noticeably reducing the total extension of the land it comprises, so as to only preserve the station belonging to the National Aeronautics and Space Administration (NASA) located on Cooper Island. The Government of Bermuda wants all the land to be returned and a new contract signed providing for the necessities of NASA.[6]

The Government of Bermuda demands from the United States that, besides withdrawing the bases, the land and areas occupied by the military facilities must be entirely cleaned, thus contributing to render the environment healthy, like the North Americans found it.

Military Bases and International Law

Many are opposed to discussing the issue of military bases at the United Nations for that organization approaches this issue from the viewpoint of colonialism and from the viewpoint of disarmament.

The issue is not currently about military bases in colonial territories that must be examined by the Committee of 24, but of those foreign military bases imposed upon independent states. However, the theme succeeded in being included in the agenda of the UN General Assembly, and was discussed by the First Committee of the UN General Assembly, one of the seven main working committees where political and security issues are discussed.

The issue of the elimination of foreign military bases in Asia, Africa and Latin America is on the agenda of the General Assembly that decided, by means of Resolution. 2165 (XXI), dated December 5, 1966, to transfer the examination of this issue to the Disarmament Committee, made up of 18 member nations, that would submit a report after deliberations. As a follow-up of the aforementioned Resolution, and via Resolution. 2344 (XXII), dated December 19,

6. Document A/AC/109/2020, dated May 2, 1995, issued by the General Assembly of the United Nations.

1967, the General Assembly reiterated the mandate of the Committee of 18 to study and submit a report about the elimination of military bases in Asia, Africa and Latin America. But the issue is at a stalemate, notwithstanding the fact that it was transferred to the Conference on Disarmament.

Resolution 2625 (XXV) approved by the UN General Assembly, on October 24, 1970, known as the "Declaration of Principles of International Law Regarding Friendly Relations and Cooperation Among States According to the UN Charter", states that:

> The territory of a state will not be the object of military occupation derived from the use of force in contravention to the Charter's provisos. The territory of a state will not be the object of territorial acquisition derived from the threat of the use of force. None of the aforementioned provisos will be interpreted in a sense that affects:
>
> a) the Charter's provisos or any international agreement prior to the Charter, in force according to international law; or
>
> b) the powers of the Security Council according to the Charter.

Throughout the process to codify international law, the United Nations have restrictively limited and applied retroactivity. Therefore, even knowing that affecting territorial integrity through military occupation or by the use of force or the threat to use force violates the principles of international law, it restricts its application to developments that occurred after the signing of the UN Charter (June 26, 1945), but providing such agreements are valid according to international law.

The Vienna Convention about law of treaties stemmed on May 23, 1969, from the UN Conference on law of treaties held in Vienna in 1969. The Convention established (Article 4) that its norms regarding treaties in effect signed on previous dates do not work retroactively, although they do not prejudge the application of any international law norm to those previously signed treaties.

Notwithstanding that those norms do not work retroactively, history points to at least the acknowledgement of the fact that such injustices had existed. Thus, on May 20, 1969, in Vienna, the aforementioned Conference also approved the "Declaration About Military, Political or Economic Coercion in the Signing of Treaties", a text included in its final record, that "solemnly [condemns] the recourse to threat or the use of any type of pressure, be it military, political or economic, by a state with the purpose of coercing another state into signing a treaty in violation of the principles of sovereign equality of all states, and of freedom of consent."[7]

At the same time, that Declaration deplored "the fact that, in the past, the states were sometimes forced to sign treaties due to various types of pressures exerted over them by other states."[8]

Resolution 2734 (XXV)—that is to say, the "Declaration on the Strengthening of International Security"—is quite significant. It was adopted by the UN General Assembly on December 16, 1970, during the 25th anniversary of the United Nations, and renewed the initiatives for peace for all humankind, security, disarmament, humankind's economic and social progress and the relations of friendship and cooperation among states. That Resolution deals with 27 issues essential for international peace and security, among them, that the states desist from any action conducive to foreign domination by force or by any other means.

We can see that a new norm of general international law (*ius cogens*) may be taking shape in the context of the development of international law, when imposed foreign military bases are deemed to be a danger for international peace and security as well as a form of colonial domination. If all that is condemned by the United Nations and, furthermore, it is internationally acknowledged that a treaty is null and must be terminated when it opposes an imperative norm of international law (*ius cogens*), it means that imposed foreign military bases must be peremptorily terminated.

The United Nations attention must be drawn permanently and effectively to the presence of foreign military bases imposed against

7. Olga Miranda Bravo, op. cit., 149.
8. Ibid.

the peoples' will, and their real threat to international peace and security.

After their defeat in Vietnam, the United States have outlined doctrines and thesis about the "defense" of vital North American interests, without risking involvement in a similar military and political situation, and military bases have an important role for these doctrines. The originally so-called "rapid deployment forces" and "low-intensity conflicts" stemmed from these theory according to which, it was necessary to station the forces as close as possible to the areas of conflict and, consequently, increase the number of North American military bases. These geographically limited conflicts, destined to achieve U.S. politico-military and socioeconomic aims, are characterized to a large extent by resorting to terrorism and subversion. The strategic planning of the defense of U.S. vital interests includes this combination since then, albeit imperialists acknowledge that it is becoming increasingly difficult to involve other governments in their military adventures, and that the peoples are increasingly rejecting the use of their territories to that end.

The First North American Naval Base Outside U.S. Territory

The U.S. naval base at Pago Pago, on Tutulla island, in Samoa, established in 1872, is a fact lost to the history of North American politics. Its establishment was made official when the United States and the Kingdom of Samoa signed the 1878 Treaty as a friendship and trade agreement, according to which the United States ensured for itself the right to keep the aforementioned base as a coaling station and, furthermore, committed itself to mediate, in order to settle on a satisfactory and solid basis, any future difference that may regrettably occur between the Government of Samoa and any other government friendly with the United States.[9]

9. U.S. Congress, 50: 1; House Ex. Doc. 238, 124-125; and V.P. Potemkin *et al.*, *Historia de la diplomacia*, II, 351-354.

The United States had other intentions: to prevent Germany and England, who also had their own interests in the archipelago, from ultimately ruling over it. In 1879, Great Britain and Germany signed friendship and trade arrangements with the Kingdom of Samoa, but in 1885, the German Consul in Samoa reached another settlement with King Malietva and hoisted the German flag on the royal hut; the United States protested this gesture and decided to implement the 1878 Agreement. The three metropolises were on the brink of war. However, the 1889 conference established a joint German-British-North American protectorate over the isles of Samoa, notwithstanding the fact that each of those three powers wanted the archipelago for itself.

In a chronicle written in New York on June 13, 1889 for the Buenos Aires newspaper *La Nación*, José Martí ponders about the imperial greed of "Uncle Sam's foreign policy:"

> [...] attempt the recognition of his bizarre theory that all land in America and the seas that surround it fall naturally under the domination of North America, whom the continent's soil and water must obey as eternal wards. Samoa would not be so interesting if the principle established by the conference could be forgotten in future cases in the countries of America or its periphery, around which European and Yankee interests clash.
>
> The United States would contend for the supremacy over Samoa, for they are neither democrats nor republicans in this regard, because the two parties equally hunger for international privileges disproportionate to the services rendered to the country from which they demand them, and to the respect that a free people must have for the freedom of others...[10]

By 1898, McKinley already had the Philippines, Guam and Hawaii; in January, 1899 he would seize the Isle of Wake. To dominate Samoa fitted perfectly with his plans to expand across the Pacific Ocean.

10. José Martí, *Obras completas*, 12, 239.

The aforementioned powers availed themselves of the death of the Samoan king and of the conflict for the succession that broke out in the archipelago, where each power had its own candidate. This situation led to internal disturbances that were naturally fuelled by the governments that wanted to appropriate Samoa.

That was the state of things when, in the autumn of 1899, Great Britain signed an agreement with Germany according to which the latter received two islands of the Samoan archipelago; one of them was the island of Upolu, whose capital is Apia; two other islands went to the United States: one of them was Tutuila, where the port of Pago Pago is located. England gave up Samoa in exchange for the island of Tonga and part of the Solomon Islands that belonged to Germany.

At the end of World War I, the 1919 Treaty of Versailles gave German West Samoa to Great Britain, that later administered it as a trusteeship together with Australia, according to a decision taken by the League of Nations.

Lastly, since January 1, 1962, and after a referendum supervised by the United Nations, the independent state of Western Samoa was established. It is a member of the UNO and in the Samoan language it is called Samoa i-Sisifo. However, Eastern Samoa is administered by the United States that still keep the Pago Pago Naval Base in place.

The history about the oldest U.S. naval base reminds U.S. of the pattern applied by the United States in the case of the Platt Amendment and the naval base at Guantánamo. The final outcome was different: we were neither a protectorate nor a colony of the United States for, thanks to the Cuban Revolution, the Republic of Cuba is now a free and sovereign state, for that was the decision defended by its sons who still fight and will continue to fight for the return of that usurped portion of their territory.

If the "gift" of the Philippines and Guam given by Spain to the United States consolidated the latter as a colonial empire in the Pacific Ocean, we must not forget that its entire colonial expansion—that had already added by annexation the Isle of Wake and the Hawaiian islands—began timidly by Samoa and its naval base at Pago Pago.

LEGAL CONSIDERATIONS ABOUT THE NULLITY OF TREATIES

Defects

The agreements that allowed the United States of America to establish a naval base at Guantánamo are plagued by numerous defects that invalidate them as legal instruments and, although Cubans consider that the unlawful North American presence in Guantánamo is a political fact and must be seen thus, we cannot but delve into the legal issues in those treaties.

That is why, after having updated the history of the developments linked to the establishment of the naval base at Guantánamo in the preceding chapters, the legal concept found in the treaties associated to it can be summarized as follows:

1. Violation of the obligations contracted and the statements made by the United States of America.

2. Violation of the freedom of consent to be bound by the treaties.

3. Lack of a mandate to oblige the Republic of Cuba.

4. Unlawfulness of the cause.

5. Violation of the legal concept of the lease.

6. Lack of good faith before, during and after the signing of the treaties.

Let us analyze in detail each of the previous issues.

Violation of the Obligations Contracted and the Statements Made

The obligations contracted according to the *Joint Resolution* dated April 20, 1898: "Cuba is and by law should be free and independent," were totally forgotten by the Treaty of Paris signed on December 10, 1898. Regarding Cuba, the United States only acquired the status of "occupation" forces, obliging themselves to abide by the norms of international law for the protection of lives and properties but, however, they not only seized them, but also, dismissing the temporality of their status, they unilaterally established in Article I of the Platt Amendment that Cuban could *never* fulfill treaties about bases, etc., bestowing upon themselves the eternal tutelage over the Cuban nation. Likewise, Cuba would *never* be able to sign such treaties with countries other than the United States.

As I mentioned earlier, even several North American congressmen denounced this arbitrariness during the debate on the amendment in the U.S. Congress.

The 1898 *Joint Resolution* stated that "Cuba is and must by law be free and independent," but the Platt Amendment was barren since its conception. Neither the *Joint Resolution* nor the Treaty of Paris were its offspring.

When the Constituent Assembly was inaugurated in Havana in 1901, Governor Wood said that "it is its duty to draft and adopt a Constitution establishing, according to the criteria of the Cuban delegates, what the relations between Cuba and the United States must be" but, simultaneously—and even before that—the Platt Amendment was in the making in Washington to be inserted as an Appendix to the 1901 Constitution, whose Article VII includes the sale or lease to the United States of the land needed for coaling and naval stations. Thus, laws were made about Cuba in Washington, that did not evince the intention of respecting the *Joint Resolution*.

Violation of the Freedom of Consent to be Bound by Treaties

Freedom of consent is a principle that determines the validity of a treaty and has a termination effect over the norm consecrated by international law (*pacta sunt servanda*) that all treaties must be fulfilled in good faith by the parties obliged by them.

Coercion exerted over the representative of a state, and coercion exerted over a state by the threat or the use of force are considered as causes for the nullity of treaties, in which case, if a treaty so affected were approved, it would lack legal validity. If a state's consent to be obliged by a treaty has been obtained through the coercion of its representatives, through threats against him by the other party, such consent is null and void. Likewise, any treaty is equally null and void if signed under threat or under the use force against the other state in such a way as to prevent it from freely consenting to oblige itself.

The experts on international law have acknowledged for centuries that a state must be exempt from all obligations regarding a treaty if it was signed when its representatives were under serious and irresistible coercion. A treaty thus signed is null *ab initio* (from its inception), not because it is a serious violation of legal principles, but also of moral principles. The Cuban members of the 1901 Constituent Assembly were not only personally coerced but also—and this was even more obvious—the nation itself, the emerging state, was under coercion.

Article 52 of the aforementioned Vienna Convention refers to the principles of international law included in the UN Charter to determine violations. It would be illogical and unacceptable that this norm was applicable only to treaties signed after the Charter or after the Convention itself. A treaty whose signature has been obtained by threat or by the use of force is null and void. The notion of "coercion" cannot be restricted solely to the acts mentioned in Article 52, for coercion can be exerted using other procedures like economic and political pressures, much more dangerous because they can be unnoticed. This was acknowledged by the UN Conference on law of treaties (Vienna, May 20, 1969) when it approved the "Declaration on Military, Political or Economic Coercion for the Signing of

Treaties," that condemned these forms of coercion and, at the same time, acknowledged and deplored their use in the past to force the signing of imposed treaties.

When the Summit Conference of Non-Aligned Countries was held in Cairo in 1964, the heads of state or government gathered there condemned economic and political pressures, and stated that the word "force"—included in paragraph 4 of Article 2 of the UN Charter—should be interpreted to encompass other procedures, like economic and political pressures.

The particular significance of consecrating this defect of consent lies in the fact that it does away with old practices that served the dominant powers well, and rejects as contrary to international law the provisos based on relations of subordination imposed under grave and unjust pressure. Because treaties express coincidence of wills in forging a legal link, the parties' free consent is essential for them to be perfect.

In the case of the treaties imposed upon Cuba so that it allowed those bases on its territory, such consent was at all times invalidated by the intimidation exerted over Cuba.

It is necessary that consent entail a free and spontaneous manifestation of the will in order for it to be legally effective. Some events may spoil the will and therefore, are insurmountable obstacles for the validity and, occasionally, even for the shaping of the agreement. Error, fraud, corruption of the representative, coercion of the representative and coercion of a state, in short, violence, are indicated as defects of consent. We will now deal only with the latter.

Violence is the physical or moral coercion exerted over a person to make him agree to a treaty. It is a cause of nullity, for fear that stems from violence invalidate the will of one of the contracting parties.

It is essential that violence be unjust and grave for it to assume the character of defect of consent and invalidate the contract.

According to the principles of international law and practice, there is violence when irresistible force and intimidation (moral violence) are used, it is the rational fear to be the victim of an imminent, grave injury that affects person or property, and is aimed at forcing the consent of the other contracting party to oblige itself by the treaty in question.

The history of the Platt Amendment, the coercion and the threats by the United States over the 1901 Cuban Constituent Assembly, the rational fear of not attaining the independence the Cubans had fought for for so long, are unquestionable proof that "consent" was brutally extolled.

The internationally renowned Cuban expert on international law Antonio Sánchez de Bustamante Sirvén says:

> It is our opinion that international public law must acknowledge as a general rule that violence or coercion exerted over a state to force it to accept an agreement, invalidate and annul consent. It is useless to refer to the inconveniences this principle may have for peace because, whereas justice often produces definitive peace, force only imposes a restless, transitory peace [...] It does not matter that pressure is material or psychological, for it suffices that in any guise it brings about as a result an act or an omission termed as voluntary but that takes place against the true will of one of the parties involved...[11]

According to Roman law, possession is qualified by its origin, says book 41 of the *Digesto*.[12] Thus, as the origin of the possession of the territory where stands the naval base at Guantánamo is unlawful because its origin is the coercion exerted over the people of Cuba by the United States, a coercion that invalidated its consent to be lawfully obliged, the1934 Treaty on the base is as spurious as the one signed in 1903.

Lack of a Mandate to Oblige the Republic of Cuba

Let us examine the capacity that the Cuban members of the 1901 Constituent Assembly may or may not have had to accept the Platt Amendment and to integrate it into the Constitution as an Appendix.

11. Antonio Sánchez de Bustamante, *Manual de derecho internacional público* (1947): 376.
12. Book 41 of the *Digesto*, collection of Roman laws by Justinian.

The capacity to sign treaties is an attribute of state sovereignty. The conditions set by the Platt Amendment for Cuba to be able to sign international treaties is an insurmountable limitation of the Republic's sovereignty. Therefore, the Amendment/Appendix could not be accepted, for its inclusion invalidated the Constitution itself. Those who wrote it, elected by the people with a specific and fixed mandate, had no authority to accept it.

The opposition of the Cuban members of the Constituent Assembly, based on the solid legal, political and moral arguments to which I have already referred, show the lack of capacity to oblige the Republic of Cuba via these delegates.

It must be recalled that the members of the 1901 Constituent Assembly were chosen to:

1. Agree upon and adopt a Constitution for Cuba.

2. Give their opinion about Cuba's relations with the United States.

3. Provide for the election of officers according to the Constitution adopted.

4. Transfer the domination and sovereignty over Cuba to the government elected according to the Constitution.

Those delegates were not elected to thwart their country's sovereignty or to draw limits over part of its territory. The additional mandate overruled the one granted by the people, it did not stem from the people's will but from the will of the North American military governor, Leonard Wood, a representative of the U.S. occupation forces and he, given this spurious authority, ordered the already elected Convention to "agree" upon the Platt Amendment.

The Treaty is void in its origin by total nullity, by the inability of the Constituent Convention, and later on, of the Cuban Government, to cede a piece of the national territory disguising this cession as a lease for an indeterminate span of time, or indefinitely.

Unlawfulness of the Cause

In order for a treaty to be valid, it is necessary that the obligations it entails have a cause, and that such a cause is not unlawful or immoral.

The cause of the lease for the base at Guantánamo is derived from clause VII of the Platt Amendment, "to place the United States in a position to maintain Cuba's independence and protect its people, as well as for its own defense..."

The cause of the aforementioned 1903 Treaty was substantially changed by the 1934 Treaty whose preamble expresses that the Treaty is based on "the wish to strengthen the links of friendship between the two countries, and to modify to that end the relations established between them by the Treaty of Relations signed in Havana on May 22, 1903..."

Whereas the cause expressed in those treaties is the strengthening of the links of friendship between Cuba and the United States, and the purpose is maintaining and protecting our independence, the original and valid cause is lacking when those links of friendship are broken by aggressive attitudes and actions of a political, economic subversive, harassing and bellicose nature that reflect a manifest and abusive animosity.

Is the U.S. Naval Base at Guantánamo that country's wish to strengthen the links of friendship with Cuba?

The unilateral and arbitrary imposition of the United States can be verified in the process to impose the Platt Amendment and the 1903 and 1934 treaties on the naval base at Guantánamo, completely devoid of consideration and with utmost contempt for a people who had fiercely fought to attain its freedom from the Spanish metropolis.

The Platt Amendment, the tool to perpetuate the U.S. occupation on our soil, disappeared years later, when the foundations for neocolonial domination had already been laid, and Cuba's dependence from the United States was not, according to their criteria, endangered, leaving the naval base at Guantánamo as a sword of Damocles swinging over our heads like a permanent threat of their hegemony, rather than for the development of links of friendship.

But if the struggle and the rejection of the people against the presence of that base were more than enough to consider the Treaty null and void, can the cause of the Treaty be considered valid after the triumph of the Revolution in 1959, despite the fact that the United States conspired against it offering the genocidal tyrant Batista all types of armament and bombs to gun down the Cuban people; after the United States severed diplomatic relations with Cuba in January, 1961—because it was them who severed those relations—and after the genocidal blockade imposed almost since the day when the Revolution triumphed?

Another law maxim refers to the fact that, when the main cause no longer exists, the things resulting from it are meaningless.[13] What was the apparent cause of the 1903 Agreement on coaling and naval stations? Let us recall its preamble: "To place the United States in a position to maintain the independence of Cuba and to protect its people, as well as for its own defense, the Government of Cuba will sell or lease to the United States the necessary land for coaling or naval stations in certain fixed places to be agreed upon with the President of the United States."

What was the cause of the 1934 Treaty? I would have to go back to this document's preamble: "The Republic of Cuba and the United States of America, driven by the wish to strengthen the links of friendship between the two countries, and to modify to that end the relations established between them by the Treaty of Relations signed in Havana on May 22, 1903…"

Neither the first nor the second cause exist: consequently, the base must cease to exist.

Violation of the Lease as a Legal Concept

In order to be valid, a treaty's aim must be licit and possible. No state can be obliged by things and rights other than those that depend upon its authority. Consequently, a treaty that violates funda-

13. Book 1 of the *Digesto*.

mental principles consecrated by the Constitution cannot have a legal value. No state can legitimately oblige itself to renounce its sovereignty over a part of its territory, albeit technically it is said that it is only a lease for an indeterminate or indefinite span of time. And this happens with the base's treaties.

Like doctor Fernando Álvarez Tabío—the eminent Cuban lawyer who specialized on constitutional issues—said in an article analyzing the case of the naval base at Guantánamo in the light of international law, the lease to which the specifications of Article III on sovereignty and jurisdiction of the 1903 Agreement on coaling and naval stations refer to "are a deceitful procedure to mock the principle of territorial integrity consecrated by Article 2 of the 1901 Constitution."[14]

I will quote next what the 1901 and 1940 constitutions say about Cuban national territory.

Article 2 of the 1901 Constitution said:

> The territory of the Republic is made up of the Island of Cuba and the adjacent islands and keys that, together with it, were under the sovereignty of Spain until the ratification of the Treaty of Paris on December 10, 1898." Note that the Isle of Pines is not mentioned due to the dispute we already referred to.

Article 3 of the 1940 Constitution said:

> The territory of the Republic is made up of the Island of Cuba, the Isle of Pines and the other adjacent islands and keys that were under the sovereignty of Spain until the ratification of the Treaty of Paris on December 10, 1898.
>
> The Republic will not sign or ratify agreements or treaties that in any way limit or harm national sovereignty or the integrity of its territory.

14. Fernando Álvarez Tabío, "La base naval de Guantánamo y el derecho internacional," in *Cuba Socialista*, 9.

When the lease of the naval base at Guantánamo was agreed upon, special emphasis was placed on Article III of the February 16/23, 1903 Agreement where "the United States acknowledge [...] the continuation of the definitive sovereignty of the Republic of Cuba over the extensions of land and water" described in the Agreement; therefore, we must state that Cuba maintains *imperium* and *dominium*—that is to say, political sovereignty and the right of property—over those portions of land and water, for it only ceded the use of and benefit from them.

When an asset is leased, one of the sides is obliged to give the other the use and benefit of such an asset for a fixed span of time, at a given price. The lessee is obliged to use that asset as it was agreed upon.

These precepts clearly refer to the following essential requisites:

- That the lease is, by nature, temporary, and that perpetuity is incompatible with the intrinsic conditions of the lease.

- That the lease always presupposes that the owner can recover the possession of and can benefit directly from the leased asset.

- That it is not licit for the solution of the lease to depend exclusively on the lessee for, according to the Treaty, the lease of that land and water by the United States is "for as long as they shall need them."

- That the asset leased is destined to the agreed use for this was the basic element of consent and the cause of the Treaty. However, the use given to the territory occupied by the base has been aggressive toward the people of Cuba and contrary to the letter of the Treaty itself.

When reviewing what happened until 1934, it becomes clear that instead of independence, it was dependence; that instead of protecting the people, it was insult, harassment, death, hunger. And after 1934, political domination, pressure, blackmail, dictatorship. The planes that bombed the territories liberated by the Cuban Rebel Army in the Sierra Maestra in 1957 and 1958 took fuel at the Guantánamo Naval Base. The bullets that killed our combatants were fired from that naval base. The naval base has been a lair for traitors, counterrevolutionaries and felons. The friendly use the agreements propose has been an aggressive use instead.

Furthermore, its use as a mere "naval base" has turned into its use as a center for military operations and intimidating gestures that go far beyond the use agreed upon, and even as a camp for Haitians, Chinese and Cuban "rafters" for migratory purposes.

Another requisite for the lease is that it must have a fixed price. The price agreed for the lease is absolutely symbolic or ludicrous, and in no way does it match what could be understood as a price befitting the magnitude of the asset leased. Although Cuba has decided not to accept any price whatsoever, for its sovereignty is neither for lease nor for sale.

In short, the Agreement for the lease of land for the bases is a legal absurdity; it is called a lease, but essentially it is not a lease.

Lack of Good Faith Before, During and After the Signing of the Treaties

Neither before nor during or after the negotiation of the base's treaties was there good faith on the part of the United States. This principle of the norm *pacta sunt servanda* was trampled by those treaties. The history of the relations between Cuba and the United States is quite eloquent in regard to this matter.

Origin Defects Prevent the Validation of the Treaties

The 1903 and the 1934 treaties about the establishment of the base are spoiled in such a way, that their validation cannot be argued because:

- The *null ab initio* regarding free consent annul them.

- The treaties cannot be understood as ratified by the mere passage of time, by tolerance or by de facto consent, for an agreement cannot be understood as confirmed unless the cause of the defect has ceased to exist, and in the case of the base's treaties the cause of the *null ab initio* is still extant.

The 1934 Treaty of Relations is a non-created treaty because it upholds one of the classes of the previous null treaties, the 1903 ones, that imposed the base upon Cuba.

The abolition of the 1903 Permanent Treaty of Relations was to be the unequivocal sign that another different agreement should rule and that all its clauses identical to the ones in the Platt Amendment would be suppressed, but it was not thus, for the clause referring to the base was not eliminated.

The maintenance of the base did not match a sincere intention of canceling the Platt Amendment. Such U.S. imperialist interference continued to live and serve North American interests, for all other rights derived from it were ensured with far less political cost by the compliant attitude of successive Cuban rulers fostered by the United States until the dawn of January, 1959.

There is no doubt whatsoever that the Platt Amendment has survived in the naval base at Guantánamo.

The Lease: A Covert Annexation

The United States could not accept the Spanish offer of appropriating the island of Cuba according to the Treaty of Paris, for there was a formal legal impediment for it: the *Joint Resolution*, and another impediment with a pharisaic image, associated to the humanitarian hue and cry sparked by the U.S. intervention in the war between Cuban and Spain.

Puerto Rico, the Philippines and Guam became U.S. possessions as war booty by virtue of the Treaty of Paris, but the Joint Resolution signed by the two chambers of the U.S. Congress in 1898 had nothing to do with those territories, for it had been drafted solely in the Cuban case. Thus, after Cuba's occupation, the North Americans prepared the scenario to replace the *Joint Resolution* by the Platt Amendment.

Occupation does not entail a transfer of sovereignty, and the Treaty of Paris only granted the United States the right of occupation regarding Cuba..

If we examine Article VII of the Platt Amendment in regard to naval and coaling stations, it says Cuba would sell or lease, and although the territory was finally leased, the United States has acted as if this lease were a form of cession of sovereignty.

Some authors like Austrian Professor Alfred Verdross, in his book *International Public Law*, establish a difference between territorial sovereignty and territorial supremacy for, due to the fact that territory is an essential element of the state, over which the state exerts its sovereignty, exercising territorial supremacy can only be legal if the territorial state authorizes it.

If the concept lease ultimately used in this treaty between the two states were assimilated to the lease contract by civil law, the result would be that the territorial state would preserve the so-called bare legal title (*nudum jus*), and that the state that exerts the territorial supremacy as occupant would have the use, benefit and full jurisdiction over such territory.

It is true that in times of war, when a foreign territory is occupied and, during the occupation, territorial supremacy is exercised but without acquiring territorial sovereignty over the occupied territory for that reason. The Nuremberg International Military Tribunal, in its ruling dated October 1, 1946,[15] confirmed this criteria. However, some consider that the concept "territorial sovereignty" stems from the Roman concept of "property" and is, therefore, an absolute right vis-à-vis all others; for that reason, the sovereign of this territory can rule over it, and even transfer it or cede it to another.

15. Letter by the International Tribunal established in Nuremberg on October 1, 1945. Quoted by Miguel A. D'Estefano Pisani, *Documentos del derecho internacional público*, I, 228.

A state that exerts territorial supremacy acts on its own behalf and not on behalf of the sovereign territorial state, although the latter preserves its sovereignty over the occupied territory. Then it could be technically considered that, because the sovereign territorial state exercises its sovereignty, it could transfer its territory to another state but, as a state that exercises territorial supremacy is located on that same territory, the territorial sovereignty state could not carry out that new cession without the consent of the state that at such a time exercises territorial supremacy.

Therefore, when there is territorial supremacy, like in the case of the lease for the naval base at Guantánamo, and albeit the 1903 Agreement on coaling and naval stations states that Cuba's sovereignty over that territory remains untouched, in practice Cuba cannot make use of it and its property rights are affected.

Finally, and regarding these comments, I want to quote what Verdross says about the definitive devolution of the territory to the territorial state:

> But even in the context of a territorial sovereignty reduced to *nudum jus* the germ of a territorial supremacy still exists, for it automatically surfaces when the occupant's territorial supremacy ceases. It must be said for truth's sake that even a territorial sovereign that cannot exercise in fact its supremacy over a given territory, continues to possess a potential territorial supremacy, for it will become real as soon as the alien supremacy disappears.[16]

According to the concepts of international law, territorial rights can be divided into two large groups: absolute rights, like sovereignty, and real limited rights like, for example, a lease.

International relations record many cases of leases; however, in the case of the naval base at Guantánamo, between Cuba and the United States, due to the fact that it is an imperfect lease, for the contract does not specify the term for its expiry, leaving it to the will

16. Alfred Verdross, *Derecho internacional público*, 207.

of one of the signatories, the two signatories were in fact transferring something more than territorial supremacy. Let us look at the following examples:

The Treaty signed by the United States and the Republic of Liberia on March 31, 1942, in the middle of World War II, granted the right to the United States to build airports in Liberia under its exclusive jurisdiction while the war lasted. These cases of territorial leases have a limited objective, for example, a military base, an airport or customs control over a border post. This limited lease of Liberian land, begun on July 14, 1941, materialized by means of the aforementioned March 31, 1942 Agreement, with the handing over of areas accessing the Robert Field airport, the maritime spot at Fisherman Lake and others, to safeguard Liberia's independence in case of an attack.[17]

As Verdross has accurately pointed out in his book, territorial sovereignty cannot be equaled to territorial supremacy:

> Territorial sovereignty is thus the right of a state to dispose of a given territory, based on international law. The territorial sovereign can exert in its territory its full dominion...
>
> On the other hand, territorial supremacy is akin to possession in right of property, for it is nothing but the dominion exerted by a state over a given space, a dominion that usually extends to the territory of the state itself, its vessels and aircraft, but that only exceptionally can also extend to foreign territories. Such an exercise can be lawful or unlawful. However, it is usually lawful based on the authorization of the territorial state.[18]

Doctor Miguel A. D'Estefano Pisani, honorable professor of the University of Havana, cites various cessions by leases in the last century when he refers to leases in international law, like:

17. *Digest of International Law*, 5, 1042.
18. Alfred Verdross, op. cit., 205.

- The one granted in 1872 by the Ottoman Empire to the Austro-Hungarian Empire over all the territory of Bosnia and Herzegovina.
- The one granted in 1878 by Turkey to Great Britain over the island of Cyprus.
- The ones—for there were several—that imperial China was forced to grant for 99 years to Germany in 1898, over the territories of Kiao Cheu (Kiaochow), and to France in 1899, also for 99 years, over Kuang Cheu.[19]

The first agreement reached by U.S. imperialism for the lease of territory in another country for naval or coaling stations was the one made with Cuba; but the one established with Panama followed immediately afterward and in the 1940s, with Great Britain. The latter included a date of expiry, but the one reached with Panama did not include such a date at first, for the original agreement expressly said it was in perpetuity. However, it was modified in 1977 by the Torrijos-Carter Treaties fixing the year 2000 for its expiry.

Therefore, of all the leases I have mentioned, only the one regarding Guantánamo continues to lack an express time limit to date.

The 1903 Agreement on coaling and naval stations between the United States and Cuba was achieved by evident coercion that invalidate said document, as I have already commented elsewhere in this book, but the United States have thought and acted as if they had acquired a right of property, *a uti possidetis eta possideatis* (as you possess, you continue to possess) in perpetuity, in full seigniory, despite the fact that the 1903 Agreement uses the legal concept of lease, but it is an imperfect lease designed to justify indefinite possession.

The Peruvian Professor Alberto Ulloa comments the effects of leases for military bases as a covert form of cession and says:

19. Miguel A. D'Estefano Pisani, *Documentos del derecho internacional público*, II, 976.

> The cases of leases are theoretically admissible and derive from the independence of the states to sign international agreements, as well as from the transferable nature of pieces of territory; but in practice, they represent an imposition of force by threat, and a fertile source of conflicts, for they are nothing but indirect forms of cession that do not hurt the state that suffers them as much as a definitive and overt dismembering.[20]

If the cession behaves thus, how much further can it go considering that the agreement was imposed against the will of the ceding state and without the right to determine its permanence or the option to terminate the treaty in question, as is the case of the naval base at Guantánamo.

The illustrious professor of the University of San Marcos, in Lima, accurately scrutinizes the Platt Amendment and states that: "Cuba was a typical case of a partial protectorate."[21] Further on, in a direct reference to the North American publicist J. Brown Scott,[22] the chairman of the International Law Institute of the United States of America, who defended at all costs in his works the benefits the Platt Amendment meant for Cuba, Professor Alberto Ulloa states that:

> Optimistic spirits in Cuba purported to interpret its international situation regarding the United States as an alliance of reciprocal benefit; the interpretation was notoriously forced, for the Platt Amendment created for Cuba a situation of dependence, a tutelage on behalf of United States' interests. On the other hand, politicians and internationalists in the United States endeavored to prove in the legal terrain that the amendment did not violate Cuba's sovereign rights.[23]

20. Alberto Ulloa, *Derecho internacional público*, 1, 247.
21. Ibid.
22. J. Brown Scott, *Cuba, la América Latina, los Estados Unidos* (1926). Quoted by Alberto Ulloa, op. cit., 1, 248.
23. Alberto Ulloa, Ibid.

If Jefferson and later Monroe expected to and longed for possessing Cuba as the cornerstone for North American expansion, the outcome of the situation was not one expected by the United States. Faced by developments in Cuba, the liberation war of 1895, and despite the 1898 Treaty of Paris, it was no longer possible to seize Cuba, it was no longer the time for overt annexation; obviously, that moment had passed, and they had to seek new formulas to sate the U.S.'s appetite for domination at the inception of the imperialist stage, whose first war was the one waged by the United States against Spain in 1898.

The 1934 Treaty and the *Rebus Sic Stantibus* Norm

The Treaty of Relations between the United States and Cuba, dated May 29, 1934, purports to replace three treaties signed by these two nations in 1903: the Agreement on coaling and naval stations and its Complementary Agreement, as well as the Permanent Treaty of Relations.

The change in the circumstances that paved the way for the signing of the aforementioned 1903 treaties, like the imposition of the Platt Amendment, and in the circumstances that brought about the 1934 Treaty of Relations—that is to say, the Good Neighbor policy—is obvious and notorious. And albeit the latter was formally valid in the beginning, it is adequate to question the validity of a treaty when the circumstances that gave it legal life have fundamentally changed. For the reality of the alleged Good Neighbor policy differs from today's reality: the continuous U.S. hostility and aggressions against Cuba since 1959.

In order to acknowledge this possibility, it is universally deemed that treaties without a date of expiry contain a tacit condition: that they will last while the circumstances existing at the time of their signature still exist and their change has not been foreseen: *rebus sic stantibus*. It is contrary to reason and to nature that treaties are signed in perpetuity.

According to international law, the norm *pacta sunt servanda* obliges states to abide by the rules created by an agreement among them, but the obligation against the will of one of the signatories, that invalidates consent, without which a legal order is unimaginable, cannot be inferred from the principle of obligation by agreement. That principle lacks an absolute value in the international order. The ruling norm *pacta sunt servanda* obliges the signatories of a treaty to fulfill the essential requisites of that treaty.

The principle *rebus sic stantibus*—that is to say, that once concluded, treaties can be modified or revoked in the light of certain circumstances—, is equal in rank and in hierarchy to the norm *pacta sunt servanda.*

Nowadays, this principle is universally acknowledged (by the scientific doctrine) and by courts of law, albeit under various names.

The application of this norm is one of the ways to terminate treaties. It consists in deeming a treaty inefficient, inapplicable or null when the circumstances that led to its signing change in such a way, that it can be said that the treaty would not have been signed if the new circumstances had existed at that time.

A fundamental change in circumstances is a principle granted the category of international law norm by the Convention on law of treaties held in Vienna, in 1969. It basically states that a treaty can be considered as terminated when the circumstances that were the essential basis for the consent of the parties to oblige themselves have changed or been modified, and that the effects of such a change can radically modify the obligations contained in the treaty or that should still "be fulfilled according to the treaty in question."

According to some authors, whenever this change of circumstances occurs, it has an extinguishing effect regarding what was agreed upon.

International practice has examples of states that have dissociated themselves from obligations contracted invoking the *rebus sic stantibus* clause, also invoked by the Permanent Tribunal for International Justice, although it is not always accepted as international law despite the fact that since the UN Convention about law of treatis was enforced, it is unquestionable that it has acquired the category of an imperative norm of international law.

The Austrian Professor Verdross analyzes in his work about international public law the invocation of the *rebus sic stantibus* clause. I quote some of his comments next:

> The autonomy of the clause can only be explained based on the assumption that after the treaty's signature, circumstances can be so essentially modified that it is out of the question to ask the parties to fulfill the agreement. From this results that our clause cannot, in general terms, be invoked in cases where it can be rescinded, for when it was included, the parties themselves bore in mind the possibility that the circumstances could change, considering that they could then rescind the treaty...
>
> An objective formulation of what was said in the previous paragraph is the decision taken by the French Chamber of Deputies on December 13, 1932, when the Treaty about debts signed with the United States was not longer applicable because it was conceived based on the assumption of collecting German war reparations...
> Likewise, at the beginning of World War II, France and Great Britain ignored the obligations assumed by virtue of Article 36, paragraph 2 of the Statute of the Permanent Tribunal of International Justice, claiming a change of circumstances...[24]

In their turn, the United States used the aforementioned clause in the same way on August 9, 1941, to free themselves from a treaty, and Verdross refers to a paper published in one of the 1942 issues of the *Juridical Yearly Report of the Inter-American International Law Society*, that quotes what the Attorney General of the U.S. Government expressly said on that date: "It is a well established principle of international law, rebus *sic stantibus*, that a treaty ceases to be binding when the basic conditions upon which it was founded have essentially changed."[25]

It is absurd to deny the change of circumstances and, to end these quotations of cases and criteria, we bring the encyclical *Summi Pontificatus*, dated October 20, 1939, where Pope Pious XII wrote:

24. Alfred Verdross, op. cit., 124-125.
25. Robert H. Jackson was the US Attorney General in 1942. *Anuario Jurídico de la Sociedad Interamericana de Derecho Internacional*, 36 (1942): 89. Quoted by Alfred Verdross, op. cit., 125.

> It has to be said that it is true that, with the passage of time and the substantial change in circumstances—unforeseen and perhaps unforeseeable at the time it was stipulated—, an entire treaty or some of its clauses can be or seem to be unjust or too onerous, or even inapplicable to one of the signatories. If this happens, a legal discussion must be timely engaged to modify whatever it is convenient to change or completely replace the established agreement.[26]

What a difference between what McKinley said in 1901 in order to not recognize the independence of the Republic of Cuba when, through Secretary of War Root, and Wood, the U.S. Governor in Cuba, the Cuban members of the Constituent Assembly were informed that, if they did not include the Platt Amendment in the Constitution, the United States would not withdraw their troops from Cuba; and the response given by the Revolutionary Government to an insolent note from Washington dated June 12, 1959!: "The Revolutionary Government assumes the authority to decide what it deems more suitable to the essential interests of the Cuban people, and does not and will not accept any indication or proposal whatsoever that tends to harm in the least the national sovereignty and dignity."[27] In 1959, Cuba was no longer the neo-colonial republic. The circumstances had undoubtedly changed.

Let us add another important fact: the absence of relations between the two countries for, in January, 1961, the Government of the United States severed diplomatic and consular relations with the Government of Cuba, that unquestionably indicates that, since then, a change of circumstances exists and, although the U.S. Government hastened to notify that they would remain in the base, the United States, by its own deed, invalidated the 1934 Treaty that claims to be based on the friendly relations between the two countries.

26. J.L. Gutiérrez García, *Doctrina pontificia,* Second Edition (bilingual), (1958): 784. Quoted by Alfred Verdross, op. cit., 125.
27. Diplomatic Note dated June 15, 1959, Archives of the Ministry of Foreign Affairs of the Republic of Cuba.

In short, it can be asserted that the February 16/23, 1903 Agreement on coaling and naval stations, a document that adopted the legal concept of the lease of the naval base at Guantánamo, is null and void since its inception, and that the 1934 Treaty is also original invalidated because it carries the invalidities of the 1903 Agreement; furthermore, it has no validity due to the behavior of the United States for, if the aim of the1934 Treaty was to strengthen the friendly links between Cuba and the United States, the North American behavior before and after the signing of that Treaty—and specially in these past decades since the triumph of the Cuban Revolution—has been the opposite: an unfriendly, aggressive and arrogant treatment toward Cuba and its people.

Does the U.S. naval base at Guantánamo contribute to the strengthening of the friendship with Cuba? What do the breaking of diplomatic, consular and commercial relations, the mercenary invasion of Playa Girón, the economic blockade, the violation of our air space, the acts of terrorism, the Torricelli Act and the Helms-Burton Act mean then?

As antagonistic to reality as the expressed purpose by the first treaty (the one signed in 1903) is the expressed purpose in the second (the one dated 1934). It is evident that there is a change of circumstances: in 1959, Cuba gained full control of its political, social and economic destiny; since then, it has not needed strollers, tutors or protection.

According to the maxim by Paulus (Julius), one of the five Roman juriconsults whose opinions were a source of law and from whom the *Digesto* quotes numerous excerpts, and *Alaric's Code* includes a summary of his *Sententiarum Receptorum libri V*: "What is initially invalid, is not validated by time."[28] Or, as the old saying teaches: "A tree born twisted will never stand straight."

Law principles acknowledge that no law is irrevocable. That is why we can assert that a treaty, assimilated into the law by the obligations they generate in linking the signatory states, is not irrevocable either, on the contrary. And it is known that it is the people upon whom the

28. "Principios de derecho-interpretación de la ley," in *Leyes civiles de Cuba y su jurisprudencia*, 187.

U.S. naval base at Guantánamo who rejected it since its inception and will continue to reject it. Therefore, that treaty can be repealed.

There is no legal argument whatsoever that justifies the permanence of the North American naval base on Cuban territory. Neither the spurious 1903 Agreement nor the deceitful and invalid 1934 Treaty can uphold the U.S. presence in Guantánamo. The occupation of the territory where stands the base in Guantánamo is a violation of the law.

Cuba's Sovereignty Over the Occupied Territory. There Are no Territorial Borders

The areas of land and water occupied by the naval base at Guantánamo, located within the limits fixed by the 1903 Agreement and ratified by the 1934 Treaty, have not, neither by fact nor by law, ceased being a part of the national territory over which the Republic of Cuba exerts its sovereignty as a free and independent state.

Nothing else can be inferred, in terms of a rational interpretation, from the text of the February 16/23, 1903 Agreement for the lease of the aforementioned areas of Cuban land and water to the United States of America, whose Article III states:

> Whereas the United States acknowledges the continuance of the ultimate sovereignty of the Republic of Cuba over the extensions of land and water described above, the Republic of Cuba consents to that, during the period in which the United States occupy said areas according to the provisos of this Agreement, the United States exerts jurisdiction and dominion over those areas with the right to acquire (under the conditions that the two Governments will later agree upon) for the United States' public purposes, any plot of land or property located in them by purchase or forced expropriation, fully compensating their owners.

By trying to adjust the incompatibility of sovereignty and dominion that stemmed from this Treaty for a lease without a timeframe or for an indefinite span of time, it could be considered that it is a situation similar to what has been called an "unequal condominium" of two states over a territory that, in this case, was the object of a lease. Note that articles I, II and III of the February 16/23, 1903 Agreement are not compatible with the legal concept lease for, according to Article II of said Agreement, the use of the areas leased is not only absolutely and exclusively restricted to the concessionaire; Article III of the Complementary Agreement dated July 2, 1903, obliges the concessionaire to prevent any person, society or association from establishing or exercising commercial, industrial or other enterprises within the areas mentioned.

The base's land and maritime area cannot be but legally considered a part of the Cuban national territory, subject to the sovereignty of the Cuban state; the lease on behalf of another sovereign state does not allow making a distinction, like some authors maintain, between the concepts sovereignty by law or "nuda sovereignty" which, in this case, would be Cuba's, and sovereignty by fact that would be exercised by the United States.[29] The French jurisconsult and professor at the Sorbonne, Paul Fauchille, without ignoring the terrible precedents set by the historic cases of Hong Kong, Macao, Kiao Tcheu (Kiaochow) and other enclaves in China, favors the theory of the "underhanded annexation."

If, on the other hand, this type of contractual territorial cessions are not only carried out but are also extinguished or resolved like any other lease in civil law—and practice bears witness to this—, there is no legal reason to doubt Cuba's right to recover that territory, for its sovereignty survives in its entirety.

If we restrict ourselves to the contract that rules over the naval base at Guantánamo, the "full jurisdiction and dominion" that, according to the terms of the February 16/23, 1903 Agreement, the United States can exercise over the leased area, must be interpreted

29. Paul Fauchille, *Traité de Droit Internationale Publique, I*, Second Part, 775.

in their material and restricted sense—that is to say, when they are indispensable in order for the United States to use and benefit from the territory according to the aims or the ends to which it was destined—, because the simultaneous and express U.S. recognition, as stated in Article III of the aforementioned agreement, of "the continuance" of the definitive sovereignty of the Republic of Cuba over the leased extensions of land and water cannot be conceived otherwise.

An eloquent fact that, in my opinion, shows the continuance of Cuba's sovereignty over the land occupied by the aforementioned naval station, is the ruling established by Article IV of the July 2, 1903 Complementary Agreement for the reciprocal return of fugitive criminals that purported to seek refuge within the leased area or in Cuban territory. The right of asylum is not recognized in principle nor, therefore, is a formal request for extradition demanded. The return must be carried out when the legitimate authority merely requests it and without establishing distinctions in regard to the nature or seriousness of the criminal deed, that can even be a contravention for which, ordinarily, extradition is not granted. In these cases, we could say that the summoned authority acts almost by delegation of the summons server.

Naturally, the behavior of the United States has been different, for the base at Guantánamo was converted by the North Americans, after the triumph of the Cuban Revolution, and purposefully acting against the sovereign rights of the people of Cuba, into a lair of felons, common criminals to whom they granted shelter and protection.

But there is another element that makes it mandatory to conclude that, according to the 1903 Agreements, Cuba's sovereignty over the areas of land and water currently occupied by the naval base at Guantánamo will always be unquestionable. I am referring to the previous eviction of its civilian population that Cuba was obliged to carry out in compliance with the stipulations in the second paragraph of Article I of the July 2, 1903 Complementary Agreement.

In order to exercise its political sovereignty in the broad sense of this concept in international law, the United States did not need Cuba to grant it the possession of assets of exclusively public dominion, that rendered indispensable the previous expropriation—according to the aforementioned Agreement—of all privately owned land and of any other estates comprised in the area to be leased. That is why Article III of the February 16/23, 1903 expressed that in the period during which the United States occupy the base, that country will exercise full jurisdiction and dominion over it, as a lessee is able to do over the leased asset, whose use thus results exclusive of all other owners or users.

If the terms in which Article III of the February 16/23, 1903 Treaty was drafted are read carefully, perhaps this idea will not seem so clear, for it seems that, together with the lease, it was attempted to transfer to the United States the right to acquire by purchase or by mandatory expropriation any land or privately owned property within the areas leased, although under conditions to be agreed upon later on by the governments of the United States and Cuba.

But the Cuban negotiators were undoubtedly aware of the enormous importance that the transference of the right to carry out mandatory expropriations on behalf of a foreign power could have for the continuance of the Republic's definitive sovereignty over such areas—as had been stipulated as a requisite *sine qua non*—, and the dangerous agreement was later modified by Article I of the July 2, 1903 Complementary Agreement, replacing it by the obligation that the Republic of Cuba solemnly contracted to acquire without delay and, naturally, on its own behalf, "all privately owned land and other estates included in those areas" that were thus brought under the direct public dominion of the Cuban state as an indispensable step prior to their being leased to the United States of America. Thus, the Republic of Cuba, abiding by the commitment imposed upon it by Article VII of the 1901 Constitutional Appendix, imposed in its turn by the Platt Amendment, prevented the alienation of a single inch of national territory and its sovereignty was, *de facto* and *de jure*, formally unharmed.

There is no territorial border according to the technical and legal meaning of the term, between the zone leased and the remaining Cuban territory, but a permanent fence that prevents all access or normal land communication between the two territories.

However, the United States does not see it thus, for an Internet report on the *1995 U.S. CIA World Fact Book*, referring to U.S. land borders includes the naval base at Guantánamo, with 29 kilometers of land border with Cuba.

The British lawyer Sir Hersch Lauterpacht, remarked about the leases of territory by one state to another that

> [...] some of these cases comprise, for most practical purposes, cessions of pieces of territory, but in strict law, these remain the property of the leasing State. Such property is not a mere fiction, as some writers maintain, for it is possible for the lease to come to an end by expiration of time or by rescission. Thus the lease granted in 1894 by Great Britain to the former Congo Free State, of the so-called Lado Enclave,* was rescinded in 1906 and the British lease of Wei-Hai-Wei in China was rescinded in 1930. On the other hand, the leases of small pieces of territory granted in 1941 by Great Britain to the United States for the use and operation of naval and airbases in Newfoundland,** Bermuda, Jamaica, St. Lucia, Antigua, Trinidad and British Guiana for a term of ninety-nine years did not involve, apart from a rigidly limited concession of certain jurisdictional rights, any surrender either of sovereignty or of the exercise thereof.[30]

The Supreme Court of the Republic of Cuba in 1934 affirmed the conviction of defendants who imported three hogs from the Guantánamo Naval Station without paying duty. The defendants had claimed that no duty was due because the hogs had already been in Cuba. The Court held, however, that "the territory of that Naval Station is for all legal effects regarded as foreign."[31]

* Bordering Congo Free State—later Belgian Congo—Uganda and the old Anglo-Egyptian Sudan.

** Now a part of Canada.

30. Hersch Lauterpacht, *Oppenheim's International Law*, 458.
31. "Juicio Guzmán y Latamble, 12 de febrero de 1934," *Jurisprudencia al día*, Penal, 35 (Cuba) 1933-34, quoted by *Digest of International Law*, 2, 217.

I have already referred to the work by the Peruvian Professor Alberto Ulloa, where he also analyzes foreign military bases. In his book, he comments on the bases established by the United States in other American countries or territories, and I will refer to the case in hand.

In 1941, due to World War II, the United States ceded various destroyers to Great Britain for the British Royal Navy in exchange for the cession of territories in the British possessions in America for military bases. When the policy for the continental defense against the Berlin-Rome-Tokyo axis was being approved, these military bases acted as a hemispheric safety belt. On the other hand, the United States reached the agreement with Cuba to establish some military bases that would be operational while the war lasted. They were all airbases, with no outlets to the sea.

Once the war was over, the United States returned these bases, among which were the ones agreed upon with England by the aforementioned exchange, and the ones they established in Cuba. Thus, the airbases in San Antonio—in the province of Havana—, in San Julián—in the province of Pinar del Río—and in the city of Camagüey, in the province that bears the same name, were returned to the Republic of Cuba on May 20, 1946. Professor Ulloa remarks about these cases that "the one in Guantánamo was not included because it is permanent since 1903."[32]

32. Alberto Ulloa, op. cit., 1, 518.

V

THE AGGRESSIONS

THE U.S. NAVAL BASE AS A CONTINUED U.S. AGGRESSION AGAINST CUBA

Use of the Base Against Cuban Popular and Revolutionary Movements

The naval base at Guantánamo has also served to support corrupt and bloodthirsty rulers upheld in Cuba by the imperialist policies of the United States, and to perpetrate criminal acts against the Cuban state and the Cuban people by common agreement between the two governments. For that reason, it is not surprising that in the various stages in which popular and revolutionary movements took place against the despotic rulers in Cuba, not only weapons but also troops came out from the base to fight the people.

As an example of the aforesaid, I will refer to two interventionist feats with the participation of troops stationed at the naval base, that occurred at two critical moments in Cuba: 1912 and 1917, respectively.

In chapter II, I have explained one of them in detail—the one that took place in 1912, with the uprising of the Colored Peoples Independent Party, later called "The Blacks' Warlet"—brutally suppressed by the Liberal Party headed by President José Miguel Gómez. U.S. troops from the base invaded various towns in the former province of Oriente, in the periphery of the cities of Guantánamo and Santiago de Cuba with the pretext of protecting the lives and properties of North Americans living there.

Also in Oriente, and due to the 1917 uprising known as "La Chambelona," carried out by members of the Liberal Party opposed to the electoral fraud that led to the reelection of President Mario García Menocal, from the Conservative Party, detachments of U.S. troops from the base were deployed to various locations in that Cuban province, using the protection of the base's water supply as a pretext.

So if Republicans and Democrats have always been the same to U.S. politics—as José Martí accurately pointed out more than one century ago—, in Cuban politics Conservatives and Liberals were also the same. They also meant the same to the United States, for what really mattered to them was to support those who, at a given time, better served U.S. interests. Thus, in 1912, the North Americans supported the Liberals to suppress the popular movement and, in 1917, they supported the Conservatives.

It was always like that. There are other similar examples. But the most significant among them is the criminal support granted by the naval base at Guantánamo to Fulgencio Batista's bloody dictatorship, as soon as the United States had the inkling that something more than a popular movement was developing in Cuba, when the armed struggle waged by Fidel Castro and his followers began to rally generalized support from the entire population. It was, without a doubt, a true Revolution.

Between 1957 and 1958, with the baseless purpose of annihilating the guerrilla war in the eastern mountains, the airplanes of Batista's tyranny—fueled at the Guantánamo Naval Base—indiscriminately strafed and bombed the rural population in the areas liberated by the Rebel Army in the Sierra Maestra.

A fragment of a report sent to Fidel Castro by Raúl Castro, the then chief of the Second Eastern Front "Frank País" of the Rebel Army, about the operations carried out in that area, is an eloquent sample of the consequences of U.S. support to the tyranny. The report was dated in Bayate, June 2, 1958. Raúl Castro said: "As it happened in previous days, the airplanes are throwing incendiary bombs given them by the Yankees at the Guantánamo Naval Base itself, and they [the Yankees] have ordered Trujillo and Somoza to give weapons to Batista for, due to the continental pressure, they are prevented from shamelessly doing so, as they used to."[1]

The Rebel Army's Military Order no. 30 was also a denunciation of the support by U.S. forces at the base to dictator Batista's indiscriminate bombings of the Cuban civilian population. The contents of this order were spread in the Message to the World Youth. The two documents were dated July 5, 1958 at the Sierra Maestra. The Message says:

1. From the author's personal archives.

> From March until May, 1958, the dictatorship's air force carried out some one hundred air raids [...], during May, the enemy air force was supplied with all kinds of bombs at the U.S. naval base [...], for that reason and thanks to that help, the dictatorship's air squadrons have been daily carrying out from 3 to 5 raids over our territories [...] suffering ceaseless bombings [...] hundreds of families have been and are still living in caves, holes and other anti-aircraft refuges, endless days of anxiety, anguish and starvation [...] hundreds of humble homes built with the sacrifice of many years of hard work have been razed to the ground.[2]

What was called "Anti-aircraft Operation" began on June 27, 1958. It was conceived by Raúl Castro, chief of the Second Eastern Front of the Rebel Army, to prevent the bombings mentioned above. This operation consisted in withholding several U.S. citizens, including 29 marines, who were heading from the base to the city of Guantánamo. Those persons were taken to the bombed areas so that they could verify such monstrous facts. Thus, the retention of these U.S. citizens served for the world to know the U.S. involvement in the massacre of the defenseless civilian population.

The North American Vice-Consul in Santiago de Cuba was obliged to meet with Raúl at the Second Front's headquarters, to verify *in situ* the accusations made by the Cuban rebel troops, as well as the support received by the tyranny's forces from the naval base at Guantánamo.

The hostages were released and U.S. authorities learned their lesson.

The U.S. Naval Base as a Spearhead Against the Cuban Revolution

With the triumph of the Cuban Revolution in 1959, as the culmination of a long popular struggle, Cuba attained its full independence for the first time; no longer the formal independence of May 20, 1902,

2. Ibid.

but true independence. From then on, the United States began to fruitlessly implement a sequence of aggressions, criminal acts and sabotages against the Cuban Revolution, besides turning the usurped Cuba territory of the naval base at Guantánamo into a permanent focus of threats, provocations and violations of the Republic's sovereignty, with the purpose of creating difficulties to the Revolution.

All types of aggressions have been perpetrated from the naval base: the violation of Cuban territorial waters and air space, insults, provocations, shots, the murder of Cuban soldiers and of Cuban workers at the base. During all these years, the Cuban Government has denounced such provocations dozens of times, not only before the Government of the United States, but also before the United Nations.

The U.S. enclave in Guantánamo has never been used to defend Cuba, as stated by the spurious 1903 Platt Treaty; nor has it been an example of the friendly relations between the two countries, as stated by the also invalid 1934 Treaty.

The U.S. naval base at Guantánamo has always been an element in the designs and operations that, for almost four decades, have been conceived and fruitlessly attempted by the United States to destroy the Cuba people's government, like the murders of its leader, Commander-in-Chief Fidel Castro, of General Raúl Castro, the second figure of the Cuban Revolution, and of other revolutionary leaders, as well as acts of sabotage and brutal terrorism.

The naval base at Guantánamo was always the detonator of purported acts of self-provocation and deployment of U.S. troops in a "justified" punitive invasion against Cuba. An example is one of the variables of the so-called "Operation Mongoose,"[3] when U.S. soldiers stationed at Guantánamo were supposed to shoot against the Cuban sentries on September 3, 1962.

In 1961, the U.S. Central Intelligence Agency (CIA) organized what they called "Operation Patty," but the Cuban State Security discovered it and, in response, planned what was called "Operation

3. Operation Mongoose, a plan conceived in November 1961 by the US Government—after the failure of the so-called "Operation Pluto" (the mercenary invasion to the Bay of Pigs, defeated at Playa Girón on April 19, 1961)— to overthrown Cuba's Revolutionary Government.

Candela." Later on, the facts were made known to the Cuban people as "Patty-Candela." The aim of "Operation Patty" was to assassinate Fidel at a public rally to be held in Santiago de Cuba to commemorate the historic date of July 26, and to also murder Raúl in Havana. The two crimes were to be committed on the same day. This action was related to a plan to "attack" the naval base as a self-provocation. The counterrevolutionary leaders, protected by the base's intelligence services, were able to infiltrate agents and weapons into Cuba.

The purported dual action would create a chaotic and critical situation in the country that, according to U.S. plans, could lead to an aggression to the base by the Cuban Army as a response to the assassination of its leaders, thus justifying an intervention by the marines—the U.S. Marine Corps—stationed at the base. Alfredo Izaguirre, the head of this operation, was arrested on June 22, 1961, a few days before the operation began. According to a report by the Brazilian journalist Claudia Furiati, Izaguirre told the Cuban State Security: "Another justification would be that the Cuban Government or somebody else attacked the base at Guantánamo [...] I believe that the United States needs a pretext to militarily intervene in Cuba [...] the naval base will be attacked and Fidel Castro will be denounced as responsible for it ..."[4]

The then Secretary of Defense of Kennedy's Government, Robert McNamara, attended the Cuba/USSR/USA Tripartite Meeting in Havana in 1992, to commemorate the 30th anniversary of the October Crisis—also known as the October Crisis—and to analyze the developments that took place then. In Claudia Furiati's book, the author refers to McNamara's reflection when answering the following question posed by the Cuban side: "And if a bombing to the naval base at Guantánamo had been provoked?" The author points out that: "McNamara hesitated: 'Well...'. The journalist says that the Cuban side continued to inquire: "Why, if you were able to blow up a ship [the "Maine"] here in the bay of Havana, and to kill your own soldiers to enter into the Spanish-Cuban War, why wouldn't you shoot against this unimportant military base?"

4. Claudia Furiati, *ZR-Rifle, El complot para asesinar a Kennedy y a Fidel Castro*, 41.

Later on, the former U.S. secretary of Defense admitted what Furiati says in her book: "I want to be honest. If I were Cuban, I would have thought the same thing. We could have invaded."[5]

The Naval Base and U.S. Aggressions Against the Cuban Economy and the Cuban Workers in that Facility

The Black Market in Cuban Currency

Since the building of the naval base began in Guantánamo, thousands of Cuban workers worked there. The Cuban workers and employees came from a country with high unemployment and underemployment rates. They were skilled and hard-working men willing to get lower wages than the ones paid to United States citizens who performed the same tasks. Caimanera, Boquerón, Guantánamo and, in general terms, other areas of the country—mainly the easternmost ones—, fed the base with civilian personnel.

When the Revolution triumphed, more than 3000 Cubans worked at the base, including women who performed menial tasks as servants, nursemaids and nannies.

Since then, the base's authorities have established a black market in Cuban currency, handled by U.S. banks, criminals and embezzlers. In short, it was money that left Cuba for the United States by various illegal means and, from the base to be exchanged for dollars by the Cuban workers, at an unofficial exchange rate. This operation had two purposes:

On the one hand:

- To try to corrupt Cuba workers, who would get more Cuban pesos when changing their dollars.

5. Ibid., 65.

- To prevent that the U.S. dollars paid as wages to the Cuban workers at the Base, which they should exchange at the official rate into Cuban pesos at an agency of the National Bank of Cuba, went to the Cuban public treasury.

And on the other hand:

- The North Americans could set in circulation large amounts of Cuban currency they had illicitly accumulated.

- Also when this black market was established at the base, the North Americans were able to reduce the expenses caused by the payment of wages to the Cuban staff.

To bring all this to a halt, the Cuban state adopted corresponding measures: It was compulsory for the Cubans working at the base to exchange U.S. dollars into Cuban pesos at the National Bank of Cuba agency opened for that purpose. They were allowed to keep 10% of the dollars they received to cater for their expenses at the base.

In an article published in October, 1961, the economist Raúl Cepero Bonilla, the then Chairman of the National Bank of Cuba, referred to the case as follows:

> It was impossible to prevent U.S. authorities from corrupting the Cuban workers at the Base by giving them the opportunity to exchange each dollar from their wages for 4 or 5 Cuban pesos. However, Comrade Fidel Castro suggested an indirect control system that put an end, as of April, 1961, to the smuggling of money at the naval base.[6]

The exchange of money remained in place until 1994 when the use and tenure of U.S. dollars was permitted; its exchange is no longer mandatory.

6. Raúl Cepero Bonilla, "El canje de billetes, un golpe a la contrarrevolución," in *Cuba Socialista*, 46.

The Fishermen and the Aqueduct

The water from the aqueduct at Yateritas, in Guantánamo, was usually supplied to the naval base, despite the many aggressions of all kinds that were launched—and are still launched—from it against Cuban free territory, as a part of the U.S. policy of harassment against Revolutionary Cuba. But Cuba took a decision about the water supply to the base after an incident in 1964.

On February 2, 1964, ships of the U.S. Navy kidnapped four Cuban fishing boats: the "Lambda 8," the "Lambda 33," the "Cárdenas 9" and the "Cárdenas 14," taking them to the naval base in Key West, in Monroe County, Florida. The fishermen were imprisoned at the jail in that county of Florida.

The 36 Cuban fishermen unduly imprisoned in the United States were subject to interrogation, coercion and insults, in ostensible violation of the U.S. and international law. They were released after the Revolutionary Government took steps that forced the United States Government to do so. One of those measures suspending the water supply to the base.

The Cuban decision was a suitable response to the unjust aggression against the Cuban fishermen kidnapped by the North Americans and taken to Florida on February 2, 1964. The Cuban Government decided to cut the drinking water supply from the Yateritas aqueduct to the base on February 6, 1964: the aqueduct faucet that supplied the base with 6.5 million gallons of water daily was closed, save for one hour each day. That water was exclusively destined for the population's consumption, for as long as the imprisonment of our innocent fishermen lasted.

However, the North Americans arrogantly decided to no longer receive the drinking water supply. Furthermore, taking as a pretext the dignified Cuban decision in response to the aggression against the fishermen, the then U.S. President Lyndon B. Johnson, on behalf of the arrogant and domineering empire, announced on February 11, among other economic aggressive measures against Cuba, the lay off of some 700 Cubans who worked at the base.

In a Note dated February 11, 1964,[7] the Cuban Revolutionary Government warned the Government of the United States that the willingness that prompted Cuba to resume supplying water to the Guantánamo Naval Base, as soon as the unjust imprisonment of the Cuban fishermen was terminated and the ships sent back—the decisive cause for the suspension decreed—was affected by more than one motive: the statements by U.S. Government officials anticipating that the resumption of the water supply would not be accepted; and the threat of laying off the Cuban workers who had traditionally worked at the base. On the other hand, the Cuban Revolutionary Government also denied in the aforementioned Note the publicized lies that Cuba sought to profit from that incident to present the issue of the base. The Cuban demand, as was clearly established in the Note, was limited to the release of the Cuban fishermen and the returning of their boats.

Notwithstanding the formal stance of the Cuban Government, U.S. authorities ordered the lay off of hundreds of Cuban workers that had spent more than 20 ears of their lives performing back-breaking tasks for the United States Government. With no respect for U.S. laws that protected their rights, and without any humane consideration whatsoever, they abruptly dismissed the workers and confiscated the accumulated pension funds, a measure added to another previous one against the Cuban workers at the base: since February, 1963, the U.S. Government had unlawfully suspended the payment of the Cuban workers pensions.

The arbitrariness of the measure adopted was thrice irritating, due to the injustice involved, to the ingratitude it exuded and to the spirit of retaliation that tainted it.

On February 19, 1964, the correspondent of the UPI news agency at the naval base at Guantánamo reported that "there is no immediate perspective of a new lay off of Cuban personnel," since "the Department of Defense has decided that it will take two years to turn the base into a garrison of a strictly military character."[8] In an interview with

7. Diplomatic Note dated February 11, 1964. Archives of the Ministry of Foreign Affairs of the Republic of Cuba.
8. Author's personal archives.

the Cuban minister of Foreign Affairs held on the afternoon of February 28, the Swiss Ambassador, whose country represents U.S. interests in Cuba, indicated that this information could be interpreted as an indirect reference to the Revolutionary Government's formal statement in the Note issued on February 11 of that same year.[9]

Later on, the drastic lay off of 204 Cuban workers, that took place in circumstances identical to the previous one, evinced that the U.S. Government had failed to heed any other consideration about this issue.

The unfriendly fact that an answer to the Cuban Government's Note was indefinitely and unaccountably deferred, raised Cuban doubts that the fishermen's imprisonment was not a fortuitous incident, but one prompted by the wish to create tensions.

Aggressions at the Workplace

The Cuban personnel at the base has been the target of U.S. aggressive maneuvers in various ways. When the U.S. Government laid off hundreds of Cuban workers who held jobs at the base, the Revolution adopted urgent measures to solve in various ways their labor or social security problems. Although they had worked for years at the base, the United States had dismissed them without paying them their dues.

But, before and after these aggressive measures against Cuban workers at the base, other acts were committed, all of which got defensive answers from the Cuban authorities. Thus, months before the kidnapping of the Cuban fishermen and the lay off of Cuban workers, the Government of the United States suspended the obligations of the U.S. insurance civil service that paid the pensions to the former workers and to the families of deceased former workers of the naval base. The North Americans based that aggression on one of the many lies that the U.S. Government spreads to justify its immoral actions. At that time, they argued the lack of guarantees on Cuba's part so that the former workers at the base and their relatives got their dues.

9. Archives of the Ministry of Foreign Affairs of the Republic of Cuba.

In consequence, considering the arbitrary suspension of the benefits that the U.S. Treasury Department was obliged to pay to the Cuban workers, and until such unjust situation was resolved and the insurance payments they were entitled to were made—something that the U.S. Government has not yet done—Resolution 9692 was issued on December 30, 1963 by the minister of Labor, stating that the Direction of Social Security of the Ministry of Labor of the Republic of Cuba must consider these workers as beneficiaries, paying them the monthly amount they had received from the United States Government. It also provided a budget totaling 300,000 pesos to pay such obligations.

Far from rectifying the situation that stemmed from the payment of retirement allocations and pensions, the United States increased its actions against the Cuban workers at the Guantánamo Naval Base. Our countrymen were placed in a situation of economic defenselessness when hundreds of them were laid off their jobs of many years there.

Faced by that U.S. labor policy against Cuban workers, the Ministry of Labor solved the case again and issued Resolution 66 on June 28, 1966. This resolution authorized granting long-term benefits as a subsidy to those Cubans who had been arbitrarily expelled and laid off their jobs at the base and that, due to their age or health, it had been impossible to find adequate jobs for them in the non-occupied territory. On the other hand, the workers that did not yet qualify in terms of age or time worked to be considered beneficiaries of Law 1100, dated March 27, 1963, were granted subsidies equal to the wages they previously received.

Again, some time later, the Ministry of Labor of the Republic of Cuba had to face the situation of these workers. Thus, that Ministry issued Resolution 81, dated November 25, 1974, which considered the decision of the United States civil service insurance of refusing or suspending payment of the benefits due to Cuban workers, to workers of other nationalities living in Cuba and to the relatives of deceased workers, without bearing in mind that some of them were already old people.

Thus, faced by such an ignoble gesture by the United States, that placed Cuban workers or their relatives in a situation of economic defenselessness, the aforementioned Resolution 81 extended Cuban social security benefits to these citizens, granting them social security benefits payable from the public funds to which, naturally, they had never contributed, for they contributed to the United States retirement funds.

Furthermore, the aforementioned Resolution also acknowledged the years those people had worked at the Guantánamo Naval Base to the effects of Cuban social security

Torture and Murder

Several crimes have been committed at the Guantánamo Naval Base against Cuban workers there. I am talking about bloody deeds, torture, horrendous assassinations. I will next mention the two most grave cases.

- On January 12, 1961, Manuel Prieto Gómez, who had been a worker at the base for over 3 years, was savagely tortured by the North Americans at the Guantánamo Naval Base for the "crime" of being a revolutionary.

- On September 30, 1961, Rubén López Sabariego, another Cuban worker, was tortured and murdered by the North Americans at the Guantánamo Naval Base.

The First Armed Aggressions Launched from the U.S. Naval Base after the Triumph of the Cuban Revolution

Next, I will list chronologically the main aggressions launched against Cuba from the U.S. naval base at Guantánamo after the revolutionary triumph. The first one chose dates back to April, 1960, months before the United States severed diplomatic relations with Cuba, on January 3, 1961.

I will not mention the mercenary invasion of the Bay of Pigs on April 1, 1961, preceded by the bombings of the airports at Ciudad Libertad, San Antonio de los Baños and Santiago de Cuba, on the 15th, that ended in defeat in less than 72 hours, on April 19, 1961, with a resounding failure for the United States.

The last fact I include here dates to barely two months before the October Crisis began, for respecting the chronological order, I will insert a section about the October Crisis, after which I will resume listing the various aggressions launched from the base.

This list of aggressions from the U.S. Naval Base in Guantánamo is not exhaustive but simply indicative, for many other aggressions have taken place all along these years. The aggressions since April, 1960 until August, 1962 are listed next.

On April 4, 1960, an aircraft from the U.S. Naval Base in Guantánamo dropped flammable material around the Buey Cabón beach, located in the former province of Oriente.

On March 20, 1961, the Revolutionary Government of Cuba protested in a Note addressed to the U.S. State Department in Washington,[10] about the provocations carried out on March 3, 4 and 5 by North American soldiers stationed at the Guantánamo Naval Base, that consisted of verbal insults, throwing stones and cans filled with flammable material and even firing shots with pistols and automatic weapons.

On March 23, 1961, 12 vessels from the Guantánamo Naval Base, among them an aircraft carrier and several smaller craft kept circling the area of Imías, on the southern coast of Oriente, while a North American cruiser opened anti-aircraft artillery fire against a Cuban airplane on that same area.

On April 9, 1961, the Revolutionary Government was forced to protest in a Note[11] addressed to the North American Government, for the successive provocations from U.S. troops stationed at Guantánamo, carried out on March 22, 23, 24, 26, 28, 30 and 31 and on April 1, 2 and 3.

10. Diplomatic Note dated March 20, 1961. Archives of the Ministry of Foreign Affairs of the Republic of Cuba.
11. Diplomatic Note dated April 9, 1961. Archives of the Ministry of Foreign Affairs of the Republic of Cuba.

On October 26, 1961, Cuban jurisdictional waters were violated by four cruisers, three submarines, five destroyers, two carriers and a tugboat of the U.S. Navy from the Guantánamo Naval Base.

On January 13, 1962, the Revolutionary Government of Cuba sent a Note[12] to the U.S. Government due to 119 new violations of Cuban territory, of which 78 were perpetrated by aircraft from the Guantánamo Naval Base.

The following was another murder perpetrated by U.S. soldiers stationed at the base. In the evening of June 11, 1962, the fisherman Rodolfo Rosell Salas set sail from the pier at Caimanera and did not come back the next day. His mates at work at the fishing cooperative went looking for him in the Guantánamo bay. His boat was spotted at a beach near the U.S. base, and in it, was the body of the fisherman, whose arms had been tied behind his back. The body evinced signs of brutal torture.

On August 13, 1962, Cuban authorities disclosed the self-aggression plans concocted at the U.S. Guantánamo Naval Base. The plan's first step was an attempt against the then Commander Raúl Castro, followed by a sham artillery attack against the base and an attack against a Rebel Army's artillery position, in a bid to provoke a large-scale armed confrontation.

The Base and the October Crisis

During the October Crisis, as part of the U.S. military mobilization aimed at invading Cuba under the pretext of the presence and installation of Soviet nuclear missiles, the naval base at Guantánamo was technically reinforced, and the number of Marines stationed there rose to over 16,000.

The base has always played an important role in the context of the U.S. blockade against the Cuban Revolution, but in the case of the October Crisis the base at Guantánamo also participated in a significant way in the illegal naval blockade set up against Cuba.

12. Diplomatic Note dated January 3, 1962. Archives of the Ministry of Foreign Affairs of the Republic of Cuba.

John F. Kennedy demanded that Nikita Jruschov withdraw the missiles and the IL-28 bombers, and reduce the number of Soviet advisors in our country for his Plattist concept could not allow the existence in Cuba—by virtue of legitimate agreements reached with another country—, of troops to defend itself, for the only ones who could enjoy "that privilege" were the North Americans, the attackers, and that was what the Guantánamo Naval Base was for.

We have selected excerpts from the concepts expounded by Commander-in-Chief Fidel Castro during the conversations that took place in Cuba between the Cuban leader and the UN Secretary General at the height of the crisis:

> It is absurd to demand the withdrawal of friendly weapons from our country, while an enemy base is left in our country. That is absolutely groundless, that is totally absurd. No one, anywhere in the world, would discuss our people's right to demand that a base be returned, to the territory where that base stands. A base where, during all these days—these days of crisis—troops were amassed to attack our country.[13]

And Fidel posed an unanswerable question: "And how are we going to be asked to withdraw friendly weapons when enemy weapons remain in the heart of our country?"[14]

He availed himself of the opportunity to place the origin of the naval base:

> The United States says it has that base by virtue of a treaty; of an agreement between the United States and a Cuba government; naturally, a Cuban government that emerged during the intervention. It was not by means of a treaty, it was by means of a unilateral agreement in the United States' Congress, by means of an amendment imposed upon our Constitution [...]

13. Fidel Castro Ruz, "Conversaciones con U Thant, Secretario General de la ONU, La Habana, 30 de octubre de 1962," in *Posición de Cuba ante la Crisis del Caribe*, in *Política Exterior del Gobierno Revolucionario de Cuba, 1959-julio de 1964*, B/4.
14. Ibid.

> warning Cuba that they would not leave Cuba unless that amendment was accepted. An amendment where the issue of the naval base was included.
>
> . . . .
>
> And if the United States has placed the world on the brink of war to demand the withdrawal of those missiles, then what right and what morals do they have to refuse to leave the territory they occupy in our country?[15]

In an appearance on national television and radio on October 23, 1962 to inform the country about the situation created by the United States, comrade Fidel told U.S.:

> And then, without any qualms, in a document of this kind, they talk about the Guantánamo Naval Base, that is a base located in our territory, and shamelessly they say they are using that base, that is to say, that they have reinforced it, to use it against Cuba. It is a wonderful warning for all countries where they currently have military bases. They are asking for a meeting of the OAS. What for? To defend a Latin American country from aggression? No, but to make it validate and support the aggression against a Latin American country. And lastly, they speak about the United Nations and they speak about nothing less than a supervision of Cuba by observers, regarding the measures that we have taken to defend ourselves.[16]

Faced by Jruschov's decision to withdraw the missiles without previously consulting or informing the Cuban Government, and by the verbal promises made by Kennedy that Cuba would not be invaded and the naval blockade would be suspended, Fidel Castro stated the Cuban Revolution's firm stance in what became known as the "Five Points," that were the most realistic analysis to that date of 1962 the U.S. policy of harassment toward Cuba, an aggressive policy that

15. Ibid., B/4-B/5.
16. Ibid., B/4.

must cease in order to attain peace and stability not only for our country, but for the Caribbean area and even for the world. Naturally, one of these fundamental Five Points is the one referred to the naval base, point number 5 of that document that states: "Withdrawal of the Guantánamo Naval Base (occupied and operated by the United States since the beginning of this century, when it was forcibly imposed upon the then mediated Cuban government), and return of the Cuban territory occupied by the United States."[17]

But these five guarantees were never taken into consideration during the negotiations between the United States and the Soviet Union. If the Soviet missiles in Cuba had really been destined to defend Cuba, its withdrawal should have guaranteed that the aggression would cease. When he was asked about the outcome of the October Crisis, Commander-in-Chief Fidel Castro answered journalist Maria Schriver that, had Cuba's stance been borne in mind, the crisis would have had a happy ending for Cuba "because no one would have been willing to wage a nuclear war over the base at Guantánamo, or over an economic blockade, or over a hostile act against a small country..."[18]

Like Fidel remarked in that interview, a few words would have sufficed to solve the crisis in a positive manner, for it was very simple: offer satisfactory guarantees to Cuba. A sentence should have been added to the agreement between Jruschov and Kennedy saying "we are willing to withdraw the missiles if the United States gives U.S. satisfactory guarantees for Cuba, if Cuba had participated in that discussion and presented the satisfactory guarantees for the country..."[19]

That was not the first time that the United States negotiated an issue related to Cuba and to Cuba's destiny ignoring Cuba. They had done so when they negotiated the Treaty of Paris with Spain in 1898, to put an end to the Cuban's war against the Spaniards. When they did the

17. *Posición de Cuba ante la Crisis del Caribe*, in *Política Exterior del Gobierno Revolucionario de Cuba, 1959-julio de 1964*, C-1.
18. Ibid.
19. Ibid.

same thing in 1962 during the October Crisis, almost 64 years later, they still refused to accept the Cuban presence in the quest for a negotiated solution under the auspices of the UN Secretary General.

After the return to New York from Havana of the UN Secretary General, Mr. U Thant, a meeting took place between the delegates of the United States and the Soviet Union, and another between the Cuban and the Soviet delegates to draft a protocol to be submitted to the Security Council and to the consideration of the Secretary General by the three countries. The United States did not accept to draft the protocol's text in Cuba's presence, therefore these two groups were separately formed; but this protocol did not even win the glory of putting an end to the crisis, thus closing the chapter begun in the Security Council, for the issue died at birth because the two parties involved had solved their problems despite Cuba. However, we bring to attention article 7 of the text—that may be a document to be recorded by history—drafted by the Group Cuba-USSR, that said: "The Government of the United States is willing to begin conversations with the Government of the Republic of Cuba about the evacuation of the Naval Base at Guantánamo."[20]

The issue was deleted from the Security Council's agenda, and that transcendental event that placed the world on the brink of war ended with this innocuous note:

> On behalf of the Governments of the United States of America and the Soviet Union we desire to express to you our appreciation for your efforts in assisting our Governments to avert the serious threat to peace which recently arose in the Caribbean area.
>
> While it has not been possible for our Governments to resolve all the problems that have arisen in connection with this affair, they believe that, in view of the degree of understanding reached between them on the settlement of the crisis and the extent of progress in the implementation of this understan-

20. Carlos Lechuga, *En el ojo de la tormenta*, 203.

ding, it is not necessary for this item to occupy further the attention of the Security Council at this time.

The Governments of the United States of America and of the Soviet Union express the hope that the actions taken to avert the threat of war in connection with this crisis will lead toward the adjustment of other differences between them and the general easing of tensions that could cause a further threat of war.[21]

Further and More Serious Aggressions against Cuba from the U.S. Naval Basc

The October Crisis was "solved" between the powers that then headed the two big contending blocs in international politics—the United States and the Soviet Union—, without bearing Cuba in mind and leaving in our soil the enclave kept by our country's worst enemy, the naval base at Guantánamo, for the felonies against this small but dignified country by the arrogant and threatening U.S. imperialism continued to be perpetrated from that base.

I will refer next to the most important aggressions since the 1962 October Crisis, in a chronological order.

On March 4, 1963, the Ministry of the Revolutionary Armed Forces issued its Denunciation 193,[22] in regard to new provocations from the soldiers stationed in the U.S. base at Guantánamo.

A letter dated April 24, 1963, addressed by the Cuban Minister of Foreign Affairs to the UN Secretary General,[23] denounced the aggressions and violations of international law committed by the Government of the United States against Cuba, a behavior, as the Note says, that "violates the Charter of the United Nations and infringes International Law." The letter summarizes some of the attacks carried out against Cuba during 1963 and early 1964, and it emphasizes among

21. *Digest of International Law*, 10, 15-16.
22. Author's personal archives.
23. Letter from the Cuban Minister of Foreign Affairs to the UN Secretary General U Thant, dated April 24, 1964. Archives of the Ministry of Foreign Affairs of the Republic of Cuba.

them the provocations, violations and unlawful acts that originated at the U.S. Naval Base in Guantánamo, that made a total of 1181 since October, 1962 until April, 1963 and that had become increasingly frequent and arrogant, evincing the purpose of worsening international tensions.[24]

At dusk, on May 14, 1964, a North American helicopter landed near the security strip that surround the base, in non-occupied Cuban territory, and the crew descended from the craft. Cuban combatant Ángel Almaguer Fonseca, on guard duty nearby, went to investigate the enemy activity and was attacked by the U.S. soldiers, who beat him on his two collar bones, his face and eyes until he was left unconscious. The combatant suffered the sequels of these wounds.

On June 9, 1964 several shots were fired from the naval base at Guantánamo against the Cuban sentries, wounding soldier José Ramírez Reyes.

On June 25, 1964, a U.S. sentry fired against Cuban soldier Andrés Noel Laurduet, seriously wounding him on the chest. The bullet punctured one of his lungs.

On July 19, 1964, U.S. soldiers stationed at the Guantánamo Naval Base fired against the Cuban sentries and murdered 18 years old soldier Ramón López Peña.

A Note addressed on July 22, 1964 by the Revolutionary Government to the UN Secretary General,[25] once again denounced the aggressions against Cuba perpetrated from the base, and listed ten points related to the following issues:

1. In a note addressed to the UN Secretary General by the Minister of Foreign Relations of Cuba, on April 24, 1964, on behalf of the Government of the Republic of Cuba, informed him about the serious situation, that evidently endangered peace in the Caribbean and, consequently, in the world, caused by the repeated provocations and aggressions carried out by the

24. Ibid.
25. Diplomatic Note from the Revolutionary Government of Cuba to U Thant, UN Secretary General, on July 22, 1964. Archives of the Ministry of Foreign Affairs of the Republic of Cuba.

United States Government's military forces stationed at the naval base that it unlawfully keeps in our territory. The Secretary General was reminded that the 1181 provocations originated at the strip of Cuban territory usurped by the Government of the United States from October, 1962 to April 19, 1964, were listed in that note.

2. After sending that Note, U.S. troops stationed at the aforementioned naval base continued to carry out similar and even more uncommon provocations. Since then to date, 851 provocations have been registered.

3. The characteristics of those provocations aimed at the members of the Cuban Border Line Battalion were increasingly grave.

4. Among the provocations by U.S. forces stationed at the naval base against our Armed Forces the criminal aggressions perpetrated against two members of the Cuban military unit in charge of defending our non-occupied territory on the border with the base must be emphasized. They were perpetrated against José Ramírez Reyes on June 9, 1964, and against Andrés Noel Laurduet on June 25 of that same year.

5. Notwithstanding the public denunciation of these most grave developments by the Cuban Government, the aforementioned provocations and aggressions far from being prevented by the Government of the United States, culminated on July 19, 1964 in a new deed that the Revolutionary Government of Cuba feels is its duty to denounce before the Secretary General, the United Nations Organization and the world public opinion. On that day, after a series of provocations and insults to members of the Cuban military unit stationed on the border line with the base, when the chief of the Cuban detachment on guard duty inspected the sentries together with his second-in-command and another three soldiers, at 19:07 hours, the North American sentries suddenly hit the ground

and at the same time fired a short burst of machine-gun fire directed toward our group of soldiers, who were ordered to take cover in a trench. When new shots were fired a few minutes afterward, the North American soldiers fatally wounded 18 years old Cuban soldier Ramón López Peña, who died 20 minutes later.

6. Shortly after, new provocations took place and at the time this Note to the Secretary General was being drafted, they had not yet stopped.

7. The UN Secretary General was told that the extreme gravity of the situation created by the provocations and the criminal aggressions against our soldiers carried out by the military forces of the Government of the United States stationed at the naval base on our territory is evinced by the death of the Cuban soldier vilely assassinated by the U.S. Marines stationed at the naval base in our country. Undeniably, this situation entails an extremely serious risk for peace and can lead, despite the sustained and patient endeavors of the Cuban Government and its Armed Forces to prevent it, in a conflict that endangers peace. Therefore, it is our Government's elementary duty to acquaint the Secretary General and the United Nations Organization about these developments and call their attention about the grave dangers they imply.

8. The Revolutionary Government of Cuba holds the Government of the United States responsible for these acts, no only because, despite the reiterated public denunciations, the diplomatic notes sent and the previous letter addressed to the Secretary General, that government has not taken a single measure to prevent them from happening again, but because by systematically and cynically denying them, it has, in fact, encouraged the perpetrators of those provocations and aggressions to continue carrying them out to the extent of even murdering a Cuban soldier.

9. The Revolutionary Government of Cuba categorically denies the version given by the State Department of the United States, daring to deny the truth of the information given by our government about the developments on July 19, 1964, and asserts that version is simple a trick to conceal the truth, although it admits that a North American sentry fired a shot, which shows that, vis-à-vis the painful circumstance of the killing of a Cuban soldier, it has not been able to completely deny the facts, and admits, for the first time, that a shot was fired by a sentry from the U.S. naval base.

10. The Revolutionary Government of Cuba thus fulfills its duty of warning the UN Secretary General and, through him, that organization and world public opinion, about the risks and increasing gravity these developments entail for peace.

Thus far the issues dealt with in the note addressed to U Thant.

But despite this categorical denunciation dated June 22, 1964, U.S. aggressions against Cuba continued.

The mass rally to commemorate the glorious 26 of July, held in 1964 in Santiago de Cuba, had a special meaning for the multitude gathered there approved on that date what became known as the "Declaration of Santiago de Cuba", that was the response of the Cuban people to the "Declaration by the 9th Advisory Meeting of the OAS" held in Washington a few days earlier. That document informed OAS member states about the severance of political, economic and all other relations with Cuba.

The "Declaration of Santiago de Cuba" has 12 points, but point number 6 specifically refers to the aggressions against Cuba from the U.S. naval base at Guantánamo, and says:

> That the Marines at the naval base at the Guantánamo bay, a Cuban territory forcefully occupied by the Government of the United States, have carried out thousands of provocations against our people of such extreme gravity that in the past few weeks, two soldiers have been wounded and one was

> killed as a consequence of the criminal and cowardly shots fired from there.[26]

On February 23, 1965, the Cuban soldier Berto Belén Ramírez was wounded by a shot fired by a Marine from the U.S. base.

On May 21, 1966, the Cuban combatant, member of the Border Line Battalion, Luis Ramírez López, aged 22, was assassinated by North American soldiers who shot him from the naval base at Guantánamo.

On June 16, 1968, the Ministry of the Revolutionary Armed Forces issued a note[27] about a certain provocation from the naval base at Guantánamo when, on the previous day, two F-8 Crusader airplanes of the U.S. Navy entered Cuba's airspace by the base's northern border, flew west of the town of Caimanera and continued to fly eastward; on that same day, another similar aircraft flew one kilometer into our airspace.

The list of the various aggressions and other acts provoked by the U.S. troops stationed at the Guantánamo naval base would be endless. However, I deem it adequate to summarize them according to the data contributed by Colonel Luis García Curaño, who holds a Ph.D. in Military Sciences, at the International Conference on Foreign Military Bases held under the auspices of the Cuban Peace Movement in Havana, in November, 1996. These data reflect that between 1962 and 1996, 8288 violations of Cuban territory (See Table 1), and 5202 provocations of various types, which make a sum total of 13,490 violations, have been carried out from the base.

The following deserve to be mentioned among the grave provocations of the past few years:

On December 7, 1989, a particularly blatant aggression was carried out. On December 7, Cubans respectfully commemorate the fall in combat against the Spanish colonialist troops, in 1896, of Lieutenant General Antonio Maceo Grajales. It is national mourning in Cuba. But this December 7, 1989 was an even more special day, for

26. "Declaración de Santiago de Cuba," in *Política Exterior del Gobierno Revolucionario de Cuba, 1959-julio de 1964*, D-9.
27. From the author's personal archives.

there was a countrywide vigil for all Cubans fallen during internationalist missions in Angola and other countries, whose remains had been brought back home. At 10:00 hours on that day, various shots were fired from Guantánamo Naval Base's Sentry Box No. 13 against sentry boxes numbers 17 and 18 of the Cuban Border Line Battalion; the bullets broke several glass windows and only by chance did Cuban soldier Luis Rodríguez Favier escape from being shot in the head. At 13:00 hours on that same day, and also from the base, several shots were fired against a bunker of the Border Line Brigade; its glass windows were broken by the shots and combatant José Ángel Batista was lucky not to have been killed.

On April 30, 1990, at 16:00 hours, several shots were fired from the base, breaking the glass windows of a sentry box of the Border Line Battalion where the combatant Marelys Morales Nieto was on guard duty. One of the bullets almost grazed her head.

Table 1: Main Violations From the Guantánamo Naval Base (1962-1996)

Type of violation	1962 to 1971	1972 to 1982	1983 to 1994	1995	1996	Total
Territorial violations	560	5	44	1	—	610
Violations of air space	5944	282	99	18	2	6345
Violations of the sea space	1251	53	11	16	2	1333
Totals	7755	340	154	35	4	8282

Table 2: Main Provocations From the Guantánamo Naval Base (1962-1996)

Type of provocation	1962 to 1971	1972 to 1982	1983 to 1994	1995	1996	Total
Throwing things to free territory	1347	13	16	—	—	1376
Shooting at free territory	755	8	20	—	—	783
Pointing guns	608	24	84	7	2	725
Verbal insults and obscene gestures	1348	80	124	—	1	1553
Spotlighting free territory	415	81	149	9	—	654
Other provocations	55	16	40	—	—	111
Totals	4528	222	433	16	3	5202

Intimidating Maneuvers

The forces stationed at the Guantánamo Naval Base were increased since the triumph of the Cuban Revolution in 1959. Some 15 North American vessels are estimated to remain at the base; under the guise of "defense" forces, the number of troops has fluctuated: there is an average of 2500 men in normal times and in times of crisis, like the 1962 October Crisis, the base increased its troops to some 5800 men over the usual numbers.

When North American forces carry out military and naval exercises like Solid Shield, Ocean Venture and Defex 2-91, the Guantánamo Naval Base forces increased by some 600 additional marines in each case.

In August, 1979, under the pretext that a Soviet brigade-type combat unit had been spotted in Cuba, President Carter ordered that the United States expanded their military forces in the region, including the Guantánamo Naval Base.

In November, 1979, due to the number of marines at the Guantánamo Naval Base, without previously submitting a report to the U.S. Congress abiding by the contents of the War Powers Resolution,[28] U.S. Congressman Paul Findley requested that the Secretary of State Cyrus Vance comply with the aforementioned Resolution and presented the report to the Congress, for he deemed that increase in numbers as "a show of force" and, consequently, the case was included among those that determined submitting such a report. Thus warned, the State Secretariat responded with a report from which I deem interesting the opinion of that Secretariat in regard to the dispatch of 1692 additional marines to Guantánamo ordered by President Carter on August 31, 1979. That report said:

> Routine training exercises have been conducted at Guantánamo in every year since the War Powers Resolution was enacted. None of these exercises has been reported to the Congress under section 4 of the War Powers Resolution because

28. "Ley Pública 93-148 dated November 7, 1973," in *Digest of International Law*, (1979): 1847.

> none has met the statutory criteria for such a report. There have been no ongoing or imminent hostilities at or near Guantánamo, and the introduction of United States forces while equipped for combat have related solely to the training of such forces.
>
> Further, we have found nothing in the Resolution's legislative history to suggest that Congress intended to require reports on training exercises in countries where United States forces were already present, but not in countries where there was no such presence.
>
> [...] The only recent training exercise at Guantánamo involving Marines in numbers approximating the figure of 1692 referred to in your letter occurred in late October and early November 1979. In that exercise, designated the Guantánamo Surface Reinforcement Exercise, a Marine amphibious unit of about 1600 personnel was transported to Guantánamo on October 17, where it engaged in routine training within the confines of the U.S. Naval Base. The unit departed, as scheduled, on November 14, 1979.[29]

It is completely false that the presence of those troops at the Guantánamo Naval Base has a defensive character; on the contrary, it is a constant danger for the security of Cuba and of the international community, for they can affect international peace and security.

In fact, the presence of those troops at the Guantánamo Naval Base has been linked with reconnaissance purposes in U.S. interventionist and intimidating operations in the Caribbean. It must be recalled that in 1991, faced by the massive exodus of Haitians, according to various sources the U.S. military forces in charge of watching out for and intercepting the Haitians' maritime movements from that naval base were approximately 8000. Likewise, in 1994, the base supported the invasion of Haiti. U.S. military aircraft that participated

29. *Digest of International Law*, (1979): 1847-1849.

on that military intervention was based at the Guantánamo Naval Base's airports.

Furthermore, the United States have not ceased using the Guantánamo Naval Base in its aggressive policy toward Cuba, and this was evinced once again in October, 1991, when the 4th Congress of the Communist Party of Cuba was being held in the city of Santiago de Cuba. At that time airplanes and helicopters from the Naval Base violated the air space over that city.

The dangerously frequent flights over Cuban territory, in violation of our air space by U.S. combat planes, are a form of violation that has always been used, as Cuba has repeatedly denounced. In March, 1988, it was known that the nuclear aircraft carrier "Theodore Roosevelt" was anchored at the Guantánamo Naval Base and, in June, 1988, planes from the aircraft carrier "Independence" flew over the towns of Boquerón and Caimanera.

Throughout the dramatic years since the triumph of the Cuban Revolution, the moments of acute crisis have alternated with times of relative but worrying calm. The use of the U.S. naval base at Guantánamo as a camp for migrants undoubtedly thwarted and upset its activity, and a change became noticeable in regard to the impossibility of carrying out training exercises due to the presence of civilians like the Cuban rafters whom the North Americans now consider and treat as undesirable. Since then, the United States have presented the Guantánamo Naval Base as a sort of base for the logistic support of the North American fleet in the Atlantic, that includes operations in the Caribbean Sea, Central and South America.

The Guantánamo Naval Base is not and will never be an innocent center; nor will it serve for the defense of the United States. Cuba has never attacked that country and does not want its territory to be involved in an imperialist military adventure in the area.

NEW TYPES OF VIOLATIONS OF THE BASE TREATIES

The Base: Concentration Camp for Émigrés

How has the United States used the naval base at Guantánamo? The 1903 Treaty stated its "noble mission" was to maintain Cuba's independence, protect the Cuban people and defend the United States. Nowadays, the base at Guantánamo does not even fulfill the strategic purposes of the military defense of the United States.

The base has only served to harm Cuba's decorum, to harbor counterrevolutionary forces, to infiltrate into the country weapons to fight against the Revolution, to concentrate troops whenever the United States has intended to intimidate the countries in the area and the Cuban people and, furthermore, it has been used as a camp for émigrés.

In an interview with the newspaper *El Sol de México* in 1993, General Raúl Castro told his interviewer when he was asked about the current military importance of the Guantánamo Naval Base for the United States:

> From a military viewpoint, Guantánamo is absolute obsolete in regard to the defense strategy of the United States. Let us say it is a "mousetrap." The base is located in a valley surrounded by mountains, where the Cuban side is stationed; in case of a conflict, it would be swiftly neutralized with a minimal number of forces. But besides that, the Pentagon knows [the base] serves no strategic purpose and that, in practical military terms, the use of its facilities is very limited for it cannot host large air-sea units and it is not even good for training troops.
>
> Add to all this another adverse element: North American soldiers consider it almost a punishment to be sent to the base, given the tensions brought about by hostility, the prolonged confinement and the unattractiveness of the stay, if

> compared with any other U.S. enclave elsewhere in the world.[30]

General Raúl Castro also referred in that interview to the tremendously provocative and dangerous character presented by the base of late:

> [...] of late, and until last year, they carried out exercises at the base that included operations for the massive reception of elements opposed to the Revolution that would supposedly try to leave the country by going into that military facility. They encouraged the crime of illegal exit via a North American official facility knowing the considerable peril for the lives of those who tried to leave Cuban territory in such a manner for, due to the fact that it is a military zone plagued by tensions, strong defensive measures have been taken and mine fields exist on both sides of the border. Acts of this nature can only be explained by their desperate quest for a detonator, for a provocation, that brought about an increase in the campaign about the violation of human rights in Cuba, and a response of unforeseeable proportions by the United States.[31]

The denunciation became a dramatic reality in the summer of 1994, when the "rafters crisis" took place. The imperialist policy of the United States triggered an uncontrolled exodus of people from Cuba, which led that country's government to set in place a protective coastguard belt to prevent those people from reaching North American territory. It is known that these acts—the illegal exits from Cuba—had always been encouraged by the United States and even highly publicized.

The design of the Clinton administration's interventionist policy toward Cuba, according to his statement of August 19, 1994, was similar in Haiti's case for the North Americans took the Haitians that left their country seeking a solution to their misery and perse-

30. Raúl Castro Ruz, "Entrevista concedida al periódico *El Sol de México*," in *Bohemia*, 24.
31. Ibid.

cutions for the Guantánamo Naval Base as part of their scheme against that Caribbean Republic. More than 45,000 Haitian émigrés were concentrated at the base, a situation that remained unchanged until mid-1995, when they were repatriated.

Cuba timely denounced the use of the Guantánamo Naval Base as a camp for Haitians:

> The Government of the Republic of Cuba vigorously protests for the unlawful use of the naval base that the United States maintain by force on the Guantánamo bay as a concentration camp for Haitian citizens.
>
> This not only violates the arbitrary, unjust and already obsolete agreements imposed during the North American military occupation in the early 20th century, that cannot be upheld against our people's sovereign will, and that are inconceivable without having previously consulted or been authorized by our country.
>
> This arbitrary use that violates a portion of the Cuban territory, to concentrate and process people who, for various reasons wish to settle in the United States, has at other times been the cause of the most firm and categorical protests from the Cuban Government.
>
> The Government of Cuba has learned that North American authorities are currently hosting at the Guantánamo Naval Base some 16,000 Haitians in inhuman, overcrowded conditions, thus violating not only the human rights of these refugees, but also gravely affecting the health, the tranquility and the stability of the Cuban towns near that U.S. military enclave.
>
> The Government of Cuba is aware of the suffering of the Haitian people and, as the international community well knows, has vigorously condemned the de facto military regime, advocating for a peaceful, just and democratic solution to the crisis it

> is undergoing, with the return of President Jean Bertrand Aristide. However, it is unacceptable for the United States to discriminatorily concentrate at the Guantánamo Naval Base the people whom they refuse to receive in their own territory.
>
> The Government of Cuba demands that the authorities of the United States put a definitive end to this illegal traffic of Haitian émigrés toward the Guantánamo Naval Base, an unjust and unlawful practice that is intolerable for it undermines Cuba's national sovereignty, and reiterates the repudiation of the Cuban people to the North American military presence in its territory, which is being used on this occasion, once again, for disgusting and hypocritical political purposes.[32]

The design used by the United States for Haitian immigrants in regard to concentrating them at the Guantánamo Naval Base was the same one they used further on for Cuban rafters. But the United States did not realize that Cuba is not Haiti, and that therefore, they cannot act unilaterally.

Never before had the North Americans declared with such force that the base's territory did not belong to the United States, but is a territory over which the United States had no sovereignty, only jurisdiction. Naturally, when they took the rafters to the base, it meant that the émigrés had not reached North American territory and, therefore, the so-called Cuban Adjustment Act[33] —that granted a privileged migratory status to the Cubans that reached U.S. territory by whatever means, specially illegal means, to be granted residence in the United States—, was not applicable to them. That prerogative was not enjoyed by other nationalities, like the Haitians, inevitably returned to Haiti, or the persecuted Mexican "wetbacks."

Since the triumph of the Revolution in January, 1959, Cubans who arrived in North American territory, and mainly those who arrived

32. "Vigorous protest issued by Cuba on the use of the Guantánamo Naval Base as a concentration camp for Haitians," in *Granma*, 1
33. Public Act 89-732 dated November 2, 1996.

illegally, were welcomed like heroes, but the generous host changed its policy and currently, since Clinton's aforementioned statement, these Cubans are also undesirable. President Clinton's August 19, 1994 statement turned the Guantánamo Naval Base into an émigrés concentration camp for the nearly 30,000 Cuban rafters.

The end is known: the "rafters crisis" concluded with the signing by Cuba and the United States of a Joint Communiqué about migratory agreements on September 9, 1994 for safe, legal and orderly migration between the two countries, and of the *Joint Declaration*, dated May 2, 1995, that complemented the previous document and established the procedure for returning to Cuba all Cuban rafters who continued trying to migrate illegally to the United States and were intercepted by North American coastguards.

The story of the Guantánamo Naval Base as a center or a camp for émigrés did not end there for, in September, 1996, it was learned that Chinese émigrés had arrived there, brought by plane from the Bermudas, after having been intercepted at sea by the North American coastguard when they tried to illegally enter into U.S. territory. These Chinese émigrés remained at the base until they were transferred to China by way of Mexico. The policy of ill-use of the Guantánamo Naval Base, in regard to its use as a camp for Cuban and foreign émigrés was confirmed by this new act.

Radio Frequencies Used by the Base

The improper use of radio frequencies is another usurpation by the base's occupants. Clause f) in article 12 of the 1976 Constitution of the Republic of Cuba, modified in 1992, rejects the violation of all states' inalienable and sovereign right to regulate the use and the benefits of telecommunications in its territory, according to universal practices and to the international agreements it has signed.

The radio-electric spectrum is a natural resource that encompasses the frequencies used by radio-electric waves that propagate through space and that we usually call "radio," regulated and controlled by the international community, by means of specialized organizations, in order to avert possible interference. The functioning of any broadcasting station must be ruled by the International Convention on Telecommunications and by the Regulations on Radio Communications, which is an annex of the aforementioned Convention, and by other regional arrangements.

Radio frequencies distributed among the states by the corresponding specialized international organization are registered by the various states in the exercise of their sovereignty and jurisdiction.

The Government of the United States registers the radio frequencies used by its naval base in Guantánamo in the International Registry of Frequencies, in the space corresponding to Cuba, thus deserving the reiterated protests and denunciations of the Cuban Government after the triumph of the Revolution.

To mention only some of the denunciations, I will go back to the World Administrative Radio Communications Conference (WARC) held in Geneva under the auspices of the International Telecommunications Union (ITU) from September 24 through December 6, 1979. The Cuba delegation presented a declaration for the Conference's Final Protocol stating that the signing and acceptance by Cuba of the Conference's Final Acts "does not mean a recognition of the notification, registration and use of frequencies by the North American Government" for its naval base in the territory of the Cuban province of Guantánamo "illegally occupied against the will of the Cuban people," a "territory usurped" by the North Americans. This declaration also asserted that the use of radio frequencies in Cuba by the United States "hindered Cuban communication services and the sovereignty of our country over the spectrum of radio-electric frequencies, which is a limited resource."[34]

The United States issued a counter-statement saying that they are in Guantánamo due to agreements in effect and that they reserved the right to fulfill the requirements of radio communications as they had done before. They referred to article III of the 1934 Treaty.

34. Manuel Yáñez Quiveiro, "Las agresiones norteamericanas contra Cuba por las frecuencias radiales," in *Agresiones de Estados Unidos a Cuba Revolucionaria*, 77.

On March 26, 1980, at the ITU 4th Plenary Session of the Regional Conference on Middle-Wave Radio Broadcasting held in Buenos Aires, in Argentina, in relation with the issue of radio broadcasting stations that operate from the North American base located in the province of Guantánamo, the Cuban delegate made the following statement:

> Consistent with the declaration of the Republic of Cuba that appears in the Final Protocol of the World Administrative Conference on Radio Communications (Geneva, 1979) and on behalf of our Administration, we reiterate to this plenary that we do not recognize the notification, registration and use of frequencies by the Government of the United States of America in part of the Cuban territory in the province of Guantánamo it occupies illegally and against the express will of the Cuban Government.
>
> The current use of radio-electric frequencies by the Government of the United States of America in the national territory of Cuba that they forcibly usurp in the province of Guantánamo, hinders radio communication services in Cuba and attempts against the sovereignty of our country over the spectrum of radio-electric frequencies.
>
> In specific regard to the use of frequencies attributed by the Regulation on Radio Communications to the Radio Broadcasting Service, the Administration of the United States in that place not only gives radio broadcasting services on the middle-wave band which is the object of this Conference, but they also transmit television programs and F/M (modulated frequency) sound track programs on the middle-wave band, thus hindering the development of national plans for these services in such bands.

> The Government of the Republic of Cuba reserves its right to take the necessary measures to safeguard its legitimate national rights and interests.[35]

The delegate from the United States answered:

> United States forces are at the Guantánamo bay, in Cuba, due to a Treaty that has been in effect for many years and continues to be an active agreement between the United States and Cuba. The United States make yearly payments to the Government of Cuba in compliance with the Treaty's provisos. That legal document grants the United States full jurisdiction and control over the areas leased according to that Treaty and over their hinterland.
> It is the opinion of the United States that transmission by radio-electric stations, including radio broadcasting stations, within the leased zone, is a necessary function of the naval station and, according to the document of the lease, jurisdiction within the leased zone includes the use of the spectrum of radio-electric frequencies.[36]

The Cuban delegate next clarified that the Cuban Government does not cash the check mentioned by the United States delegate, because it believes that the territory where the base stands belongs to Cuba and should be returned to it.[37]

THE BORDER LINE BRIGADE

The history of the U.S. Naval Base at Guantánamo could not be written without granting pride of place to the Border Line Brigade, made up by heroic Cuban combatants on the Motherland's front line of defense.

35. Ibid., 76.
36. Ibid., 76-77.
37. Ibid., 77.

In the years 1960, 1961 and 1962, the Guantánamo zone was quite active in the fight against counterrevolutionary bands, and the area next to the base was attended by the military post at Caimanera and by the post at Boquerón, two very small garrisons. Therefore, it was decided that the integrated revolutionary forces should be formed, including the Rebel Army, the National Revolutionary Police, the State Security Department and the National Revolutionary Militias, among others, to confront the enemies of the Revolution whose lair was located at the base.

The naval base played an important role in the context of Operation Pluto, designed by the United States for the mercenary action in Playa Girón, for it would be the beachhead and starting point for other aggressions against the Republic of Cuba.

Although Commander Demetrio Montseny (Villa) was the district's chief, it was Lieutenant David Pérez Concepción who was in charge of organizing the first unit of the Eastern Army on the limits with the base. Training of the men who would form the Border Line Battalion—soldiers from the Rebel Army, members of the Union of Rebel Youths, peasants and militiamen—began late in May, 1961 in the schools set up in the areas close to the base, like those at Vilorio and Macambo.

On the night of November 8, 1961, the trained personnel, already established as a battalion, was transferred to the points chosen for the defense devices and at dawn on November 9, under the nose of the U.S. troops, our soldiers were already positioned. The defensive front line was thus set up, as a sort of protective ring connected to the forces of the Guantánamo Division, to prevent the assault of the U.S. troops against the city of Guantánamo, if they dared do so.

The Cuban forces stationed facing the naval base became a brigade in September, 1964, whose first chief was the then Commander—currently Brigadier General—Demetrio Montseny (Villa). The border line battalion is known as "BON fronterizo" in Cuba, where the word contraction "BON" has became in a term.

I was honored to visit the Border Line Brigade twice some years ago, to speak to that group of brave young men, with a deep love for their Motherland, about the legal issues related to the base treaties, the unlawfulness, the forcible occupation of that piece of the Motherland's soil. The integrity and firmness of those young men, and of the older men as well, who remain for two years in this battlefront, is an everlasting memory to me.

Whoever comes to the Border Line Brigade feels obliged to think about the dear and honored names of the combatants who gave their lives in this trench, who live in the hearts of Cuban revolutionaries. Those are the cases of the combatants assassinated by U.S. troops stationed at the naval base: Ramón López Peña, 18 years old and Luis Ramírez López, 22 years old; of the ones who had to face counterrevolutionary U.S.-led invasions in areas near the base: Maximiliano Domínguez Domínguez, 18 years old, José Rafael Pérez Cutiño, 20 years old, and Luis de la Rosa Callamo, 20 years old. Other combatants from the Border Line Brigade have fallen in the call of duty near the base. They were mentioned by Raúl Castro in the moving words I shall quote later on.

The belongings and the beds those fallen combatants are kept in the Border Line Brigade's dormitories as if they still were in active service. They are taken care of on a daily basis.

General Raúl Castro Ruz, in a speech delivered at the ceremony to commemorate the proclamation of the socialist character of our Revolution and the Day of the Militiaman, held at the Mariana Grajales Revolution Square in Guantánamo, on April 16, 1994, said:

> It is a cause of deep satisfaction to commemorate, in compliance with the Decree issued by the State Council, the heroic combatants and civilian workers of the Border Line Brigade who have placed their lives at risk many times doing their duty, or have been mutilated in the minefields on the strip bordering the territory unlawfully occupied by the United States. Today, we award the Order Antonio Maceo, post mortem, to those who fell on those risky missions: First Lieutenant Arturo Ruiz Martínez and privates Raúl Milanés Labrada, Roberto Navarro Hernández and Wilber Vázquez Gamboa.

Those young men who died in the prime of their lives, are worthy followers of privates Ramón López Peña and Luis Ramírez López who, in previous decades were killed by the treacherous bullets fired from the other side of the fence; the sacrifice of those wounded or mutilated forever; the harsh tests undergone by thousands of combatants and officers who have successively done the Motherland's guard duty during the 30 years since this Border Line Unit was created, facing dangers and suffering from the front line tensions; all that is the high price we are forced to pay for the existence of that foreign military base on a portion of our soil.

Since the triumph of the Revolution we have asserted and reiterated that that base was forcibly imposed upon the Cuban people, and we demand that it be dismantled and returned to Cuba. Its permanence, despite our people's express will and the claims of its legitimate government, violates all the norms of international law. It is a brutal act of arrogance of the empire.

Nowadays, that base is obsolete from the military point of view, and is an unnecessary expenditure that North American taxpayers must pay for.

To reduce its unsustainable military budget, the United States are dismantling dozens of facilities on their territory and abroad. However, they maintain this base as a hotbed of constant provocation and humiliation against Cuba.

We will never renounce our sovereign right over that piece of our island, of our national territory.[38]

38. Raúl Castro Ruz, "Discurso en el acto conmemorativo por la proclamación del carácter socialista de nuestra Revolución y el Día del Miliciano, efectuado en la Plaza de la Revolución Mariana Grajales in Guantánamo, on April 16, 1994," quoted by Felipa Suárez and Pilar Quesada, in *A escasos metros del enemigo*, 203-204.

VI

TERMINATION OF THE TREATY. VINDICATION OF THE OCCUPIED TERRITORY

Legal Considerations about the Termination of the Treaty on the Naval Base at Guantánamo

Whenever I have dealt with the issue of the naval base at Guantánamo, I have been asked if it is true that the North Americans will leave on the year 2002, that is to say, 99 years from 1903; and when I answer that perhaps on that date they will no longer need it, the question about the termination of the 1903 and 1934 treaties or, to put it better, of the illegal occupation, inevitably crops up.

Inexorably, sooner or later the United States must dismantle the base and return its territory to Cuba, but that presupposes a good faith stance on the occupant's part and paying attention to the demands of a people and the favorable opinion of the international community, as the Second Conference of Heads of State or Government of Non-Aligned Countries held in Cairo in 1964 expressed. The Conference considered that the maintenance by the United States of America of the naval base at Guantánamo, in Cuba, despite the will of the Cuba Government and people, and also despite the provisos in the "Declaration of the 1961 Belgrade Conference", is a violation of Cuba's sovereignty and territorial integrity. The Cairo Conference also considered that the Cuban Government has stated to be willing to resolve its dispute with the Government of the United States of America about the military base at Guantánamo on an equal footing. Therefore, the Second Conference of Non-Aligned Countries requested from the North American Government to hold negotiations with the Government of Cuba to evacuate that military facility.

By way of a speculation, I think that the end of the U.S. occupation of the territory of Guantánamo could be analyzed under any of these three options, to wit:

- The abandon by the United States (unilateral action).
- A negotiation between Cuba and the United States (bilateral action).

- The presentation of the case before the International Court of Justice (multilateral action).

My references to the 1903 Treaties on the base, both the Agreement for coaling and naval stations, the Complementary Agreement, the Platt Amendment and other documents, pursue the idea of conveying these antecedents to the reader, but in a legal confrontation over the issue of the base, and according to incidental statements by the United States, the basic element they would wield would be the 1934 Treaty. But that is their mistake: ignoring that the 1934 Treaty went back to the 1903 Agreement and, consequently, dragged its defects of consent into itself, which is tantamount to saying that there was not consent, but coercion, blackmail and other similar evils.

The termination of a treaty requires, in the first place, the application of the provisos of said treaty and, therefore, each of the elements expounded in the document must be examined. I will approach in detail next the two ways allowed by the 1934 Treaty for its termination, and I will refer later on to the third option.

Unilateral Action

"For as long as they need it" and "as long as it is not abandoned" are sentences from the February 16/23, 1903 and May 29, 1934 treaties between Cuba and the United States. Article III, second paragraph of the latter says: "as long as said Naval Station at Guantánamo is not abandoned by the United States of America..." According to that Treaty's letter, one of the ways to repeal the leasing rights of the United States is that *motu propio*, by its own will, by itself, without any consultation or warning, that nation left the base. Unilateral action—that the United States leave it—is therefore appropriate for terminating the agreement about said base.

To date, there has been no hint that the United States are thinking about leaving the base at Guantánamo; consequently, it is not worthwhile to speculate about it. Besides, to act is up to them. It would only take to withdraw the territory occupied by the base, dismantle it and pack their belongings. That would be the most sensible action.

Bilateral Action

Another way to terminate the agreements on the naval base at Guantánamo is firstly expressed in the section about this issue included in the 1934 Treaty. It is noticeable that the beginning of the first paragraph in Article III of this Treaty clearly says: "Until the two contracting parties agree to modify or repeal the provisos of the 1903 Agreement."

I understand that the idea expressed in this sentence does not imply the termination of the occupation of the territory. Were the United States thinking perhaps about a new, more modern form of agreement, like the treaties that country signed since 1940 about military bases in foreign territories? I think that the idea of abandoning, that is to say, the unilateral action foreseen in the 1903 agreements and ratified by the 1934 Treaty is the one that survives in this sentence: "as long as said Naval Base at Guantánamo is not abandoned by the United States." For that reason, it would be worth while to explain here that when "the 1934 Treaty" is mentioned, it implies what regards the base in the 1903 agreements. Thus, it would not be absurd to speak about the "1903/1934 Treaty or Agreement."

The 1969 Vienna Convention on law of treaties establishes that a state may not contend a cause to annul or terminate a treaty if after knowing about such a violation it has expressly communicated that:

- The treat is valid or,
- It is still in effect or,
- Its application continues or,
- It has been verified in such a way that it must be deemed it has acquiesced to the validity of the treaty or to its continued enforcement or application, according to the case in question.

I ask my self if the United States could at some point claim the continuity of the application of the Treaty on the base due to the simple fact that its troops remain in it, notwithstanding the defects and violations of that treaty by the North American side. I also ask myself whether that undesired permanence could mean Cuba's acquiescence and, consequently, a sort of validation that left without effect the demand that the treaty be annulled due to said originating defects of consent in the agreement. However, it is publicly and well known that the Cuban people never consented to that undesirable presence, imposed upon it, apart from the violation of the Cuban constitutional norm, approved by a popular referendum that repudiated it and declared it unlawful and null.

A grave violation—understood as such the violation of an essential proviso for the purpose or finality of the treaty, and also a fundamental change of circumstances (*rebus sic stantibus* norm) that radically modifies the scope of the obligations yet to be fulfilled by the treaty—, can cause the termination of a treaty.

The insane Helms-Burton Act, a monstrosity engendered by the United States against Cuba, applied in March, 1996, that meddles in everything "human and divine" regarding Cuba, could not resist the temptation of predetermining when the issue of the Guantánamo Naval Base can be faced by the Government of the United States with the Government of Cuba and, consequently, the North Americans unilaterally modify in said act the 1903/1934 Treaty that they themselves state is in effect.

Let us recall that the aforementioned treaty refers the termination of the lease to the will of the United States: "for as long as they need it." Now, "thanks" to Section 201 (12) of Chapter II of the Helms-Burton Act, the Government of the United States would have to be "ready to begin negotiations" with a Cuban Government they liked, that is, that fitted their "democratic" pattern. The alleged usefulness of the base to determine it is still needed, according to the treaty, is irrelevant since March 1996, when the Helms-Burton Act was implemented. Now it is up to a Cuban Government to Washington's liking.

Therefore, by mandate of said act—imperial will that prevails over the so-called "Treaty"—by the unilateral decision taken by one of the two parties, although the base may become an annoyance, as it in fact is, for the stated purposes of the Treaty, although North American taxpayers must continue to suffer for the increase in their taxes to pay for the mess created by the aberrant Helms-Burton Act in general terms and, particularly, to keep the naval base at Guantánamo, the hands of the United States Government will be tied in the implementation of the Treaty.

The Helms-Burton Act ruling is one more proof that the presence and the permanence of the naval base in Guantánamo is an act imposed by the United States with no legal backing whatsoever and, therefore, the will of the Cuban people is not taken into consideration. Since its inception, the naval base was a unilateral decision taken by the United States, and this last link confirms it once again.

The sponsors of the Helms-Burton Act that, in a shameless and indecent fashion purport to turn Cuba into a protectorate, to make the Republic disappear, to annex it to the Federal State of the stars and stripes, must remember this truth that answers with brilliant thinking of José Martí, the Apostle: "Cubans, sometimes indomitable by dint of rebelliousness, are as harsh toward despotism as they are courteous toward reason. Cubans are independent and moderate and proud. They are their own masters and they want no masters. Whoever intends to saddle them will be shaken off."[1]

Multilateral Action

According to Article 35 of the Statute of the International Court of Justice, the Court is open to all party states and, according to Article 93 of the United Nations Charter, all members of the organization are, *ipso facto*, parties to the Statute of the Court. Cuba, therefore, as a member of the United Nations and, consequently, as a party to the Court, can present its demands before the international organization that deals with law issues. However, to present a case to the Court it must be decided that the Court is competent. Cuba has

1. José Martí, "Personas y Patria," in *Obras completas*, 2, 277.

stated that it does not accept the Court's compulsory statute. Consequently, in order to take a case before the court, both Cuba and the United States have to be in agreement, for at this time neither of the two states accepts the previous obligation of submitting their disputes for solution to the International Court.

According to Article 38 of the Court's Statute, if the state against which the request is made has not accepted the controversy presented before the Court by the plaintiff state, the request or demand will not be registered, and no procedure will be initiated until the state against which the request was made accepts the competence of the Court in regard to the issue in question. However, the Court will make that request known to the defendant state. The Court's competence in regard to contentious issues depends of the acceptance of the litigating states of the initiation of the process.

Another important question is the nature of the dispute, that has to be a legal and not a political one. Only in exceptional cases have political disputes been accepted when they endanger international peace and security. The plaintiff state must establish the Court's competence and the fact that there exists a dispute of a legal character. Due to the fact that neither Cuba nor the United States acknowledge the obligatory competence of the Court, they will have to reach an agreement to previously accept that it is competent in this regard.

I have referred to some primary issues regarding the previous and elementary procedure before the Court, without delving further in this question.

To take a bilateral dispute before the Court, both parties have to agree to submit to its jurisdiction, and it must be proved that all other peaceful means to solve the controversy—specially negotiations, mediation, conciliation, etc.—have been tried to no avail.

In repeated statements by the Government of the Republic of Cuba regarding treaties that invoke the International Court of Justice for the solution of controversies stemming from them, our country has referred to a solution by means of negotiations, and does not accept the compulsive application of the jurisdiction of the aforementioned Court.

The Cuban stance vis-à-vis the compulsory statute of the Court is based on its controversial performance in cases regarding the interests of underdeveloped countries.

Only with its decision in favor of Nicaragua in its dispute against the United States, did the International Court of Justice issue a significant ruling on June 27, 1986, when it declared the U.S. interference in the internal affairs of the Republic of Nicaragua. This ruling favorable to Nicaragua made the United States determine to retire from the Court, besides unfulfilling the adverse ruling in its usual arrogant manner.

The Court can also advise about any legal issue at the behest, for example, of the Security Council or the UN General Assembly, but such rulings are not mandatory.

Caution and Thoughtfulness

The Guantánamo Naval Base is not a thing of the past, but of the present and the future; therefore, the interpretation about the possible application of international norms, principles or opinions about the termination of the Treaty regarding the base must be done with caution and thoughtfulness. To choose between the peaceful option or the military option to solve the case of the Guantánamo Naval Base demands a high dose of discernment and caution for the concerned parties may not be the only ones to be directly involved. The question in such thorny issues like the aggression against a small country by a more powerful one, does not entail philosophizing or theorizing. An in-depth analysis of the entire phenomenon and its consequences are the best way to face such issues.

Cubans have been wise enough to pose the Guantánamo issue to themselves as the solution of a conflict with the United States without resorting to the *ultima ratio*, that is to say, to bellicose actions typical of monarchs and empires.[2] A military option to try to solve the dispute about the dismantling of the Guantánamo Naval Base and the

2. *Diccionario latino-español de jurisprudencia*, 983.

return of its territory to the people of Cuba would entail grave consequences for the international community.

The North American expert Roland H. Linden offers an opinion in this sense when he analyzes the Cuban issue and says: "A military option to solve the dispute over the Guantánamo Naval Base would entail disastrous consequences for the entire international community."[3]

As I said before, the Republic of Cuba has not ratified the Vienna Convention on the 1969 law of treatis and, given that the situation of treaties without a date of expiry is dealt with by said Convention, I think that it would be interesting to make some remarks in that regard.

It is a general norm of law that treaties without a date of expiry are terminated according to their provisos or at any time, with the consent of the parties involved, as is expressed in Article 54 of the Vienna Convention.

Article 56 of the aforementioned Convention addresses the denunciation of a treaty lacking provisos for its termination. It is a *sine qua non* requisite for the denunciation or withdrawal of such treaties that they establish it was the intention of the parties concerned to admit the possibility of a denunciation, or that the right to denounce the treaty may be inferred from the nature of the treaty itself.

In the case of the 1934 Treaty, it does not evince the possibility of a denunciation by the Cuban side, for the expiry of the treaty is in the hands of the other party concerned ("for as long as it is needed").

According to some authors' criteria, the problem of the Guantánamo Naval Base should be dealt with by the nations of the world, as the Austrian lawyer Christoph Schreuer stated: "The case of the naval base at Guantánamo has become increasingly thorny and virulent given the time elapsed and the fact that international law and the community of nations have not played the role that befit them."[4]

3. Roland H. Linden, *Cuba and East Europe in the 1990*, 17.
4. Christoph Schreuer, *Die internationalen Organizationen*, (Salzburg University Press: 1989): 154. Quoted by Nicolaus Keller, *Deliberaciones jurídicas internacionales sobre la Base Naval de Guantánamo en Cuba*, 24.

In his turn, Arthur Mach also refers to the issue of the North American base at Guantánamo in his work *La Science Moderne et ses Theories*, from which I deem very interesting the following remark: "Our contemporarity seems impotent to solve some grave problems of international public law, and we are astonished by unquestionable truths that only need a little good faith and sense of classical justice to be solved, as is the case of the naval base at Guantánamo in Cuba."[5]

I also call the attention upon the opinion of the North American expert David Covers, a professor at Harvard University, who said the following about the occupation by his country of a portion of Cuba's territory:

> Only the cases worsened by time, without an apparent solution, like the case of the naval base at Guantánamo, in which the interest of the international community is involved, acquire certain diffusion when it seems that the injustice of those who for decades have not understood is going to explode, and now no one wants to face and solve once and for all the pending disputes."[6]

The Ecuadorian expert Reinaldo Valarezo states in regard to the case of the base at Guantánamo: "If international law norms are left aside, there will be no hope of solving this conflict before this century ends, and the way will not be paved for future applications in other fields of litigation."[7]

The North American expert Jan K. Black also refers to the issue of Guantánamo, and offers this valuable opinion: "The solutions for the case of the naval base at Guantánamo in the framework of international law have to be valid at present and not be seen as something to be solved in the future."[8]

5. Arthur March, *La Science Moderne et ses Theories*, 338-340.
6. David Coves, *The Choice of Law Process*. Speech delivered at his investiture as Professor Emeritus at Harvard University, (Harvard Press: 1996). Quoted by Nicolaus Keller, op. cit., 29.
7. Reinaldo Valarezo García, *Manual de derecho internacional*, 13.
8. Jan K. Black, *Area Handbook for Cuba*, 352.

It sometimes happens that a theory valid to solve a conflict at a given moment becomes obsolete or its application to a seemingly similar case can be completely inadequate. Analogy is worthless in international law, and so are formulas. Guantánamo is a very specific case.

Although many countries have supported Cuba with statements in its just demand to recover that strip of land snatched away from Cuba by imperial greed, the idea of participation has not yet arisen in regard to the conflict over the naval base at Guantánamo for, whether we like it or not, all of U.S. are involved in an issue that affects sovereignty and territorial integrity and, consequently, one of the main principles of the United Nations. A *laissez-faire*, *laissez-passer* stance is, therefore, out of the question.

Cuba and its people have received not only the support and the solidarity of various governments and international organizations, but also of figures who, as individuals, have asked the Government of the United States to return the usurped territory occupied by the Guantánamo Naval Base to its legitimate owner. Such is the case of the letters dated July 12, 1996, addressed by Guillermo Torriello García, former Minister of Foreign Affairs of Guatemala, representative of his country at the foundation of the United Nations, signatory of the San Francisco Charter in 1945, and chairman of Our America's Anti-imperialist Tribunal, to Warren Christopher, Secretary of State of the United States, and to the heads of states and governments who participated in the Third Iberian-American Summit held in San Salvador de Bahía, in Brazil, on July 15-16, 1993.

Claim Over the Occupied Territory. Sovereign Will and Decision of the Cuban People

Since the Cuban people attained its true independence and full sovereignty with the revolutionary triumph on January 1, 1959, it continued to bravely demand the return of the portion of its territory usurped by the United States.

However, at a very complex time in the relations between the United States and Cuba, when it was known—as was proven later when the information from the Pentagon was declassified—, that the North Americans were concocting a self-aggression, that is to say, a simulation of a Cuban aggression against the base, in order to have an excuse to openly attack Cuba, the Revolutionary Government clearly stated that we would never attack the base. Thus, Commander Fidel Castro said during the Labor Day commemoration held in Havana, on May 1, 1964:

> There are other, older problems, like the problem of the base. The base was there when the Revolution triumphed, it is an old problem from half a century ago; we have stated here what our position is regarding the problem of the base, we have stated that we will never resort to force to solve the problem of the base, and that has always been the position of the Revolutionary Government. Because we know those shameless imperialists, we have followed the policy of not giving them any pretext for their plans. The problem of the base is an old problem, and we can take whatever time is necessary to discuss and resolve it; because it is a problem, an old evil that the Revolution found when it came to power...[9]

The Cuban people rejected the unlawful occupation of our territory in Guantánamo by the United States, and it was thus proven when 97.7% of the voters approved the February 24, 1976 Constitution, whose Article 10 (Article 12 of the modified 1992 Constitution) states: "The Republic of Cuba repudiates and considers illegal and null the treaties, pacts or concessions agreed upon in unequal terms so that ignore or diminish its sovereignty over any possession of the national territory."

Thus, the people ratified its original repudiation of the treaties about the Guantánamo Naval Base and, consequently, the United States

9. Fidel Castro Ruz, "Discurso conmemorativo por el Primero de Mayo, La Habana, 1964," in *Política exterior del Gobierno Revolucionario de Cuba, 1959-julio de 1964*, B-5.

must leave that territory unlawfully occupied against the will of the Cuban people.

General Raúl Castro, in the aforementioned interview, granted to the newspaper *El Sol de México*, ratified the cautious and wise policy of the Revolutionary Government in regard to the Guantánamo Naval Base:

> We will not act irresponsibly about this matter, but we will not give up our absolutely firm stance demanding our sovereign right over that piece of our country's soil.
> As I recently said at the city of Guantánamo, a few kilometers away from that facility, to us the U.S. military base is a dagger stuck on the side of the Motherland. And we intend to draw it out peacefully and in a civilized manner. The demand for the return of the territory of the base is not only Cuba's unanimous claim, but also a clamor of world public opinion.[10]

It is difficult to summarize in a few pages the violations, aggressions and punitive behavior that dagger stuck on our Motherland's soil meant and still means. But in order to fasten in the readers' minds what I have been saying in the previous pages, I can emphasize the following:

- It is well known that the February 16/23, 1903 Agreement and its July 2, 1903 Complementary Agreement, as well as the sequel of those two documents, the May 29, 1934 Treaty, about the occupation by the United States of land and water at the Guantánamo bay and its periphery, where the Guantánamo Naval Base stands, in relation to its origin, manner and maintenance has been and is repudiated by the people of Cuba.

- The violation by the United States of America of their own obligations—stemming from the *Joint Resolution* dated

10. Raúl Castro Ruz, "Entrevista concedida al periódico *El Sol de México*," in *Bohemia*, 24.

April 19, 1898, and contracted in the Treaty of Paris, dated December 10, 1898—, by imposing upon the people of Cuba, by coercion, against its will and without any hindrance, at a time when Cuba was militarily occupied by North American troops, a unilateral resolution approved by the Congress of the United States of America (the Platt Amendment), a foreign law that allowed the North Americans to assume the right to occupy certain sites of Cuba's national territory for coaling or naval stations.

- The violation by the United States of America of the principles consecrated by international law, that must rule all international negotiations, on equal footing, in good faith, by means of the expression of the parties' free consent to oblige themselves, and respecting and observing what was agreed upon. In fact, the United States of America, both in regard to the Platt Amendment and to the Permanent Treaty of Relations dated May 22, 1903, the Agreement on coaling and naval stations of February 16-23, 1903 and its Complementary Agreement of July 2, 1903, coerced the Government of Cuba by threatening to use force in all its guises—military, political and economic—, to impose upon it, as it did, those same aforementioned instruments.

- The profound and repeated violation by the United States of America of the cause and object of the Permanent Treaty of Relations (May 22,1903), the February 16/23, 1903 Agreement, its Complementary Agreement (July 2, 1903) and the Treaty of Relations (May 29, 1934).

- The full sovereignty of the Cuban people and the inalienable right of the Cuban state to the integrity of its territory.

- The firm position of the people and the Government of Cuba to avoid provocations that may endanger international peace and security, and their warning to the North

Americans that they be sane enough so as not to overstep their mark, because they know well what the military effect of that base against Cuba is, and the fact that, for this reason, their presence rather responds to a political decision, and to imperialist arrogance in not complying with our people's legitimate demands.

- International solidarity with the just demand of the Cuban people that the piece of its territory unlawfully occupied by the United States be returned. Cuba has not been alone, will not be alone in this struggle: its sons' courage goes hand in hand with the solidarity of the best of humankind.

- Since the triumph of the Cuban Revolution, the people of Cuba has reiterated and continues to reiterate its irrevocable right to vindicate the usurped territory, and has demanded and still demands that the Government of the United States of America adopt all necessary measures to effectively vacate the portion of Cuban territory it unlawfully occupies in Guantánamo, leaving it at the free and absolute disposal, use and benefit of the Republic of Cuba.

And we can also tell them in their own language, so it is clearly understood: *Yankee, go home!* Thus they can get rid of the burden of infamy they shouldered ever since they imposed upon us the occupation of a piece of our territory where their undesirable naval base now stands.

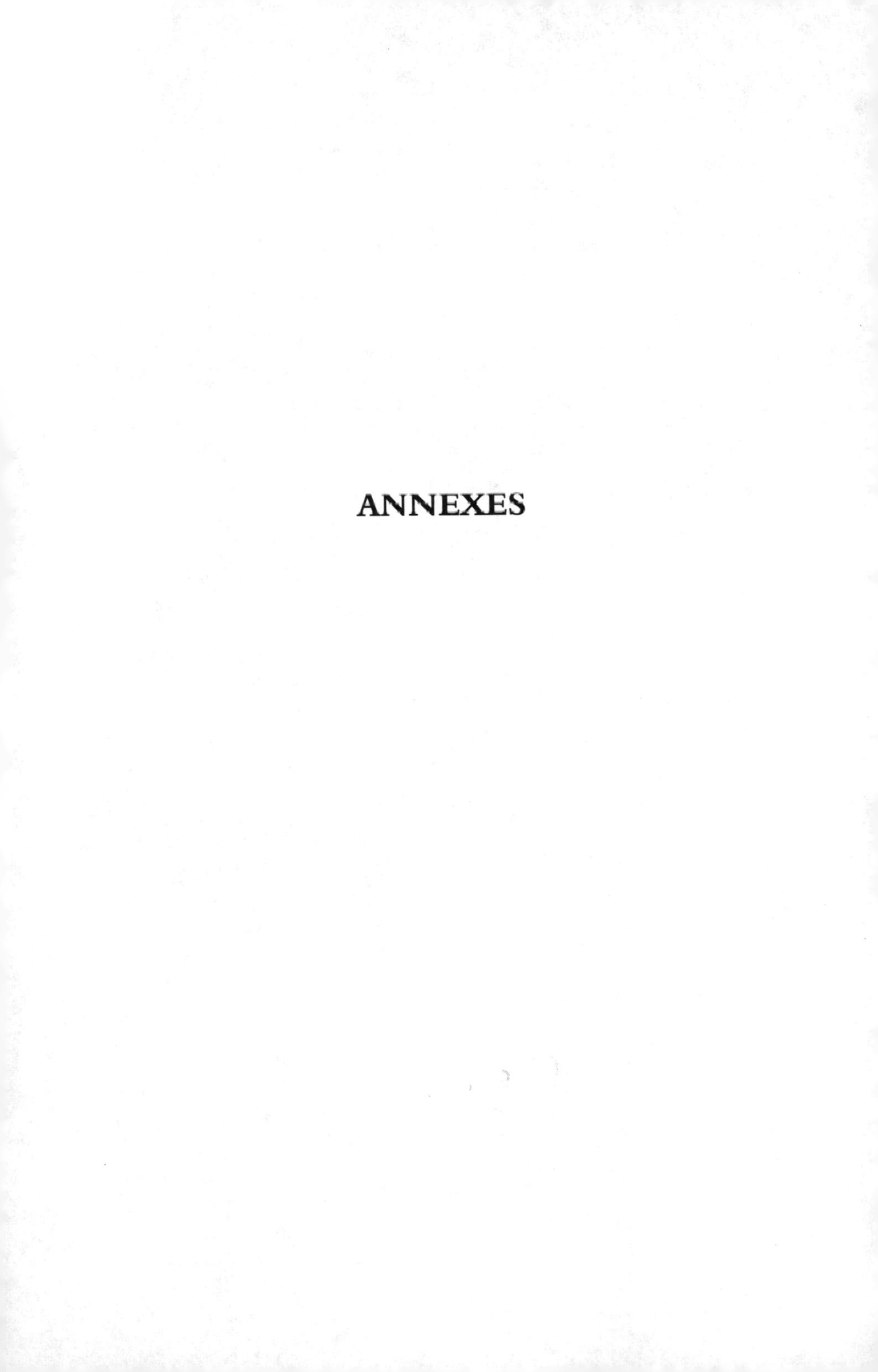

ANNEXES

ANNEX 1

JOINT RESOLUTION*

Approved by the North American Congress on April 1st, 1989. Sanctioned by President McKinley on April 20, 1898

Whereas the abhorrent conditions which have existed for more than three years in the island of Cuba, so near our own borders, have shocked the moral sense of the people of the United States, have been a disgrace to civilization, culminating as they have in the destruction of a United States battle ship, with two hundred and sixty-six of its officers and crew, while on a friendly visit in the harbor of Havana, and can no longer be endured, s has been set forth by the President of the United States in his message to Congress of April eleventh, eighteen hundred and ninety-eight, upon which the action of Congress was invited.

Therefore, resolved by the Senate and House of Representatives of the United States of America in Congress assembled,

First. That the people of the island of Cuba are, and of right ought to be, free and independent.[1]

Second. That it is the duty of the United States to demand, and the Government of the United States does hereby demand, that the Government of Spain at once relinquish its authority and government in the island of Cuba and withdraw its land and naval forces from Cuba and Cuban waters.

Third. That the President of the United States be, and he is, directed and empowered to use the entire land and naval forces of the United States, and to call into the actual service of the United States

* Text taken from Elbert J. Bentont: *International Law and Diplomacy of the Spanish-American War*, Baltimore, The Johns Hopkins Press, 1908, 97-98.

1. The words "and that the Government of the United States hereby recognizes the Republic of Cuba as the true and lawful government of the island" were stricken out.

the militia of the several States, to such extent as may be necessary to carry these resolutions into effect.
Fourth. That the United States hereby disclaims any disposition or intention to exercise sovereignty, jurisdiction or control over said island, except for the pacification thereof, and asserts its determination when that is accomplished, to leave the government and control of the island to its people.[2]

2. Foreign Relations, 1898, 763.

ANNEX 2

TREATY OF PARIS

Treaty of Peace between Spain and The United States of America on December 10, 1898

Her Majesty the Queen Regent of Spain, in the name of her August Son Don Alfonso XIII, and the United States of America, desiring to end the state of war now existing between the two countries, have for that purpose appointed as Plenipotentiaries:
Her Majesty the Queen Regent of Spain,
Don Eugenio Montero Ríos, President of the Senate;
Don Buenaventura Abarzuza, Senator of the Kingdom and ex-Minister of the Crown;
Don José de Garnica, Deputy to the Cortes and Associate Justice of the Supreme Court;
Don Wenceslao Ramírez de Villa-Urrutia, Envoy Extraordinary and Minister Plenipotentiary at Brussels; and
Don Rafael Cerero, General of Division.
And the President of the United States,
William R. Day, Cushman K. Davis, William P. Frye, George Gray and Whitelaw Reid, citizens of the United States;
Who, having assembled in Paris, and having exchanged their full powers, which were found to be in due and proper form, have, after discussion of the matters before them, agreed upon the following articles:

ARTICLE I

Spain relinquishes all claim of sovereignty over and title to Cuba.
And as the island is, upon its evacuation of Spain, to be occupied by the United States, the United States will, so long as such occupation shall last, assume and discharge the obligations that may, under international law, result from the fact of its occupation, for the protection of life and property.

ARTICLE II

Spain cedes to the United States the island of Porto Rico and other islands now under Spanish sovereignty in the West Indies, and the island of Guam in the Marianas or Ladrones.

ARTICLE III

Spain cedes to the United States the archipelago known as the Philippine Islands, and comprehending the islands lying within the following lines:

A line running from west to east along or near the twentieth parallel of north latitude, and through the middle of the navigable channel of Bachi, from the one hundred and eighteenth (118th) to the one hundred and twenty-seventh (127th) degree meridian of longitude east of Greenwich, thence along the one hundred and twenty seventh (127th) degree meridian of longitude east of Greenwich to the parallel of four degrees and forty-five minutes (4°45') north latitude, thence along the parallel of four degrees and forty five minutes (4°45') north latitude to its intersection with the meridian of longitude one hundred and nineteen degrees and thirty-five minutes (119°35') east of Greenwich, thence along the meridian of longitude one hundred and nineteen degrees and thirty-five minutes (119°35') east of Greenwich to the parallel of latitude seven degrees and forty minutes (7°40') north, thence along the parallel of latitude seven degrees and forty minutes (7°40') north to its intersection with the one hundred and sixteenth (116th) degree meridian of longitude east of Greenwich, thence by a direct line to the intersection of the tenth (10th) degree parallel of north latitude with the one hundred and eighteenth (118th) degree meridian of longitude east of Greenwich, and thence along the one hundred and eighteenth (118th) degree meridian of longitude east of Greenwich to the point of beginning.

The United States will pay to Spain the sum of twenty million dollars ($20,000,000), within three months after the exchange of the ratifications of the present treaty.

ARTICLE IV

The United States will, for the term of ten years from the date of the exchange of the ratifications of the present treaty, admit Spanish ships and merchandise to the ports of the Philippine Islands on the same terms as ships and merchandise of the United States.

ARTICLE V

The United States will, upon the signature of the present treaty, send back to Spain, at its own cost, the Spanish soldiers taken as prisoners of war on the capture of Manila by the American forces. The arms of the soldiers in question shall be restored to them.

Spain will, upon the exchange of the ratifications of the present treaty, proceed to evacuate the Philippines as well as the island of Guam, on terms similar to those agreed upon by the Commissioners appointed to arrange for the evacuation of Porto Rico and other islands in the West Indies, under the Protocol of August 12, 1898, which is to continue in force till its provisions are completely executed.

The time within which the evacuation of the Philippine Islands and Guam shall be completed shall be fixed by the two Governments. Stands of colors, uncaptured war vessels, small arms, guns of all calibres, with their carriages and accessories, powder, ammunition, livestock and materials and supplies of all kinds, belonging to the land and naval forces of Spain in the Philippines and Guam, remain the property of Spain. Pieces of heavy ordinance, exclusive of field artillery in the fortifications and coast defences, shall remain in their emplacements for the term of six months, to be reckoned from the exchange of ratifications of the treaty; and the United States may, in the meantime, purchase such material from Spain, if a satisfactory agreement between the two Governments on the subject shall be reached.

ARTICLE VI

Spain will, upon the signature of the present treaty, release all prisoners of war and all persons detained or imprisoned for political offenses, in connection with the insurrections in Cuba and the Philippines and the war with the United States.

Reciprocally, the United States will release all persons made prisoners of war by the American forces, and will undertake to obtain the release of all Spanish prisoners in the hands of the insurgents in Cuba and the Philippines.
The Government of the United States will, at its own cost, return to Spain and the Government of Spain will, at its own cost, return to the United States, Cuba, Porto Rico and the Philippines, according to the situation of their respective homes, prisoners released or caused to be released by them, respectively, under this article

ARTICLE VII

The United States and Spain mutually relinquish all claims for indemnity, national and individual, of every kind, of either Government or of its citizens or subjects, against the other Government, that may have arisen since the beginning of the late insurrection in Cuba and prior to the exchange of ratifications of the present treaty, including all claims for indemnity for the cost of the war.
The United States will adjudicate and settle the claims of its citizens against Spain relinquished in this article.

ARTICLE VIII

In conformity with the provisions of Articles I, II and III of this treaty, Spain relinquishes in Cuba and cedes in Porto Rico and other islands in the West Indies, in the island of Guam, and in the Philippine Archipelago, all the buildings, wharves, barracks, forts, structures, public highways and other immovable property which, in conformity with law, belong to the public domain, and as such belong to the Crown of Spain.
And it is hereby declared that the relinquishment or cession, as the case may be, to which the preceding paragraph refers, cannot in any respect impair the property or rights which by law belong to the peaceful possession of property of all kinds, of provinces, municipalities, public or private establishments, ecclesiastical or civic bodies, or any other associations having legal capacity to acquire and possess property in the aforesaid territories renounced or ceded, or of private individuals of whatsoever nationality such individuals may be.
The aforesaid relinquishment or cession, as the case may be, inclu-

des all documents exclusively referring to the sovereignty relinquished or ceded that may exist in the archives of the Peninsula. Where any document in such archives only in part relates to said sovereignty, a copy of such part will be furnished whenever it shall be requested. Like rules shall be reciprocally observed in favor of Spain in respect of documents in the archives of the islands above referred to. In the aforesaid relinquishment or cession, as the case may be, are also included such rights as the Crown of Spain and its authorities possess in respect of the official archives and records, executive as well as judicial, in the islands above referred to, which relate to said islands or the rights and property of their inhabitants. Such archives and records shall be carefully preserved, and private persons shall, without distinction, have the right to require, in accordance with law, authenticated copies of the contracts, wills, and other instruments forming part of notarial protocols or files, or which may be contained in the executive or judicial archives, be the latter in Spain or in the islands aforesaid.

ARTICLE IX

Spanish subjects, natives of the Peninsula residing in the territory over which Spain by the present treaty relinquishes or cedes her sovereignty, may remain in such territory or may remove therefrom, retaining in either event all their rights of property, including the right to sell or dispose of such property or of its proceeds; and they shall also have the right to carry on their industry, commerce and professions, being subject in respect thereof to such laws as are applicable to other foreigners. In case they remain in the territory, they may preserve their allegiance to the Crown of Spain by making, before a court of record, within a year from the date of the exchange of ratifications of this treaty, a declaration of their decision to preserve such allegiance, in default of which declaration, they shall be held to have renounced it and to have adopted the nationality of the territory in which they may reside.
The civil rights and political status of the native inhabitants of the territories hereby ceded to the United States shall be determined by the Congress.

ARTICLE X

The inhabitants of the territories over which Spain relinquishes or cedes her sovereignty shall be secured in the free exercise of their religion.

ARTICLE XI

The Spaniards residing in the territories over which Spain by this treaty cedes or relinquishes her sovereignty shall be subject in matters civil as well as criminal to the jurisdiction of the courts of the country wherein their reside, pursuant to the ordinary laws governing the same; and they shall have the right to appear before such courts, and to pursue the same course as citizens of the country to which the courts belong.

ARTICLE XII

Judicial proceedings pending at the time of the exchange of ratifications of this treaty in the territories over which Spain relinquishes or cedes her sovereignty shall be terminated according to the following rules:

1. Judgements rendered either in civil suits between private individuals, or in criminal matters, before the state mentioned, and with respect to which there is no recourse or right of review under the Spanish law, shall be deemed to be final, and shall be executed in due term by competent authority in the territory within which such judgements should be carried out.

2. Civil suits between private individuals which may on the date mentioned be undetermined, shall be prosecuted to judgement before the court in which they may then be pending or in the court that may be substituted therefor.

3. Criminal actions pending on the date mentioned before the Supreme Court of Spain against citizens of the territory which by this treaty ceases to be Spanish, shall conti-

nue under its jurisdiction until final judgement; but such judgement having been rendered, the execution thereof shall be committed to the competent authority of the place in which the case arose.

ARTICLE XIII

The rights of property secured by copyrights and patents acquired by Spaniards in the island of Cuba, and in Porto Rico, the Philippines and other ceded territories, at the time of the exchange of the ratifications of this treaty, shall continue to be respected. Spanish scientific, literary and artistic works, not subversive of public order in the territories in question, shall continue to be admitted free of duty into such territories, for the period of ten years, to be reckoned from the date of the exchange of the ratifications of this treaty.

ARTICLE XIV

Spain shall have the power to establish consular offices in the ports and places of the territories the sovereignty over which has been either relinquished or ceded by the present treaty.

ARTICLE XV

The Government of each country will, for the term of ten years, accord to the merchant vessels of the other country, the same treatment in respect of all port charges, including entrance and clearance dues, light dues, and tonnage duties, as it accords to its own merchant vessels, not engaged in the coastwise trade.

This article may at any time be terminated on six months notice given by either Government to the other.

ARTICLE XVI

It is understood that any obligations assumed in this treaty by the United States with respect to Cuba are limited to the time of its occupancy thereof, but it will, upon the termination of such occupancy, advise any Government established in the island to assume the same obligations.

ARTICLE XVII

The present treaty shall be ratified by Her Majesty the Queen Regent of Spain, and by the President of the United States by and with the advice and consent of the Senate thereof; and the ratifications shall be exchanged at Washington within six months from the date hereof, or earlier if possible.

In faith whereof, we, the respective Plenipotentiaries have signed this treaty and have hereunto affixed our seals.

Done in duplicate at Paris, the tenth day of December, in the year of Our Lord one thousand eight hundred and ninety-eight.

(Signed by)

Eugenio Montero Rios	William R. Day
B. de Abarzuza	Cushman K. Davis
J. de Garnica	William P. Frye
W. R de Villa Urrutia	George Gray
Rafael Cerero	Whitelaw Reid

ANNEX 3

THE PLATT AMENDMENT

Approved by the North American Senate on February 27, 1901, by the North American Chamber of Representatives on March 1st, 1901, and Sanctioned by President McKinley on March 2, 1901

I

That the government of Cuba shall never enter into any treaty or other compact with any foreign power or powers which will impair or tend to impair the independence of Cuba, nor in any manner authorize or permit any foreign power or powers to obtain by colonization or for military or naval purposes or otherwise, lodgment in or control over any portion of said island.

II

That said government shall not assume or contract any public debt, to pay the interest upon which, and to make reasonable sinking fund provision for the ultimate discharge of which, the ordinary revenues of the island, after defraying the current expenses of government shall be inadequate.

III

That the government of Cuba consents that the United States may exercise the right to intervene for the preservation of Cuban independence, the maintenance of a government adequate for the protection of life, property and individual liberty, and for discharging the obligations with respect to Cuba imposed by the Treaty of Paris on the United States, now to be assumed and undertaken by the government of Cuba.

IV

That All acts of the United States in Cuba during its military occupancy thereof are ratified and validated and all lawful rights acquired thereunder shall be maintained and protected.

V

That the government of Cuba will execute, and as far as necessary extend, the plans already devised or other plans to be mutually agreed upon, for the sanitation of the cities of the island, to the end that a recurrence of epidemic and infectious diseases may be prevented, thereby assuring protection to the people and commerce of Cuba, as well as to the commerce of the southern ports of the United States and the people residing therein.

VI

That the Isle of Pines shall be omitted from the proposed constitutional boundaries of Cuba, the title thereto being left to future adjustment by treaty.

VII

That to enable the United States to maintain the independence of Cuba, and to protect the people thereof as well as for its own defense, the government of Cuba will sell or lease to the United States lands necessary for coaling or naval stations at certain specified points to be agreed upon with the President of the United States.

VIII

That by way of further assurance the government of Cuba will embody the foregoing provisions in a permanent treaty with the United States.
Note: It was approved with the same words by the Constituent Commission on June 12, 1901 as a Constitutional Appendix with the following text:

WHEREAS the Constitutional Convention of Cuba, on June 12, 1901, adopted a Resolution adding to the Constitution of the Republic of Cuba which was adopted on the twenty-first of February 1901, an appendix in the words and letters of the eight enumerated articles of the above cited act of the Congress of the United States.

ANNEX 4

AGREEMENT ON COALING AND NAVAL STATIONS (FEBRUARY 16/23, 1903)

AGREEMENT

Between the Republic of Cuba and the United States of America for the lease (subject to terms to be agreed upon by the two Governments) to the United States of lands in Cuba for coaling and naval stations.

The Republic of Cuba and the United States of America, being desirous to execute fully the provisions of Article VII of the Act of Congress approved March second, 1901, and of Article VII of the Appendix to the Constitution of the Republic of Cuba promulgated on the 20th of May, 1902, which provide:

"Article VII. To enable the United States to maintain the independence of Cuba, and to protect the people thereof, as well as for its own defense, the Cuban Government will sell or lease to the United States the lands necessary for coaling or naval stations, at certain specified points, to be agreed upon with the President of the United States."

have reached an agreement to that end, as follows:

ARTICLE I

The Republic of Cuba hereby leases to the United States, for the time required for the purposes of coaling and naval stations, the following described areas of land and water situated in the Island of Cuba:

1st. In Guantanamo (see Hydrographic Office Chart 1857). From a point on the south coast, 4.37 nautical miles to the eastward of Windward Point Light House, a line running north (true) a distance of 4.25 nautical miles;

From the northern extremity of this line, a line running west (true), a distance of 5.87 nautical miles;

From the western extremity of this last line, a line running southwest (true), 3.31 nautical miles;
From the southwestern extremity of this last line, a line running south (true), to the seacoast.
This lease shall be subject to all the conditions named in Article II of this agreement.

2nd. In Northwestern Cuba (see Hydrographic Office Chart 2036).
In Bahia Honda (see Hydrographic Office Chart 520b).
All that land included in the peninsula containing Cerro del Morrillo and Punta del Carenero situated to the westward of a line running south (true) from the north coast at a distance of thirteen hundred yards east (true) from the crest of Cerro del Morrillo, and all the adjacent waters touching upon the coast line of the Ave described peninsula and including the estuary south of Punta del Carenero with the control of the headwaters as necessary for sanitary and other purposes.
And in addition all that piece of land and its adjacent waters on the western side of the entrance to Bahia Honda included between the shore line and a line running north and south (true) to low water marks through a point which is west (true) distant one nautical mile from Pta. del Cayman.

ARTICLE II

The grant of the foregoing Article shall include the right to use and occupy the waters adjacent to said areas of land and water, and to improve and deepen the entrances thereto and the anchorages therein, and generally to do any and all things necessary to fit the premises for use as coaling or naval stations only, and for no other purpose.
Vessels engaged in the Cuban trade shall have free passage through the waters included within this grant.

ARTICLE III

While on the one hand the United States recognizes the continuance of the ultimate sovereignty of the Republic of Cuba over

the above described areas of land and water, on the other hand the Republic of Cuba consents that during the period of the occupation by the United States of said areas under the terms of this agreement the United States shall exercise complete jurisdiction and control over and within said areas with the right to acquire (under conditions to be hereafter agreed upon by the two Governments) for the public purposes of the United States any land or other property therein by purchase or by exercise of eminent domain with full compensation to the owners thereof.
Done in duplicate at Habana, and signed by the President of the Republic of Cuba this the sixteenth day of February 1903

(signed) T. Estrada Palma

Signed by the President of the United States on the twenty third day of February, 1903

(signed) Theodore Roosevelt

ANNEX 5

COMPLEMENTARY AGREEMENT OF THE ABOVE JULY 2ND, 1903 AGREEMENT ON COALING AND NAVAL STATIONS

The Republic of Cuba and the United States of America, being desirous to conclude the lease of areas of land and water for the establishment of naval or coaling stations in Guatánamo and Bahía Honda the Republic of Cuba made to the United States by the Agreement of February 16/23, 1903, in fulfillment of the provisions of Article Seven of the Constitutional Appendix of the Republic of Cuba, have appointed their Plenipotentiaries to that end:

The President of the Republic of Cuba, José M. García Montes, Secretary of Finance and acting Secretary of State and Justice.
And the President of the United States of America, Herbert G. Squiers, Envoy Extraordinary and Minister Plenipotentiary in Havana who, after communicating to each other their respective full powers, found to be in due form, have agreed upon the following Articles:

ARTICLE I

The United States of America agrees and covenants to pay to the Republic of Cuba the annual sum of two thousand dollars, in gold coin of the United States, as long as the former shall occupy and use said areas of land by virtue of said Agreement.
All private lands and other real property within said areas shall be acquired forthwith by the Republic of Cuba. The United States of America agrees to furnish to the Republic of Cuba the sums necessary for the purchase of said private lands and properties and such sums shall be accepted by the Republic of Cuba as advance payment on account of rental due by virtue of said Agreement.

ARTICLE II

The said areas shall be surveyed and their boundaries distinctly marked by permanent fences or inclosures. The expenses of construction and maintenance of such fences or inclosure shall be borne by the United States.

ARTICLE III

The United States of America agrees that no person, partnership or corporation shall be permitted to establish or maintain a commercial, industrial or other enterprise within said areas.

ARTICLE IV

Fugitives from justice charged with crimes or misdemeanors amenable to Cuban law, taking refuge within said areas, shall be delivered up by the United States authorities on demand by duly authorized Cuban authorities.

On the other hand, the Republic of Cuba agrees that fugitives from justice charged with crimes or misdemeanors amenable to United States law, committed within said areas, taking refuge in Cuba territory, shall on demand, be delivered up to duly authorized United States authorities.

ARTICLE V

Materials of all kinds, merchandise, stores and munitions of war imported into said areas, for exclusive use and consumption therein, shall not be subject to payment of customs duties nor any other fees or charges, and the vessels which may carry same shall not be subject to payment of port, tonnage, anchorage or other fees except in case said vessels shall be discharged without the limits of said areas; and said vessels shall not be discharged without the limits of said areas, otherwise than through a regular port of entry of the Republic of Cuba when both cargo and vessel shall be subject to all Cuban Customs laws and regulations and payment of corresponding duties and fees.

It is further agreed that such materials, merchandise, stores and munitions of war shall not be transported from said areas into Cuban territory.

ARTICLE VI

Except as provided in the preceding Article vessels entering into or departing from the Bays of Guantánamo and Bahía Honda within the limits of Cuban territory shall be subject exclusively to Cuban laws and authorities, and orders emanating from the latter in all that respects port police, Customs or Health, and authorities of the United States shall place no obstacle in the way of entrance and departure of said vessels except in case of a state of war.

ARTICLE VII

The lease shall be ratified and the ratifications shall be exchanged in the City of Washington within seven months from this date.
In witness whereof, We, the respective Plenipotentiaries, have signed this lease and hereunto affixed our Seals.
Done at Havana, in duplicate, in Spanish and English, this second day of July, nineteen hundred and three.

(signed) José M. García Montes

(signed) H. G. Squiers

ANNEX 6

1904/1925 TREATY ON THE ISLE OF PINES EXECUTED BETWEEN THE REPUBLIC OF CUBA AND THE UNITED STATES OF AMERICA

The Republic of Cuba and the United States of America, being desirous to give full effect to the sixth Article of the Provision in regard to the relations to exist between Cuba and the United States, contained in the Act of the Congress of the United States of America, approve March second, nineteen hundred and one, which sixth Article aforesaid is included in the Appendix to the Constitution of the Republic of Cuba, promulgated on the 20th day of May, nineteen hundred and two and provides that "The island of Pines shall be omitted from the boundaries of Cuba specified in the Constitution, the title of ownership thereof being left to future adjustment by treaty;" have for that purpose appointed as their Plenipotentiaries to conclude a treaty to that end:
The President of the Republic of Cuba, Gonzalo de Quesada, Envoy Extraordinary and Minister Plenipotentiary of Cuba to the United States of America; and
The President of the United States of America, John Hay, Secretary of State of the United States of America;
Who, after communicating to each other their full powers, found in good and due form, have agreed upon the following Articles:

ARTICLE I

The United States of America relinquishes in favor of the Republic of Cuba all claim of title to the Island of Pines situated in the Caribbean Sea near the southwestern part of the Island of Cuba, which has been or may be made in virtue of Articles I and II of the Treaty of Peace between the United States and Spain, signed at Paris on the tenth day of December eighteen hundred and ninety-eight.

ARTICLE II

This relinquishment, on the part of the United States of America, of claim of title to the said Island of Pines, is in consideration of the grants of coaling and naval stations in the Island of Cuba heretofore made to the United States of America by the Republic of Cuba.

ARTICLE III

Citizens of the United States of America who, at the time of the exchange of ratifications of this treaty, shall be residing or holding property in the Island of Pines shall suffer no diminution of the rights and privileges which they have acquired prior to the date of exchange of ratifications of this treaty; they may remain there or may remove therefrom, retaining in either event all their rights of property, including the rights to sell or dispose of such property or of its proceeds and they shall also have the right to carry on their industry, commerce and professions being subject in respect thereof to such laws as are applicable to other foreigners.

ARTICLE IV

The present treaty shall be ratified by each party in conformity with the respective Constitutions of the two countries, and the ratifications shall be exchanged in the City of Washington as soon as possible.

IN WITNESS WHEREOF, we the respective Plenipotentiaries have signed this treaty and hereunto affixed their seals.
Done at Washington, in duplicate, in Spanish and English, this second day of March one thousand nine hundred and four.

(Signed) Gonzalo de Quesada (Seal)

(Signed) John Hay (Seal)

ANNEX 7

TREATY OF RELATIONS BETWEEN THE REPUBLIC OF CUBA AND THE UNITED STATES OF AMERICA MAY 29, 1934

Franklin D. Roosevelt, President of the United States of America. To All to Whom These Presents Shall Come, Greeting:

KNOW YE, that whereas a Treaty of Relations between the United States of America and the Republic of Cuba, was concluded and signed by their respective Plenipotentiaries at Washington on the twenty-ninth day of May, one thousand nine hundred and thirty-four, a true copy of which treaty is word for word as follows:

The United States of America and the Republic of Cuba, being animated by the desire to fortify the relations of friendship between the two countries and to modify, with this purpose, the relations established between them by the Treaty of Relations signed at Habana, May 22, 1903, have appointed, with this intention, as their Plenipotentiaries:

The President of the United States of America, Mr. Cordell Hull, Secretary of State of the United States of America, and Mr. Sumner Welles, Assistant Secretary of State to the United States of America; and

The Provisional President of the Republic of Cuba, Señor Dr. Manuel Márquez Sterling, Ambassador Extraordinary and Plenipotentiary of the Republic of Cuba to the United States of America;

Who, after having communicated to each other their full powers which were found to be in good and due form, have agreed upon the following articles:

ARTICLE I

The Treaty of Relations which was concluded between the two contracting parties on May 22, 1903, shall cease to be in force, and is abrogated, from the date on which the present Treaty goes into effect.

ARTICLE II

All the acts effected in Cuba by the United States of America during its military occupancy of the island, up to May 20, 1902, the date on which the Republic of Cuba was established, have been ratified and held as valid; and all the rights legally acquired by virtue of those acts shall be maintained and protected.

ARTICLE III

Until the two contracting parties agree to the modification of the agreement in regard to the lease to the United States of America of lands in Cuba for coaling and naval stations signed by the President of the Republic of Cuba on February 16, 1903, and by the President of the United States of America on the 23rd day of the same month and year, the stipulations of that agreement with regard to the naval station of Guantánamo shall continue in effect. The supplementary agreement in regard to naval or coaling stations signed between the two Governments on July 2, 1903, also shall continue in effect in the same form and on the same conditions with respect to the naval station at Guantánamo. So long as the United States of America shall not abandon the said naval station of Guantánamo or the two Governments shall not agree to a modification of its present limits, the station shall continue to have the territorial area that it now has, with the limits that it has on the date of the signature of the present Treaty.

ARTICLE IV

If at any time in the future a situation should arise that appears to point to an outbreak of contagious disease in the territory of either of the contracting parties, either of the two Governments shall, for its own protection, and without its act being considered unfriendly, exercise freely and at its discretion the right to suspend communications between those of its ports that it may designate and all or part of the territory of the other party, and for the period that it may consider to be advisable.

ARTICLE V

The present Treaty shall be ratified by the contracting parties in accordance with their respective constitutional methods; and shall go into effect on the date of the exchange of their ratifications, which shall take place in the city of Washington as soon as possible.
IN FAITH WHEREOF, the respective Plenipotentiaries have signed the present Treaty and have affixed their seals hereto.
DONE in duplicate, in the English and Spanish languages, at Washington on the twenty-ninth day of May, one thousand nine hundred and thirty-four.

(Seal) Cordell Hull
(Seal) Sumner Welles
(Seal) M. Márquez Sterling

AND WHEREAS, the Senate of the United States of America by their resolution of May 31 (Legislative day, Monday, May 28), 1934 (two-thirds of the Senators present concurring therein), did advise and consent to the ratification of the said treaty;
NOW, THEREFORE, be it known that I Franklin D. Roosevelt, President of the United States of America, having seen and considered the said treaty, do hereby, in pursuance of the aforesaid advise and consent of the Senate, ratify and confirm the same and every article and clause thereof.
IN TESTIMONY WHEREOF, I have caused the seal of the United States of America to be hereunto affixed.
DONE at the City of Washington this fifth day of June, in the year of our Lord one thousand nine hundred and thirty-four and of the Independence of the United States of America the hundred and fifty-eight.

(Seal) Franklin D. Roosevelt

By the President:
(Signed) William Phillips

GRAPHICS

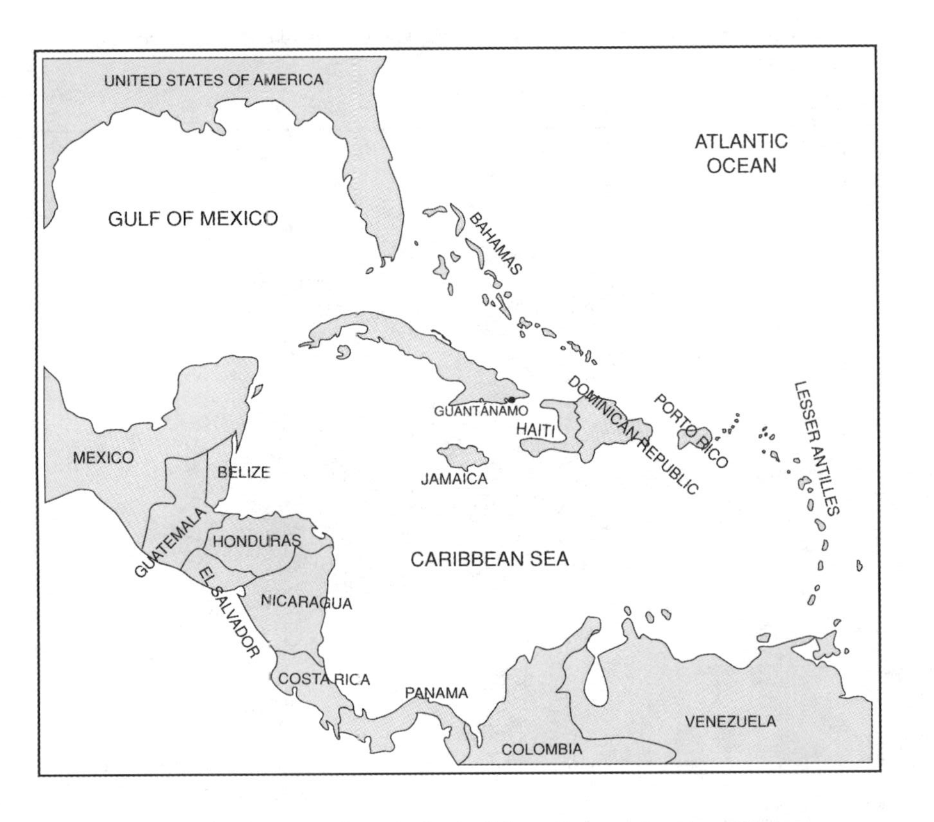

Site of the U.S. Naval Base in the Caribbean. Strategic location of Cuba.

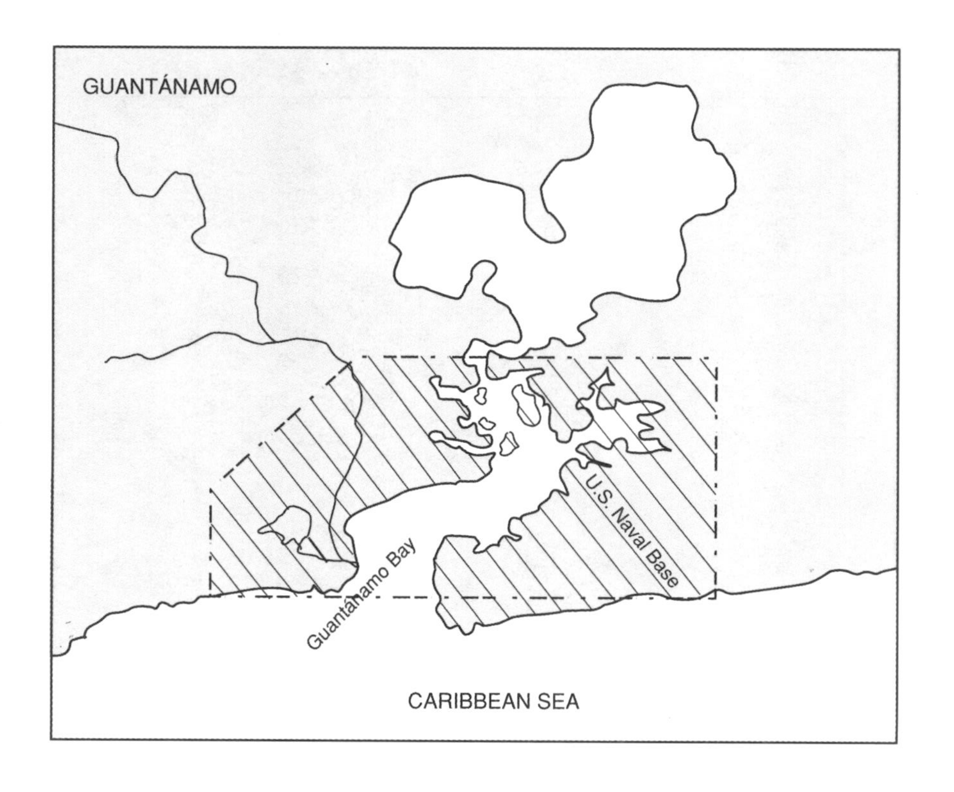

Outline delimiting the area illegally occupied by the U.S. Naval Base in Guantánamo.

S. M. la Reina Regente de España, en nombre de Su Augusto Hijo Don Alfonso XIII, y los Estados Unidos de América, deseando poner término al estado de guerra hoy existente entre ambas Naciones, han nombrado con este objeto por sus Plenipotenciarios, á saber:

S. M. la Reina Regente de España á:

Don Eugenio Montero Rios, Presidente del Senado;

Don Buenaventura de Abarzuza, Ministro que ha sido de la Corona, Senador del Reino;

Don José de Garnica, Diputado á Cortes, Magistrado del Tribunal Supremo;

Don Wenceslao Ramírez de Villa-Urrutia, Enviado Extraordinario y Ministro Plenipotenciario en Bruselas;

Her Majesty the Queen Regent of Spain, in the name of her August son Don Alfonso XIII, and the United States of America, desiring to end the state of war now existing between the two countries, have for that purpose appointed as Plenipotentiaries:

Her Majesty the Queen Regent of Spain,

Don Eugenio Montero Rios, President of the Senate;

Don Buenaventura de Abarzuza, Senator of the Kingdom and ex-Minister of the Crown;

Don José de Garnica, Deputy to the Cortes and Associate Justice of the Supreme Court;

Don Wenceslao Ramirez de Villa-Urrutia, Envoy Extraordinary and Minister Plenipotentiary at Brussels, and

Copy of the first page of the Treaty of Paris (1898).

-dente de los Estados Unidos de acuerdo y con la aprobacion del Senado; y las ratificaciones se canjearán en Washington dentro del plazo de seis meses desde esta fecha, ó antes si posible fuese.

En fé de lo cual, los respectivos Plenipotenciarios firman y sellan este tratado.

Hecho por duplicado en Paris, á diez de Diciembre del año mil ochocientos noventa y ocho.

Eugenio Montero Ríos

B. de Abarzuza

J. de Garnica

W. R. de Villa Urrutia

Rafael Cerero

President of the United States, by and with the advice and consent of the Senate thereof; and the ratifications shall be exchanged at Washington within six months from the date hereof, or earlier if possible.

In faith whereof, we, the respective Plenipotentiaries, have signed this treaty and have hereunto affixed our seals.

Done in duplicate at Paris, the tenth day of December, in the year of Our Lord one thousand eight hundred and ninety-eight.

William R. Day

Cushman K. Davis

Wm. P. Frye

Geo. Gray

Whitelaw Reid

Copy of the last page (9) of the Treaty of Paris (1898).

Convenio

Entre la República de Cuba y los Estados Unidos de América, para arrendar á los Estados Unidos (bajo las condiciones que habrán de convenirse por los dos Gobiernos) tierras en Cuba para estaciones carboneras y navales.——

—

Deseando la República de Cuba y los Estados Unidos de América ejecutar en todas sus partes lo prevenido en el Artículo VII de la Ley del Congreso que fué aprobada el 2 de Marzo de 1901 y en el Artículo VII del Apéndice á la Constitución de la República de Cuba promulgada el 20 de Mayo de 1902, en los cuales se dispone que:——

Agreement

Between the Republic of Cuba and the United States of America for the lease (subject to terms to be agreed upon by the two Governments) to the United States of lands in Cuba for coaling and naval stations.——

—

The Republic of Cuba and the United States of America, being desirous to execute fully the provisions of Article VII of the Act of Congress approved March second, 1901, and of Article VII of the Appendix to the Constitution of the Republic of Cuba promulgated on the 20th of May, 1902, which provide:——

Copy of the first folio of the Agreement on Coaling and Naval Stations (February 16/23, 1903).

dente de la República de Cuba, hoy día diez y seis de Febrero de 1903.	dent of the Republic of Cuba this the sixteenth day of February 1903.

T. Estrada Palma.

Firmado por el Presidente de los Estados Unidos hoy día veinte y tres de Febrero de 1903.	Signed by the President of the United States on the twenty third day of February 1903.

Theodore Roosevelt

Copy of the last folio of the Agreement on Coaling and Naval Stations (February 16/23, 1903).

FRANKLIN D. ROOSEVELT,

President of the United States of America.

TO ALL TO WHOM THESE PRESENTS SHALL COME, GREETING:

KNOW YE, That whereas a Treaty of Relations between the United States of America and the Republic of Cuba, was concluded and signed by their respective Plenipotentiaries at Washington on the twenty-ninth day of May, one thousand nine hundred and thirty-four, a true copy of which treaty is word for word as follows:

The United States of America and the Republic of Cuba, being animated by the desire to fortify the relations of friendship between the two countries and to modify, with this purpose, the relations established between them by the Treaty of Relations signed at Habana, May 22, 1903, have appointed, with this intention, as their Plenipotentiaries:	Los Estados Unidos de América y la República de Cuba, animados por el deseo de fortalecer los lazos de amistad entre los dos países y de modificar, con ese fin, las relaciones establecidas entre ellos por el Tratado de Relaciones firmado en la Habana el 22 de mayo de 1903, han nombrado con ese propósito, como sus Plenipotenciarios:
The President of the United States of America; Mr. Cordell Hull, Secretary of State of the United States of America, and Mr. Sumner Welles, Assistant Secretary of State of the United States of America; and	El Presidente de los Estados Unidos de América;al Señor Cordell Hull, Secretario de Estado de los Estados Unidos de América y al Señor Sumner Welles, Subsecretario de Estado de los Estados Unidos de América; y
The Provisional President of	El Presidente Provisional

Copy of the first folio of the Treaty of Relations (May 29, 1934).

EN FE DE LO CUAL, los Plenipotenciarios respectivos han firmado el presente Tratado y han estampado sus sellos.

HECHO por duplicado, y en los idiomas español e inglés, en Washington el día veinte y nueve de mayo, de mil novecientos treinta y cuatro.

IN FAITH WHEREOF, the respective Plenipotentiaries have signed the present Treaty and have affixed their seals hereto.

DONE in duplicate, in the Spanish and English languages, at Washington on the twenty-ninth day of May, one thousand nine hundred and thirty-four.

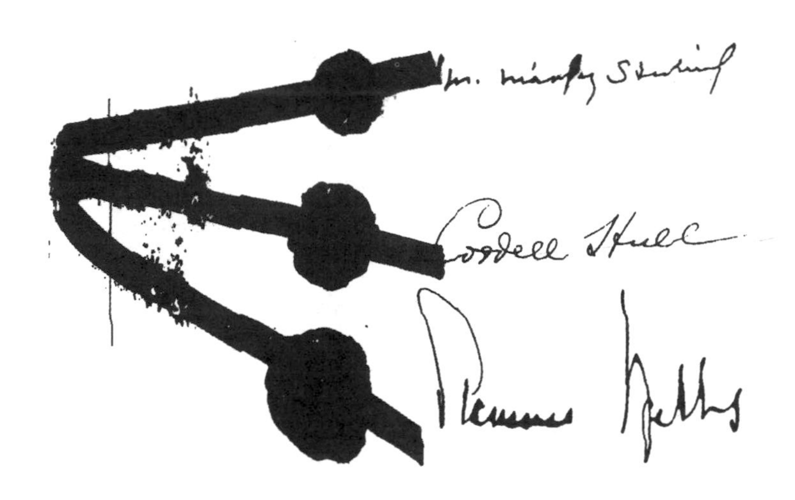

Copy of the last folio of the Treaty of Relations (May 29, 1934).

U.S. Naval Base Area.

Air view of the residential area of the U.S. Naval Base.

Entry to the U.S. Naval Base through the land door.

U.S. marines performing body search to Cuban workers at the U.S. Naval Base.

sierra 26 maestra

Organo Oficial del Movimiento 26 de Julio -Editado en el Exilio-

VOLUMEN I | MIAMI, FLORIDA | Julio 1958

SUPLEMENTO

REQUISITION

Commanding Officer, Naval Station

8 May 1958

HOLD MATERIAL FOR PICK-UP BY CUBAN NAVY

Suplemento

Grafico

Copy of the Sierra Maestra *newspaper: Graphic record of airplanes of Batista's tyranny being supplied at the U.S. Naval Base.*

Doorway to the free territory of America.

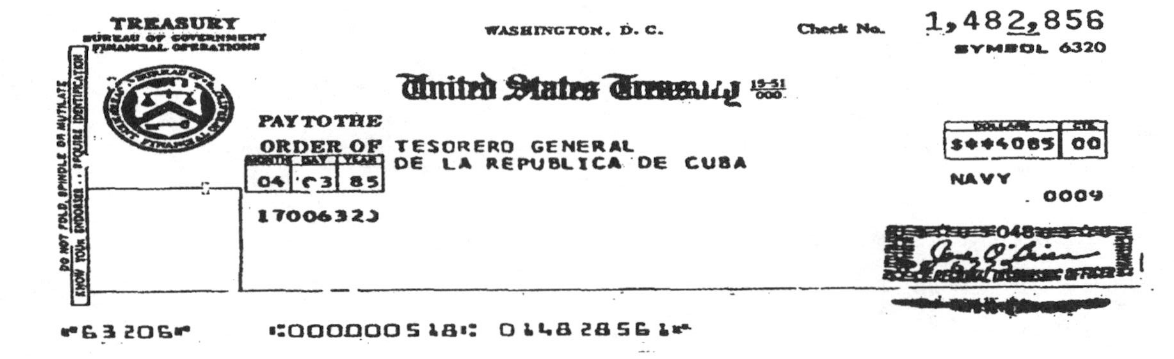

TREASURY
BUREAU OF GOVERNMENT FINANCIAL OPERATIONS

WASHINGTON, D. C.

Check No. 1,482,856
SYMBOL 6320

United States Treasury 15-51/000

DO NOT FOLD, SPINDLE OR MUTILATE
KNOW YOUR ENDORSER . . REQUIRE IDENTIFICATION

PAY TO THE ORDER OF TESORERO GENERAL DE LA REPUBLICA DE CUBA

MONTH	DAY	YEAR
04	03	85

DOLLARS	CTS.
$**4085	00

NAVY
0009

17006323

⑈63206⑈ ⑆000000518⑆ 01482856⑈

Copy of one of the checks issued for the lease of the U.S. Naval Base in Guantánamo. They are kept in Cuba and have not been collected as an evidence for the history of the illegal usurpation of part of the Cuban territory.

BIBLIOGRAPHY

Almodóvar Salas, Tomás. "Apuntes del derecho diplomático y consular." Lectures delivered at the Foreign Service Institute, Ministry of Foreign Affairs, Havana, 1976.

Álvarez Tabío, Fernando. "La base de Guantánamo y el derecho internacional." *Cuba Socialista* I, (2); II, (11), (October, 1961 and July, 1962).

Antokoletz, Daniel. *Tratado de derecho internacional público.* 5th ed. Buenos Aires: Librería y Editorial La Facultad, 1951.

Archives of the Ministry of Foreign Affairs of the Republic of Cuba.

Black, Jan K. *Area Handbook for Cuba.* 2d ed. Washington, D.C.: Government Printing Office.

Bravo Correoso, Antonio. *Cómo se hizo la Constitución de Cuba.* Havana: 1928.

Castro Ruz, Fidel. "Conversaciones con U Thant, secretario general de la ONU, La Habana, 30 de octubre de 1962." In *Posición de Cuba ante la Crisis del Caribe.* Havana: Comisión de Orientación Revolucionaria, diciembre de 1962. Taken from *Política Exterior del Gobierno Revolucionario de Cuba, 1959-julio de 1964.* Havana: Ministry of Foreign Affairs, 1964.

———————. "Discurso conmemorativo por el Primero de Mayo, La Habana, 1964." Taken from *Política Exterior de Cuba, 1959-julio de 1964.* Havana: Ministry of Foreign Affairs, 1964.

Castro Ruz, Raúl. "Entrevista concedida al periódico *El Sol de México.*" *Bohemia,* May 14, 1993.

———————. "Discurso en el acto conmemorativo por la proclamación del carácter socialista de nuestra Revolución y Día del Miliciano, efectuado en la Plaza de la Revolución 'Mariana Grajales' en Guantánamo, el 16 de abril de 1994." Taken from Felipa Suárez and Pilar Quesada. *A escasos metros del enemigo.* Havana: Ediciones Verde Olivo, 1996.

Cepero Bonilla, Raú. "El canje de billetes: un golpe a la contrarrevolución." *Cuba Socialista* I, (2),: October, 1961.

"Cronología de agresiones." In *Agresiones de Estados Unidos a Cuba Revolucionaria.* Havana: Sociedad Cubana de Derecho Internacional, Editorial de Ciencias Sociales, 1989.

D'Estefano Pisani, Miguel A. *Documentos del derecho internacional público.* Havana: Editorial de Ciencias Sociales, Instituto Cubano del Libro, 1980.

Diccionario enciclopédico hispano-americano. Barcelona: Montaner y Simón, Ed., n.d.

Diccionario enciclopédico ilustrado. Barcelona: Editorial Sopena S.A., 1977.

Diccionario enciclopédico UTEHA. Mexico: Unión Tipográfica Editorial Hispano Americana, 1951.

Diccionario latino-español de jurisprudencia. Madrid: Editorial Reus, 1992.

"Enérgica protesta de Cuba por utilización de la base de Guantánamo como campo de concentración de haitianos." *Granma,* August 11, 1994.

Fauchille, Paul. *Traité de Droit Internationale Publique.* 1922.

Figueroa, Javier and Carlos García Santa Cecilia. "16 de febrero de 1998, el año en que España perdió su imperio." *El Mundo,* February 16, 1998.

Furiati, Clara. *ZR-Rifle: El complot para asesinar a Kennedy y a Fidel Castro.* Havana: Si-Mar S.A., 1995.

Griñán Peralta, Leonardo. *Maceo.* Havana: 1937.

Guerra Sánchez, Ramiro. *La Guerra de los Diez Años.* Havana: Instituto Cubano del Libro, 1972.

Jenks, Leland H. *Nuestra colonia en Cuba.* Havana: Edición Revolucionaria, 1966.

Keller, Nicolau. "Deliberaciones jurídicas internacionales sobre la Base Naval de Guantánamo en Cuba." Graduation dissertation in International Law for the University of Vienna. Olga Miranda Bravo (Tutor). Spanish version, 1995.

Lauterpacht, Hersh. *Oppenheim's International Law,* 8th ed., 1955.

Lechuga, Carlos. *En el ojo de la tormenta.* Havana: Si-Mar S.A., 1995.

Linden, Roland H. *Cuba and East Europe in the 1990.* Washington, D.C.: 1993.

López Civeira, Francisca. "La política del Buen Vecino y su aplicación en Cuba." In *Historia de las relaciones de Estados Unidos con Cuba. Selección de Lecturas.* Havana: Facultad de Filosofía e Historia de la Universidad de La Habana, Ministerio de Educación Superior, 1985.

March, Arthur. *La Science Moderne et ses Theories.* Paris: Editorial Gallimard, 1955.

Martí, José. *Obras completas.* Havana: Editorial Nacional de Cuba, 1965.

Miranda Bravo, Olga. "Algunas consideraciones histórico-jurídicas sobre la ocupación ilegal del territorio cubano de la base naval yanqui en Guantánamo." *Revista Cubana de Derecho* 38, 1989.

Pichardo, Hortensia. *Documentos para la historia de Cuba.* Havana: Editorial de Ciencias Sociales, 1971.

Potemkim, V.P. *et al. Historia de la diplomacia.* Mexico: Editorial Grijalbo, 1967.

"Principios de derecho-interpretación de la ley." In *Leyes civiles de Cuba y su jurisprudencia.* Havana: Editorial Lex, 1951.

Public Law 93-148 November 7, 1973 and *89-732*, November 2, 1996.

Roa García, Raúl. *Retorno a la alborada.* Villa Clara: Editora del Consejo Nacional de Universidades, Universidad Central de Las Villas, 1964.

———————. *Aventuras, venturas y desventuras de un mambí.* Havana: Editorial de Ciencias Sociales, 1970.

———————. *La Revolución del 30 se fue a bolina.* Havana: Editorial de Ciencias Sociales, 1973.

Roca Calderío, Blas. "El golpe de estado del 20 de marzo." In Francisca López Civeira. *Historia de las relaciones de Estados Unidos con Cuba. Selección de Lecturas.* Havana: Facultad de Filosofía e Historia de la Universidad de La Habana, Ministerio de Educación Superior, 1985.

Roig de Leuchsenring, Emilio. *Ideario cubano: Máximo Gómez.* Havana: 1936.

————————. *Cuba no debe su independencia a los Estados Unidos.* 3d ed., Havana: Ediciones La Tertulia, 1960.

————————. *Historia de la Enmienda Platt.* 3d ed. Havana: Editorial de Ciencias Sociales, 1974.

Roosevelt, Franklin Delano. Inauguration speech at the swearing in ceremony on March 4, 1933. In "Buen Vecino." In "Parte III, Glosario." In *Prontuario Diplomático.* Havana: Ministry of Foreign Affairs of the Republic of Cuba, 1963.

Saco, José Antonio. *Contra la anexión.* Havana: Editorial de Ciencias Sociales, 1974.

Sánchez de Bustamante, Antonio. *Manual de derecho internacional público.* 4th ed. Havana: Talleres Tipográficos La Mercantil, 1947.

Schriver, María. *Misiles en el Caribe: Entrevista de Fidel Castro para la NBC.* Havana: Editora Política, 1993.

Torrás, Jacinto. "Las relaciones comerciales y económicas entre Cuba y Estados Unidos de América." *Revista de Comercio Exterior* 4 (July-September, 1963) 4.

Ulloa, Alberto. *Derecho internacional público.* 4th ed. Madrid: Ediciones Iberoamericanas, S.A., 1957.

UN General Assembly. *Documento A/AC/109/2020.* May 2, 1955.

U.S. Congress. 50:1; House, Ex. Doc. 238.

U.S. Department of State. *Digest of International Law.* Washington, D.C.: 1963.

Valarezo García, Reinaldo. *Manual de derecho internacional.* Universidad Nacional de Loja, 1984.

Verdross, Alfred. *Derecho internacional público.* Madrid: Biblioteca Jurídica Aguilar, 1972.

Yáñez Quiveiro, Manuel. "Las agresiones norteamericanas contra Cuba por las frecuencias radiales." In *Agresiones de Estados Unidos a Cuba Revolucionaria.* Havana: Sociedad Cubana de Derecho Internacional, Editorial de Ciencias Sociales, 1989.

NAME INDEX

A

B

C

D

E

F

G

K

L

M

N

O

P

Q

R

S

T

U

V

W

Y

Z

Este libro se terminó de imprimir en el
mes de febrero de 2001, en los talleres gráficos
de Quebecor Impreandes, Bogotá, Colombia.
La edición consta de 2.000 ejemplares .